Freight Trains pass on the Horseshoe Curve, USA

Planning Freight Railways

eds Nigel G Harris & Felix Schmid

Published by A & N Harris
43a Palace Square
Crystal Palace
London
SE19 2LT

British Library Cataloguing in Publication Data

Planning Freight Railways
   1. Railways
   I. Harris, N. G.   II. Schmid, F.

Printed in Great Britain by
Hobbs the Printers Limited
Brunel Road
Totton
Hampshire
SO40 3WX

ISBN 0 -9529997-1-4

Acknowledgements

Cover photographs are from Freightliner (front cover, and top picture on back cover), EWS (middle picture, back cover) and Exel Logistics (bottom picture, back cover), with wagon drawings from VTG. Any pictures not acknowledged are from the authors' collections.

In addition to those credited for with text or illustrations, help has come from a wide variety and colleagues within the industry. Lynne Duric designed the cover whilst Richard Morris drew various diagrams. Paul Cosgrove wrote the case study on supermarket logistics. More general help has come from Tony Berkeley of the Rail Freight Group, Steve Turner and Maciej Chwatow of Network Rail, Peter Holland of Amec, and Douglas Medrisch and Dan Smart of the Railway Consultancy.

Lastly, we thank our families and friends for supporting us.

Nigel G Harris
Crystal Palace, London

Felix Schmid
Chorlton-cum-Hardy, Manchester
July 2003

Foreword

As congestion gets relentlessly worse and the hottest summer on record confirms the inexorable rise in global warming, the imperative of getting more freight on rail has never been more urgent. UK business desperately needs an effective rail alternative to beat road congestion and avoid the costs and deteriorating service it brings. If we fail to make the necessary breakthrough the UK will become a European backwater with global shipping lines abandoning UK ports and global companies investing elsewhere, in places with transport links fit for the twenty first century. Governments worldwide have to face up to their responsibilities to reduce harmful emissions, and moving from less to more environmentally friendly modes of transport is as important as increasing the contribution from sustainable energy sources, such as wind farms.

To many transport users and providers rail freight has in the past appeared complicated, opaque and difficult to use. Road transport (highly competitive, efficient, increasingly environmentally aware, cheap and favoured by Government), has provided a simple easy-to-use solution for the last four decades. However, congestion, the EU working time directive, driver shortages, environmental concerns and the real prospect of increasing costs are about to change all that. While rail freight will never be as simple as road freight, especially when used in combined transport, it need not be any more complicated or difficult than supply chains involving shipping, air-freight or multiple road legs with intermediate storage, load consolidation or processing.

Planning Freight Railways cuts through the complexity to present rail freight - the providers, the economics and the technicalities - in a clear, easy to understand way, suitable for both transport practitioners and policy makers as well as students. Focussing on rail freight today, and with bang up to date examples of current practice and the latest developments, Planning Freight Railways provides a clear explanation of the nature of rail freight and hence of where and how it can be used effectively in modern supply chains.

A proper understanding of the rail freight business is the first step for businesses looking to evolve their transport arrangements and Planning Freight Railways makes an important contribution to that understanding.

Julia Clarke
Director, Freight,
Strategic Rail Authority, 1999-2002

Contents

1 Introduction

Problems such as road congestion and restrictions on drivers' hours are increasingly challenging the use of lorries as the main method of freight distribution in Britain. As a result, more and more companies are thinking of using rail. However, there is very little published material available (either for students or practitioners) which sets out the issues in any detail. Exceptions include the "Rail Freight Guide" produced by the Freight Transport Association, and the material contained on Network Rail's website at *www.freightcommercial.co.uk/fg_new2/contents/contents.asp*, but both of these are necessarily summary in their treatment of various issues.

We have therefore taken up the challenge of rectifying this situation with this handbook, produced in consultation with key players. It covers both the early planning stages, and (we hope) sufficient detail of railway operations and economics to guide readers towards implementable solutions to their freight transport problems.

After the background to the subject contained in chapter 2, chapters 3-5 cover the business framework within which rail freight decisions have to be made. Chapters 6-11 provide the context for the technical specification of solutions to different applications, ranging from heavy-haul to the freight multiple unit. Chapters 12-16 describe the operational practicalities of implementing particular solutions, whilst chapter 17 attempts to give an indication as to which of those solutions are likely to be profitable.

Although much of the book covers the British situation, we have included other examples from around the world, showing best practice wherever it is. We have taken on board contributions from a wide range of specialists, in an attempt to reflect the differing outlooks held within the industry. In order to bring this material together in an ordered fashion, we have had to combine material from different contributors, and any errors are therefore our responsibility.

2 The History of Rail Freight and Today's Environment

Felix Schmid, University of Sheffield

2.1 Freight Railways and Freight on Rail

Most railways in the world (at least in terms of route km) are concerned primarily with the carriage of freight. The important freight role of the rail mode is often neglected since passenger services dominate main line railway operations in many European countries (e.g., Britain) and in parts of Asia (e.g. Japan), especially in urban areas. Freight railways can make a substantial contribution to the welfare of society by allowing the efficient and effective movement of goods over long distances with a limited impact on the environment. A well-loaded freight train requires about one eighth of the energy required to move the same goods by road, thanks to the low friction and the stiff interface between wheel and rail. A high capacity rail freight route also requires only a fraction of the space taken up by a highway with an equivalent capacity because of the much higher load per unit length and the ability to form consists up to 5km long. Conversely, road haulage theoretically requires a full braking distance between any two vehicles.

The market share of the rail mode has been declining worldwide since the 1960s, perhaps with the exception of long haul freight in the USA, China and, to some extent, in Russia. All the same, several highly specialised operations have shown substantial growth towards the end of the 20th century, as can be found in chapter 6. However, the major reasons for the general decline have been quoted as poor reliability, punctuality and extended transit times. There are encouraging signs though of a recovery of market share in some areas, to an extent because of the reducing performance of rail's main competitors: road traffic and air transport both suffer from congestion and some 'air-freight' is already moving by rail between major hubs in Europe.

Railways must re-establish themselves as the carrier of choice by the adoption of better planning, more appropriate technologies and the development of new operational methods, including closer integration with other modes of transport and much better use of information technology and modern equipment. The present text on planning freight railways is focused on providing some of the tools required to respond to the challenges facing freight railways. To understand better the context of freight by rail, a historical introduction is followed by a brief overview of the current state of railways in

Europe and an assessment of the most important drivers for change and the conditions for success.

2.2 Early History of (Freight) Railways (to ca 1850)

The history of railways is tied to the history of land transport of raw materials and finished goods. Before the emergence of railways, land transport had been slow and unreliable. Ride quality and service were generally poor and caused problems for the movement of both freight and passengers. All the same, the Roman emperors, for example, relied almost entirely on land transport for the expansion of their sphere of influence, with soldiers walking or riding while provisions of all types were supplied by cart. Luxury goods were transported along the Roman roads in both directions, based on a well-developed transport logistics system. Today's railway can thus be seen as the result of an incremental process which started in Antiquity, culminating in the smooth steel wheel on steel rail system which eventually revolutionised land transport.

Evidence from archaeological investigations indicates that both early Greek and Roman roads featured grooves on some stretches. These were not just ruts but properly engineered tracks which served to guide vehicles, intentionally created using stonemasons' tools. While this was not a very important feature on ancient Greek roads where two-wheel vehicles dominated, it was important on Roman roads in mountainous areas. On narrow ledges, e.g. on the old Hauenstein pass in Switzerland and the approach to the Petit St. Bernard Pass, the heavy four-wheel carts supplying the Roman armies had to be guided, that is, the motion had to be restricted to one degree of freedom. This was necessary to minimise the width of the roads and because the pivoted front axle (bogie) was only invented in the Dark Ages, that is, several hundred years after the Roman period. The guidance function inherent in railways was therefore established more than 2000 years ago.

The most significant early "railway" was the famous Diolkos [1] or railed way across the Isthmus of Corinth, built under Periander (the ruler of Corinth) in the 6th Century BC and rising from sea-level to 75m. It was built to avoid the treacherous passage around Cape Malea at the southern tip of the Peloponnese. Not just goods but also small numbers of ships were transported across the Isthmus on this "railed way" which was at least 8.5km long. The track "gauge" was between 157cm and 167cm but with grooves wide enough to accept vehicles of either gauge.

Roman gold miners in Portugal used "railed ways" in the Três Minas mine, with passing loops and a groove gauge of about 1.2m [1]. Unfortunately though, there is no evidence for a link between today's railway track gauges and the distance between the grooves on Roman Roads, as explained by Pawluk:

3

Intentional ruts are an interesting feature of some ancient Roman roads. While there are some ruts that developed from general use, there are others that are purposeful, between 6 and 30 centimeters deep, with sharp edges shaped by a pick or a point and hammer. Such ruts seem to have been used to guide wagons on difficult stretches of the road (Chevalier 89).

These ruts do not necessarily indicate the widths of the wheel-base of Roman vehicles, "for one can not be sure that the ruts form a true pair" (Margary 21-2). Adam says that the ruts would give the impression of the standardization of the distance between wagon wheels. "However, although an average of roughly 1.3 meters has been arrived at, the wide variations mean that a precise typology cannot be established". [quoted from 2]

Pawluk quotes three authors [3,4,5] while the writer of this section has found conflicting evidence elsewhere, variously stating that the Romans used 1000mm, 1067mm and 1435mm gauges or that the grooves were purely a result of wear caused by the passage of many wheels.

The next step in the development of the railway occurred as a result of the expansion of mining in the mountainous areas of Central Europe, in the 15th and 16th century. German miners even brought the technology to Britain's Lake District in about 1560 [6]. It was found that it was much easier and more economical to move ore and coal using carts running on wooden rails (Trämel – hence the term tramway) rather than poor quality earth tracks. Carts could be pushed by children and unskilled people thanks to the guidance provided by the rails and heavier loads could be hauled because of the reduced friction of wooden wheels running on wooden tracks. A second physical characteristic of the rail mode of transport had thus been discovered, low friction.

The earliest overland railway in Britain was probably the colliery line connecting Strelley colliery to Wollaton in Nottinghamshire, operational by 1604. Railways serving collieries were established in Shropshire by the following year and on Tyneside by 1608. In the 18th century they were increasingly found in ironworks, quarries and foundries, and at any large construction sites – such as lighthouses and factories – where building materials had been brought in by rail. Even before the wrought-iron rail and the steam locomotive ushered in the 'railway age' in the 1830s, Britain had many thousands of miles of railway. [quoted from 6]

The discovery of wrought iron allowed the development of metal tyres and so-called plate-ways where strips of metal were fixed to the wooden rails to reduce both friction and wear. Broken rails though were frequent, so the system was really only suitable for human and animal powered freight transport. The development of cast iron rails by the foundries in Coalbrookdale in 1776 and, subsequently, the invention of carbon steel provided the final feature which allowed the rail mode of transport to become established as an economical and reliable means of transporting goods and people: the ability to minimise energy use and provide a smooth running surface thanks to the stiff interface provided by the steel wheel running on a steel rail. Added to this was the ability to distribute loads over a large surface area, even on poor ground, thanks to the rails transferring the forces to sleepers and ballast.

Early railways were thus constructed for the carriage of goods rather than the conveying of passengers. The low friction associated with the rail mode offered great advantages at a time when traction power was provided by horses and people. A comparison of the rates of the Peak Forest Tramway in Derbyshire with that of road haulage provides a good example: a movement of two tons over a distance of 5 miles cost 1s 2d (14d) by tramway in 1808, whereas the hire of a two-horse and cart team was charged at 8s (96d) to haul the two tons over the same distance, that is, nearly 7 times the cost of the tramway [7].

The speed of horse drawn and stationary steam engine hauled rail vehicles had not been sufficient to compete with the performance of coaches on the good quality toll roads built towards the end of the 18th century[1]. Thus, mixed traffic railways for passenger and freight could develop only once steam-powered locomotives became a reliable option. Traditionally, therefore, the creation and development of the rail mode of transport has been inaccurately credited to people like Trevithick and Stephenson. However, their contribution was invaluable since mechanical power expanded rapidly the capability of a system which had been developed over hundreds of years without gaining widespread adoption.

2.3 The Heyday of Freight by Rail (1850-1900)

From about the middle of the 19th century, international trade was no longer confined to luxury products, such as tea and silk. New markets emerged because the main colonial powers extended their control from the early coastal occupation inland and because large-scale farming and cattle operations became features of both South America and the American West. At the same time, Britain and America rapidly developed into the world's major producers of industrial goods. Reducing transport cost and the shorter and more reliable transit times offered by steamships encouraged this massive expansion of markets. As a result, the movement of raw materials and finished products began to flourish throughout the world.

[1] Many of these existed in both Britain and Germany in the 18th and 19th century and were also known as turnpike roads where charges were levied as a function of the type and quantity of cargo or the number of people carried. Turnpike companies were the fore-runners of railways since they demonstrated to financiers that investment in transport infrastructure could be profitable

Manufacturers required vast quantities of raw materials, often brought by ship from overseas (cotton, wool, iron ore, copper etc.), while emerging new markets for industrial products were an important feature of colonialism. Nationally, agricultural activity had moved beyond self-sufficiency and the industrial workforces in the cities needed supplies of food while industrial and domestic users ordered ever-increasing quantities of coal from the mines. Most large flows of goods, whether national or international, were carried by rail for the whole or important parts of almost any haulage operation.

Most of the railways existing today were built in the mid to late 19th century to respond to these new demands, mostly on a private basis, at a time when labour and other resources were comparatively cheap. Thanks to the relative ease with which parliamentary powers could be obtained in Britain and other liberal economies, lines were built to carry particular freight flows rather than being planned to handle centrally identified flows of general merchandise. Competing railway companies would often build separate connections to major traffic generators, such as coalmines and steelworks. Many of these traffic hubs and associated flows have since disappeared and with them the raison d'être of a substantial number of railway lines.

Mixed traffic railways were constructed in many parts of the world, with a peak of activity between 1845 and 1890. Freight transport in this context was successful – as long as the scheduling of fast passenger services was not allowed to interfere with the timely operation of freight trains. However, by 1880 passenger services were regularly scheduled to run at 100km/h and freight trains were relegated to off-peak hours, unless dedicated tracks could be made available. Only mail services tended to be operated to the same schedules as passenger trains.

Labour was generally plentiful and workers were expected to have relatively modest needs. Even large flows of goods were thus usually transported in baled or bagged form, either because the producers and shippers were used to this or because of the distribution requirements of many small end-users. Transhipment was time and labour intensive but this was not a serious problem because the relative cost of road movement was so high.

Rail freight reached even remote parts of Europe thanks to early agreements about the operation of wagons across national borders or multiple transhipments from one mainline railway to another. So-called light railways and narrow gauge feeder lines serving rural areas then effected the final distribution in collaboration with local road haulage using horsepower.

2.4 Developments in Europe from 1900 to 1950

National and international trade grew phenomenally from the 1890s, partly thanks to rapid population growth, the result of better health and migrations, and partly thanks to growing specialisation and international division of labour. Whilst the major period of construction of new railways had come to an end by then, major progress was achieved through better use of the existing routes, with faster, heavier and longer trains, through increasing the number of tracks and by segregating different traffics and allocating lines according to speed. On the freight side, the introduction of air-braked wagons brought about major capacity increases and cost-reductions. However, growth slowed as a consequence of the First World War and the world recession in its wake, resulting in closures of marginal railway operations and the abandonment of some routes.

Throughout continental Europe, private railways had been strongly regulated, from the beginning, to avoid exploitation of monopoly power (for instance, 'common carrier' obligations were often imposed, forcing the railways to provide rates for all types of traffic) and also to safeguard their role as a national asset in case of war. Common carrier obligations were very onerous since they required railways to have available a large variety of different types of rolling stock as well as large fleets of wagons and even lines only used rarely. Examples of this include Swiss Railways' sugar beet traffic and the grain trafffic in the USA. Most networks were nationalised in the early 1900s or shortly after the First World War, either to increase state control of transport provision or to prevent the wholesale abandonment of socially necessary services. Britain's railway system was one of the exceptions to this rule since private ownership was seen as a more effective tool for containing cost and enhancing services. Nationalisation of the 'big four' private operators took place only in 1948, to allow the rehabilitation of a railway network ravaged by the effort of the Second World War.

Freight services on rail played a major role in both World Wars 1 and 2 and were thus a prime target for bombardment from the air and attacks on the ground. Many nationalised railway systems suffered badly during the two world wars, with large parts of the networks destroyed by 1945. However, both the Marshall Plan and national investment led to the major European networks being rebuilt to modern standards, with substantial electrification programmes. Britain started its own modernisation programme in the early 1950s, but the very substantial funds were not applied as part of a strategic plan for the long-term development of the network. Much of the investment was therefore wasted on uneconomic routes and services. This pattern was not exclusive to Britain since some other European railways were similarly rehabilitated after World War 2, without due concern for the viability of individual routes and services.

2.5 From the 1950s to the 1990s

Although the rail mode of transport had dominated the freight scene for nearly 100 years, from 1850 to the 1950s, its market share in Britain and elsewhere started to decline rapidly after World War 2 due to competition from

Picture courtesy of Milepost 92½

Figure 2.1 Steam-hauled Mixed Freight Train

more convenient and flexible road transport and due to the initially poor state of the railway infrastructure and rolling stock after the war years. Motorised road transport, developing from about 1910, had proved its worth during the wars and started to grow despite a relatively poor road network. Rapidly though it benefited from the new roads and motorways which were built as part of the infrastructure renewal after the World War 2.

The British modernisation plan was largely abandoned in the 1960s as a consequence of the Beeching report which was based on an analysis of the revenues generated by all parts of the railway network. Beeching found that about 30% of the network carried around 75% of the combination of tkm[2] and pkm. The renewal of the freight fleet was an important casualty of this development even though the closure of a large number of branch lines and

---

2 tkm = tonne km, the sum of the distances carried of all goods, pkm = passenger km, the sum of the distances of all passenger journeys.

duplicated routes achieved more prominence. However, Beeching also created the concept of inter-modal traffic by introducing the movement of International Standards Organisation (ISO) containers on specialised fast freight trains.

The creation of viable businesses had been one of the main objectives of nationalisation in most European countries. State ownership though reduced the ability of managements to adapt to changing markets since railways became part of the mechanisms for controlling labour markets and for satisfying social needs. Rail's costs increased as staff expectations rose while the cost base of its competitors reduced. The major (private) railways of the United States abandoned most passenger services in the 1960s to concentrate on their profitable freight operations. This was a consequence of the particular geography of the US and also of the urbanisation patterns adopted: airlines and coaches took over long distance passenger services while the private car more or less eliminated the need for regional services. In contrast to the United States, Europe remained the domain of the mixed traffic railway where intercity services, local stopping trains and freight operations of different types shared the same infrastructure. As a result, conflicts between different train types became a regular problem on European railways. From the 1960s onwards, the desire to reduce journey times to enable rail to compete with the rapidly developing car and air modes, served to aggravate the capacity and compatibility problems on the mixed traffic railway. In many ways the networks became too complex to manage effectively (see chapter 17 for a further consideration of the costs associated with complexity).

The post World War 2 boom had led to a resurgence of freight traffic on rail in many European countries but this did not allow railways to retain their share of the rapidly expanding overall transport market. Rail's European freight market share fell from 32% to 13% between 1970 and 2000. This decline was masked to some extent by the near exponential growth of the transport market as a whole, so that absolute volumes carried stayed constant or did not fall spectacularly. In Britain, by 1994, the railways' share had fallen to 6% of the freight tonne km (Ftkm) carried by all modes.

Throughout the 1970s and 1980s, the railways of Europe became less and less efficient, partly because network size and cost base remained at high levels while both volumes and rates dropped. At the same time, with the growing integration of the European common market, the importance of freight transport grew and thus the pressure to address the poor performance of the railways' freight operations.

Notwithstanding these problems, rail freight is of great importance in specific markets in Europe and in many areas outside Europe. This is to a large extent the result of specialisation or the availability of particular flows e.g. iron ore. American freight railways continue to form the logistics backbone for the world's largest economy and much of the coal used to fuel power stations

9

around the globe travels by rail for part of its journey from mine to power station, as is the case for the Wyoming coal basin in the USA.

2.6 European Commission Intervention

In the late 1980s, transit times for European rail freight flows were highly uncompetitive, with some long-distance flows from northern to southern Europe averaging less than 20km/h – although this speed is largely apocryphal. Through its Directive 91/440[3], the European Commission forced the European railways to face the realities of the transport market place. The directive placed an obligation on national governments to eliminate any anti-competitive behaviour of railway companies and to put in place structures which allow licensed railway undertakings access to the rail networks of individual states on a non-discriminatory basis.

As a result of the implementation of 91/440 and its successor directives by national governments, many railway operators no longer have direct control over the infrastructure they use. All the same, they are entirely dependent on its specification, quality and availability. Instead of direct control over this essential resource, railway undertakings now have to rely on contractual arrangements.

Sweden pre-empted the requirements of Directive 91/440 in 1988 by creating a state-owned infrastructure owner and manager, Banverket, and by awarding operating contracts to its state railway company (SJ) and to other organisations. Britain chose the avenue of privatising the infrastructure, its maintenance and train operations as separate businesses. Other governments chose less radical approaches to reorganisation but the need for reducing operating subsidies to railways has resulted in staff reductions and outsourcing almost everywhere. Indeed, the need to reduce costs has also resulted in abandoned and simplified infrastructures throughout the European Union.

In the UK, rail privatisation was chosen as the answer to the requirements of 91/440, with Railtrack becoming the owner of the infrastructure [8]. Train operations, maintenance and renewal activities were also privatised. The process resulted in 25 passenger Train Operating Companies (TOCs) and several freight businesses. As later developments showed, this approach did not represent an efficient method for introducing competition. In a study of system size of European railways, Preston (1993) showed that the optimum number of units for managing an operation the size of Britain's railways was about three. This is close to the figure of five adopted by British Rail in the early

---

3 European Commission Directive 91/440 requires the separation of infrastructure and operations. The minimal acceptable form of separation is the creation of separate accounts for the provision of the infrastructure and that of passenger and freight services. Subsidies must not distort the economic balance between modes of transport and international tenders must be called for the provision of subsidised services.

1990s, but very different from the 100 or so individual companies actually created by privatisation.

In Germany and Sweden, many new operators are emerging, demanding access to the network. The example of Switzerland though points in a different direction: the country still has a large number of small operators, often vertically integrated. However, with effect from the year 2000, major consolidation of activities has been taking place, led by Swiss Federal Railways (SBB) which is still state owned. This operator has taken over the wagonload traffic of most standard gauge 'private'[4] railways in the country to become more competitive. Many analysts believe that Europe cannot support more than four large freight operators and several state owned railways are creating alliances or are taking over businesses outside their borders. The freight arm of Deutsche Bahn, for example, took over freight services on the Dutch and Danish networks using the Railion brand while SBB started an operation in northern Italy in 2002.

Perhaps the most important Directive for the freight industry is 95/18/EC which sets common criteria for the licensing of railway undertakings established in the European Union. This was adopted by the Council of Ministers in 1995. To obtain an operating licence, the railway undertaking must meet a number of specific conditions, including requirements in respect of good reputation, financial standing and professional competence, plus the ability to accept civil liability. From March 2003, such a licence gave access to the 50,000 route-km of the Trans European Rail Freight Network (TERFN) and from 2008 access will be open to the whole of the European rail network.

Directive 95/19, also part of the implementation package of 91/440, is important from the perspective of the infrastructure managers since it defines the basic principles and procedures governing the allocation of main-line infrastructure capacity between alternative users, including open access operators, in order to facilitate the development of new services. It also specifies the criteria for setting rail infrastructure charges.

2.7 Britain's Railway Infrastructure and its Management

Although originally very large, by the 1980s Britain's railway infrastructure had been pared back to the essential, both in terms of route length and the provision of diversionary facilities, sidings and terminal connections. Whilst this was attractive from a management as well as a maintenance volume point of view, it created risks for service stability. Very limited numbers of passing loops

---

[4] The Swiss railway network consists of about 3000km owned and operated by SBB, about 700km of standard gauge lines, owned by counties, communities and individual share-holders but largely state funded, and ca. 1400km of narrow gauge railways with similar ownership. In accounting terms, SBB has been divided into infrastructure management and train operations to comply with 91/440, but both from part of a state owned corporation.

and long single track sections (e.g. the branch line from Burnley to Colne) no longer allow the recovery from disruptions in train movements and make the re-introduction of freight services almost impossible on some routes. Access for maintenance is a significant problem because of the lack of diversionary routes.

The railway infrastructure in Britain had been managed largely on the basis of affordability and the minimum level of investment which would allow the continued operation of existing services, from the 1960s. It was designed to satisfy limited traffic and operational requirements rather than to provide a flexible response to shippers' and passengers' needs. The availability of resources determined the ability to operate services and indirectly affected their cost.

When the British railway system was privatised, the whole of the railway infrastructure[5] was vested in Railtrack, the company formed specifically for this purpose. It was then sold in a public share offering which raised approximately £4,000m for the government. Railtrack was guaranteed an income based on track access payments from the train operators. The framework for calculating the charges was designed to generate adequate funds to cover the maintenance and renewal cost[6] and to leave a profit margin of 8% for the institutional and individual shareholders.

Railtrack assumed ownership of all the assets of the operating railway (tracks, stations, electrification, signalling systems, access roads) while the British Rail Property Board (BRPB) retained ownership of non-operational assets, such as disused freight yards and old railway alignments where no future use was foreseen at the time of incorporation[7]. Some safeguards were put in place to ensure that land with potential use for future railway operations was not sold off.

Railtrack was given the task of managing the railway infrastructure in 1994 in the expectation that passenger traffic flows would remain more or less constant, that freight traffic would continue to decline in line with the decline of heavy industry in the UK. Its financial structure and incentive regime were therefore designed to achieve optimum performance from a slowly reducing network. The main future roles of the railways were expected to be in commuter traffic for the major conurbations and in providing some intercity links, effectively a pure passenger operation.

---

5 The railway infrastructure includes the structures (bridges, tunnels and stations), embankments, track-bed, tracks and signalling systems.
6 The expectation was that renewal would generally be to present day equivalent standard, e.g. several mechanical (lever frame) signal boxes would be replaced by a power signal box with remotely controlled solid state interlockings.
7 Increased passenger and freight traffic could encourage re-openings of such routes but the obstacles to doing this are formidable. Re-opening a disused route will almost invariably require a Transport and Works Act order.

On its formation, Railtrack inherited a railway infrastructure in reasonable but by no means good condition. It had been maintained under a strict rule-based regime which ensured that no route was treated preferentially over another. Any work though which took place was to a very high standard. The maintenance and renewals activity was defined on the basis of the type of traffic using the route and the design speed but it took no account of actual usage and other conditions, the track in the Severn Tunnel, for example, was renewed every 7 years, regardless of its condition.

In Autumn 2001, Railtrack was placed in administration by the British government because it was in breach of its licence, not having been able to contain costs in the wake of the Hatfield accident which was caused by faulty infrastructure. The company had also failed to put in place a credible asset register and associated maintenance system. In late 2002 its assets were bought by Network Rail, a company limited by guarantee which is notionally independent of the government.

Network Rail manages and controls the use of all running lines and operates directly 15 of the major stations while the rest are managed by the lead operator of the station. The lead operator charges other users of a station for the services provided but Network Rail agrees the timetable and thus the platform occupation with all the operators as part of the time-tabling process.

2.8 Operations on The Privatised Network in Britain

Freight Services
The freight network was split into national groups of services including Freightliner (the operator of intermodal and container services), Rail Express Systems (RES) which covered Royal Mail services and Railfreight Distribution (RfD), the operator of Channel Tunnel freight. The majority of services though was allocated to three bulk haul businesses to ensure competition, namely, LoadHaul, TransRail and MainLine. However, these organisations as well as RES and RfD were all taken over by English Welsh and Scottish Railway, then owned by Wisconsin Central Transportation Corporation and venture capital providers. Freightliner was taken over by its management, who have been both innovative and successful, and have subsequently diversified into trainload freight operations, with higher returns. Direct Rail Services (DRS), owned by British Nuclear Fuels, emerged as a small open access operator running nuclear flask trains and operating some coal trains on behalf of EWS. GB Railfreight is the only significant new entrant, operating first infrastructure maintenance and subsequently trainload freight services, in a competitive environment. However, at the time of going to press, two further companies are setting up freight operations.

Passenger Services
At the time of privatisation, the passenger network was split into 25 geographically based services or service groups and these were auctioned off to the highest bidder, that is, the potential operator who offered either the lowest net subsidy over the franchise period or the highest net payment to the treasury. The Gatwick Express operation, for example, is a single service franchise and its operator National Express, the coach operator, has to pay an annually increasing fee for the privilege of running the franchise for a period of seven years. Central Trains, another franchise awarded to National Express, receives an annually declining subsidy from the Strategic Rail Authority (previously the Office of Passenger Rail Franchising (OPRAF)).

Franchises were advertised for tender purposes with a minimum service commitment which was normally based on about 80% of the service being provided by British Rail (BR) during the last equivalent timetable period (summer or winter). In most cases there were also clear time-windows given during which specified service levels had to be provided. This was a process described as "protecting services", but has the impact of reducing the timetable flexibility available for freight services. Passenger operators can move their protected services by a few minutes to suit their own needs or those of the infrastructure provider but they cannot re-arrange the timetable wholesale. Only on routes with very few services were the schedules protected in their entirety.

Franchisees were invited to offer a package of improvements over and above the protected service levels. Most franchises ended up offering 100% or more of the pre-existing services, with the additional trains timed to capture as much additional custom as possible while making maximum use of the rolling stock required to cover their franchise commitments. Franchisees had to make further commitments with respect to investment in rolling stock, stations and passenger information systems, depending on the duration of the franchise and the current state of the rolling stock operated by British Rail (BR) over the routes. However, the increasing passenger train mileage, supported by increasing passenger numbers, has also put pressure on rail freight operations. By the end of 2002, many franchises were losing money due to the poor performance of the network post-Hatfield. During 2003, the Strategic Rail Authority (see section 2.9) therefore began to renegotiate franchises, either lengthening or shortening their duration, and injecting new funds.

One of the objectives of the creation of the rolling stock leasing companies (ROSCOs) was the injection of new private funding into the acquisition of rolling stock with a life of 40 years. Individual train operating companies (TOCs) were unable to make financial commitments of this nature due to the short duration of their franchises. In the event, new rolling stock has been financed from a number of sources: existing ROSCOs, vehicle manufacturers and banks and big leasing companies operating worldwide. These companies are also available to provide finance for financing freight rolling stock.

2.9 Government and other Official Bodies involved in Rail Transport in Britain

Strategic Rail Authority

The Strategic Rail Authority (SRA) was created by the incoming Labour government in 1997 to combine the activities of the Office of the Passenger Rail Franchising Director (OPRAF) and the residual tasks of the British Railways Board. It is responsible for ensuring that the minimum passenger service requirements for every route in Britain are covered. It obliges train operating franchisees to run a defined number of trains per day, at times which are fixed with some lee-way. Additional trains are run at the franchisee's discretion on a commercial basis but can be removed from the timetable if the SRA feel that this is in the national interest to do so (e.g. if they are prejudicing network-wide punctuality levels). The SRA also awards targeted grants for local initiatives, the construction of terminals and for the transfer of freight from road to rail where this is in the public interest.

In 2003, the SRA started to develop a so-called capacity utilisation strategy to address reliability and punctuality problems on a route by route basis. Although this is focused on passenger services, it is also designed to allow more freight trains to be run, e.g. on the West Coast Main line. Effectively, the SRA have re-invented the UIC's old rule that only 75% of theoretically available capacity should be used to allow for irregularity. This is enshrined in the Capacity Utilisation Index or CUI which is being defined for all the main routes.

Office of the Rail Regulator

The Office of the Rail Regulator (ORR)'s primary function is to regulate Network Rail, the monopoly provider of railway infrastructure. This includes assessing its investment needs, maintenance strategies and charging regime. ORR also protects the interests of passengers and freight shippers.

Railway Safety and Standards Board

The Railway Safety and Standards Board (RSSB), established on 1 April 2003, is a not-for-profit company owned by the railway industry. It is limited by guarantee and is funded by a levy on train operators, infrastructure managers and other organisations involved in Britain's railway system. RSSB is responsible for maintaining and updating Railway Group Standards in consultation with all stakeholders in the industry. It audits the compliance of Railway Group members with their safety cases and with Railway Group Standards. Its role is also to monitor railway safety and to provide leadership in the development of the long-term safety strategy and policy for the UK railway industry.

Department of Transport, Local Government and the Regions
The Department of Transport, Local Government and the Regions (DETR) is responsible for the promulgation of all legislation relating to transport matters and also calls in projects for public enquiries. It handles applications for new works under the Transport and Works Act regulations. The Secretary of State for the Department approves or rejects these on the basis of a report and advice by the planning inspector. In 2002, for example, the application to build the London International Freight Exchange (LIFE) near Heathrow was turned down because of a concern about loss of Green Belt – see chapter 16 for more detail on this.

Health and Safety Executive
In legal terms, all forms of guided transport tend to be regulated by government agencies. In Britain, this task has been devolved to Her Majesty's Railway Inspectorate (HMRI), a part of the Health and Safety Executive (HSE). Unlike other such bodies, HMRI does not issue absolute rules but offers guidance on best practice. It has, in the past, also provided resources for accident investigation, but this function passed to a new Rail Accidents Investigations Board. HMRI's role also has to adapt to changing European regulations.

Rail Freight Lobbying Groups
For a number of years, the Rail Freight Group has provided a forum for rail freight users to share best practice, ideas and experience. The secretariat lobbies on behalf of their interests – for instance, in highlighting reductions in freight paths where the CUI is too high or in promoting grants for terminals and operations.

Also active in this area are the Railway Forum (containing members of the rail passenger sector, as well as rail freight) and the Freight Transport Association (representing freight across all modes).

2.10 Current European Contexts for Freight on Rail

European railways are being opened up for competitive operation. A number of private local freight operations already exist (for instance, Häfen und Güterverkehr Köln or HGK and Rail4chem in Germany) but increasingly these involve cross-border traffic. The furniture manufacturer and distributor Ikea, for example, is a licensed rail freight operator and runs its own trains from Sweden to Germany, Switzerland and Hungary, using traction provided by others. National railways may now also operate freight trains into other countries; indeed, Eurotunnel have recently announced their intention to do so as well. Internal rail freight within European states is being opened to so-called cabotage in 2006, allowing an operator from country A to offer internal services in country B.

International Union of Railways (UIC)
The Union Internationale des Chemins de Fer is a worldwide association of railway operators and infrastructure owners based in Paris. UIC is the international body for rolling stock and operations standards and for the co-ordination of international research. Its European group co-operates closely with the European Commission on interoperability issues. Interoperability is the term used to describe a framework of technologies and processes which allows rolling stock and trains from one network to operate on another without impediment or changes to traction systems and staff. See section 11.3 for an example of current obstacles.

European Commission
Through its Directive 91/440 the European Commission forced railways to face the realities of the transport market place. The Directive places an obligation on national governments to eliminate any anti-competitive behaviour of railway companies and to put in place structures which allow access by licensed railway undertakings to the rail networks of individual states. 91/440 was supplemented by further Directives, focusing on the implementation of open access, e.g. 95/18/EC on the licensing of railway undertakings. The high-speed Trans-European Network (TENs) routes are covered by the Interoperability Directive 96/48/EC which has little relevance for conventional freight services but will be relevant for future freight services on high-speed lines. However, the Conventional Interoperability Directive 2001/16/EC applies to the conventional network and was introduced into national legislation from 2003. Both Directives are implemented by means of Technical Standards for Interoperability (TSIs). Directives 2001/12/EC, 2001/13/EC and 2001/14/EC (OJ L 75 of 15 March 2001) are opening up the international freight market between 2003 and 2008. They lay down rules on licensing, allocation of infrastructure capacity, and charging for use thereof.

2.11 Successful Freight Operations

The success of rail freight is largely independent of the track gauge and other limiting technical features, such as the type of traction. On standard gauge, for example, BHP Iron Ore (formerly Mount Newman Mining) in the Pilbara region of Australia operates ore trains of 36,000t, formed of 240 wagons with an axle load of 37.5t. Trains can be 3km long and a single driver at the front controls all locomotives by radio. The Sishen Saldhana railway in South Africa is a classic heavy haul freight railway operating on 3'6" gauge track, the standard for the country, with 20,000t trains. Queensland Railways operate trains of a similar size over 100s of km in their coal corridors (see Figure 6.2). Rheinbraun AG in Germany operates an extensive network of standard gauge coal mining railways electrified at 6000V 50Hz, with a maximum speed of 50km/h, axle loads of 35t and haulage distances of less than 50km. Chapter 6 contains a more detailed review of heavy haul operations.

It is a characteristic of these example situations that the railway operations are essential for the main commercial activities of a parent company or of a major customer and the services are therefore not required to compete on a purely economic basis. In many situations, rail is the only mode of transport which can satisfy the business requirements.

Although there are many freight success stories, rail operators also have to face up to major problems which are largely caused by government regulation, changing markets and ever more aggressive competitors. Rail freight is faced with problems in markets for which it is not ideally positioned and in situations where its management does not control all aspects of the operation. There are thus four key factors which must be understood to achieve success:

- The economic characteristics of the market being served;
- The level of operational control which can be exercised;
- The physical assets which are available to the company; and
- The influence of national government and European Union regulation.

Success is founded on good performance in all these areas and thus requires accurate situational analyses and highly qualified staff at all levels.

References

1. Lewis, M.J.T., 'Railways in the Greek and Roman World', pp.18-19, Early Railways, Papers from the 1998 First International Early Railways Conference in Durham, The Newcomen Society, London, 2001.
2. Pawluk, A., 'The Construction and Makeup of Roman Roads', Ancient Roman Technology electronic handbook at the University of North Carolina, USA, 1997.
3. Adam, Jean-Pierre. 'Roman Building: Materials and Techniques', London: B.T. Batsford, 1994.
4. Chevalier, Raymond. 'Roman Roads'. Berkeley: California UP, 1976.
5. Margary, Ivan. 'Roman Roads in Britain', London: John Baker, 1973.
6. Gwyn, D., 'Engines of Change', Feature in British Archaeology, Issue 65, June 2002.
7. Ripley, D., 'The Peak Forest Tramway', Oakwood Press, Oxford, 1989
8. Harris, N G & Godward, E W, 'The Privatisation of British Rail', pp. 84-93 & 104-107, The Railway Consultancy Press, London, 1997 (161pp).
9. Hagenbüchle, W, 'Enge herrscht auf den Strassen', Neue Zürcher Zeitung und Schweizerisches Handelsblatt, vol. 222, 8.1.2001.

3 Business Planning

Allen Marsden, EWS

There is an understandable perception that privatisation of the rail industry in Britain has caused its fragmentation and thus made it complicated and difficult for the end-user to deal with. The reality is that more independent parties now exist than before but that they are learning to work with each other well enough to encourage new customers. Alternative freight transport modes are not without their own organisational complexities and have many similarities with rail. For rail freight, the players can be divided into five main groups: train operators, providers of rolling stock, infrastructure providers, terminal owner/operators and, finally, end-users. This chapter considers each of these in turn, followed by some thoughts on the way in which they work together, the impacts of costs and government policy on each. Although this chapter examines the British context specifically, the key players tend to be similar in many other countries.

3.1 Train Operating Companies
The core activity of freight railways is the transport of freight. Since privatisation of British Rail under the 1993 Railways Act, the operation of freight trains has been in the hands of Freight Operating Companies (FOCs). The principle of open access allows an organisation to become a FOC by satisfying the requirements of the Rail Regulator (ORR). Today, four FOCs operate freight trains on the UK network: English Welsh & Scottish Railway (EWS), Freightliner Limited, GB Railfreight and Direct Rail Services (DRS):

- English Welsh & Scottish Railway is the largest FOC and serves a wide range of market sectors, operating throughout the UK network and via the Channel Tunnel, to and from the continent.
- Freightliner Limited operates a network of services conveying intermodal containers, linking several UK deep sea ports with inland terminals. Freightliner has a separate organisation, Freightliner Heavy Haul Limited, which serves bulk freight markets.
- GB Railfreight Limited is part of the GB Railways Group plc and serves both bulk freight and intermodal markets.
- Direct Rail Services Limited is a subsidiary of BNFL and specialises in the movement of irradiated nuclear fuel but also serves the general merchandise market.

These FOCs are the equivalent of road hauliers and, like the latter, they own or lease their resources, in this case, locomotives and wagons.

The structure of operating companies
The need to combine both national coverage with product specialisation led British Railways, later British Rail, to adopt a succession of organisational structures for its freight business. Operating and engineering functions lend themselves to a regionally-based geographical structure, albeit with a high degree of centralisation, as in the case of the EWS Customer Care Delivery Centre (CSDC). However, during the latter years of British Rail, a market-based structure was successfully introduced. This saw the establishment of the "Trainload Freight" organisation with its product-specific sectors of Coal, Metals, Construction and Petroleum, each responsible for its own portfolio of customers on a national basis. This specialisation was particularly suited to customers that did business on a national scale and which had single, national contracts with British Rail. It was reinforced by the allocation of the locomotive fleet and maintenance depots on a sector basis and by the application of sector-specific corporate identities to locomotives and other equipment. After a brief pre-privatisation interregnum when Trainload Freight was divided into three independent regional companies, EWS came into existence and reintroduced the concept of sectorisation for its marketing team.

However, EWS chose not to adopt sectorisation for its locomotives and wagons and instead allocates and manages them on a fleet by fleet basis, albeit controlled on a regional basis. This approach affords efficiency gains since fewer "spare" locomotives are required with one single fleet compared with a number of smaller dedicated fleets. Against this is set the risk that the lack of market-specific or local identities may reduce the commitment of staff to keeping the job going – a significant factor when locomotives are ageing, requiring high maintenance, and are being used intensively to serve demanding customers. Since today's EWS fleet is largely modern and standardised, delivering high-levels of availability and reliability, the company has not felt it necessary to "dedicate" locomotives to individual markets, flows or customers.

It should be added that one virtue of a geographic structure for the marketing function is that individual managers are able to "network" in their areas and pick up business leads, a valuable ability when contacts such as port managers may be "generalists" themselves. EWS has a number of appointments who are responsible for all business sectors in a specific region, working in addition to but closely with the sector-specific marketing teams.

In determining the structure of the train operator, there is, then, a balance to be made between geography and specialism, to which there is no generic solution.

3.2 Rolling stock

FOC customers often make their own wagon provision and, like the TOCs, may either own or lease these resources. A small number of leasing companies offer a range of wagons, including GE Capital, Nacco (UK) Limited and VTG Lehnkering AG. Prior to privatisation, various factors including the (un-)availability of investment funds caused British Rail to encourage some of its customers to provide new wagons, while providing them for others. In the aggregates and petroleum product markets, customers invested in new equipment but in coal and metals, British Rail was allowed to provide its own new wagons. To a large extent, this division of responsibilities continues: between them, EWS and Freightliner Heavy Haul provide virtually all the wagons required to move coal and have both recently invested in new equipment. In petroleum and construction, all new wagon investment has been made by customers.

Locomotives are generally provided by FOCs but there is the important exception of Mendip Rail Limited (MRL), which provides both locomotives and wagons for the haulage of aggregates on behalf of Foster Yeoman Limited and Hanson Aggregates. MRL does not provide its own traincrew nor track access, however. The electricity generator National Power took the opportunity under the 1993 Railways Act to establish an in-house rail freight operation which provided locomotives, wagons and traincrew and obtained track access in order to move coal to its power stations. In March 1998, this operation was sold to EWS and no other rail freight customer has emulated NP's example.

There are a range of potential methods of operation, using different types of rolling stock. Chapter 5 sets out some of the strategy underlying which type might be appropriate, whilst chapters 6–11 examine different operations and the wagon types which are suitable.

3.3 Infrastructure

In addition to the provision of haulage, rolling stock and terminal facilities, an essential component of rail freight is the infrastructure. Following the privatisation of British Rail, the UK railway network was vested with Railtrack which was subsequently floated as a plc. In 2003, it was succeeded by Network Rail, a not-for-dividend company. This is the rail equivalent of the UK's road network of public highways, controlled by the Highways Agency (trunk roads) and numerous local authorities (non-trunk roads). Conditions of access to the railway network are established by the 1993 Railways Act and regulated by the Office of the Rail Regulator. Essentially, FOCs – like their passenger counterparts – require a Safety Licence, issued by the ORR, which also approves the Access Agreements between FOCs and the rail infrastructure provider.

How the freight customer and operator get their train planned across the infrastructure network is considered in chapters 12 – 14.

Figure 3.1 Mendip Rail Class 59 on an aggregates train at Crystal Palace

Terminals
Terminal or railhead provision is relatively straightforward and again, is anal-
ogous to that in road-based logistics. Many end-users of rail freight have dedicated rail facilities on their own premises, connected to the main UK railway
network. Examples include power stations, collieries, quarries, oil refineries and
aggregates terminals. Ownership of the rail facility is almost invariably with
the same party that owns the site as a whole – and not necessarily the rail
customer. This is the case at coal mines (deep and opencast) where the "carriage-paying party" is the power generator.

Those customers without their own rail access make use of remote railheads via intervening road haulage. These railheads are usually owned by
specialist companies, often in the logistics sector, such as the Potter Group
which owns and operates rail-served warehousing and freight handling facilities at three of their regional distribution sites (Ely, Selby and Knowsley).
Nearly forty UK ports have "shared-user" rail freight facilities, usually with

direct access to wharfage. The port-owning company Associated British Ports (ABP) also owns and operates the intermodal railhead at Hams Hall near Birmingham. Other such "shared-user" railheads are owned and operated by FOCs, generally inherited from before privatisation. Freightliner Limited owns "Intermodal Logistics Centres" at Manchester, Coatbridge, Leeds, Birmingham and Liverpool as well as four smaller facilities. EWS owns a number of railheads including facilities in the West Midlands, Manchester and central Scotland. Planning for terminals and their design are issues discussed in chapters 15 and 16.

3.4 Assembling the package

As with the organisation of other transport modes, the relationship between the end-user of freight transport and the supplier will vary.

Bulk freight customers generally have their freight moved in dedicated trainload sized consignments and often contract directly with FOCs; usually the customer is the supplier or manufacturer itself rather than the end-user. One exception is in electricity generation where (as mentioned above) it is the power generators that employ FOCs to move coal to their power stations, rather than the coal producers. Another is the automotive industry where specialist logistic companies contract to move new cars on behalf of the manufacturers.

Less than trainload customers frequently deal through intermediaries rather than directly with the FOCs, particularly where intermodal units are concerned. FOCs act as wholesalers of capacity on shared-user trains and sell it to freight forwarders and logistic companies which in turn retail to end-users. These arrangements are similar to those that are found in air freight and road-based groupage. For instance, the Scottish logistics company W H Malcolm offers space to end-users on trains which it subcontracts to DRS to run daily in each direction between Grangemouth and the DIRFT terminal at Daventry.

The important issue is that customer and railway adopt an appropriate arrangement, and share a common understanding of what it is they are trying to achieve. If a 'Just-In-Time' approach is required, then this must apply as much in the warehouse as in the factory – and it must apply to road competitors too. In some cases, the road haulage sector meets JIT criteria by arriving at the factory early, and waiting outside, but this does not quite equate to the continuous 'flow' of materials that the JIT philosophy is supposed to suggest. As is highlighted in chapter 7, different customers have different requirements, but reliability features highly for most of them and, provided that this can be achieved, many are indifferent as to the method of production.

3.5 Costs and Prices

The transport of freight on a large scale over a national railway network is a complex process involving a wide variety of rolling stock, locomotives, terminals, infrastructure, specialised personnel and various support functions, including maintenance and overhaul. This is reflected in the cost structure of the operating companies and influences the way in which haulage rates are devised. As an industry with a high proportion of fixed overheads shared across all or many activities, marginal operating expenses form a smaller part of total costs than is the case elsewhere. It has been questioned whether the predecessors of today's freight operating companies ever fully understood their cost structures or were able to spread overheads across their activities in a realistic way. It is fair to say that, under British Rail, Trainload Freight developed an effective cost model which guided rate quotations and helped ensure that the business was viable. EWS has built upon this experience and makes extensive use of cost models. Clearly, the cost of operating a given flow will depend on the supply of key resources: in many cases, some resources (such as wagons and terminals) are provided by the customer or by third parties, as discussed elsewhere; this will be reflected in the quoted rate.

One significant cost component – the access charge for use of the national track network – has recently been placed in the public domain by the Office of the Rail Regulator following comprehensive revision of the charges. This new system is relatively complex, with charges based on a combination of variables including train speed, axle-load, route, time of day and bogie type. Routing and time of day reflect an element of congestion charging, an issue which may confront road hauliers in future but which applies to rail freight operators today.

Transforming costs into rate quotations is not solely a matter of applying the cost-model and adding a mark-up or of pitching bids at the market price. The movement of larger volumes of freight by rail involves a number of issues unrelated to price, although many are ultimately reflected in financial terms. Some examples:

- Commitment. When freight operating company resources are effectively under-written by a contract, the customer may be asked to pay some of the rates as a fixed charge irrespective of volume. This guarantees a minimum income to the freight operator.
- Duration of contract. Long-term business gives freight operators the comfort of a more predictable income stream which in turn allows greater certainty when budgeting and investing, and can be acknowledged by lower rates. Conversely, some short-term "spot" business may be handled with resources that might otherwise be under-utilised, particularly if the customer is able to be flexible in its requirements. In these circumstances, a lower rate may be quoted which seeks to recover only some fixed costs.
- Performance. Rail's competitiveness is viewed in terms of service quality as well as price. Quality of service is measured in various ways, typically in punctuality and reliability. With rail freight customers having to meet

the exacting standards of their own clients, so-called penalty clauses set time-keeping and cancellation targets for freight operating companies, with "fines" in the form of rebates for sub-standard performance. This is not necessarily a one-way process: some contracts provide financial incentives on customers to encourage right-time departures.

These factors help to explain why rail freight operators may be less able to give rate quotations as quickly as road hauliers are sometimes alleged to. It is perhaps fair to state that few hauliers would be prepared to give instant quotations for flows of the size and duration typically handled by rail. However, the rail industry still has scope for improvement in the speed of quotation, especially for international traffics, where liaison with other railways is required.

3.6 Government Spatial Development Policy

The context in which rail freight business planning takes place is set by the Government's top-down transport and land-use planning policy. For Britain, this is laid out in the 1998 White Paper and its daughter documents, notably including "The Ten Year Plan". In essence, one of several solutions to the problems of road congestion and environmental pollution is the greater use of rail to move freight – with the target of an 80% increase in volume over the decade to 2010. This policy translates into a range of guidance notes to regional and local government planners. Although Planning Policy Guidance (PPG) notes 11 and 12 are relevant, the most important is PPG13 "Transport" (published by the DETR in March 2001) which encourages that railhead sites and railway track-beds be safeguarded from non-rail development and for new industry and warehousing to be situated beside railway lines. Guidance on Full Local Transport Plans (LTPs) was issued in March 2000 by the DETR and encourages local authorities to support non-road modes of freight transport.

3.7 Rail Freight Grants

Originally established under the 1968 Transport Act, public support has been made available by successive governments to encourage freight to use rail instead of roads. This has been justified on the basis of the variation between the respective external environmental impacts of road and rail. It is argued that the true costs of the noise, exhaust emissions, visual intrusion and vibration caused by lorries are not met by the carriage-paying party but by society as a whole – making road haulage rates unfairly low when compared with rail (which generates less external impact).

Today, public support aimed at striking a balance between the true costs of road and rail takes the form of Freight Facilities Grants (FFGs) and Track Access Grants (TAGs), administered on behalf of the Department for Transport by the Strategic Rail Authority's (SRA's) Freight Grants Unit. FFGs help to meet some of the fixed costs of a freight flow, such as terminal facilities, handling equipment and railway wagons and take the form of a one-off payment in arrears to help secure to rail a guaranteed volume of freight over a period of time (usually three years or more). TAGs are also paid in arrears but help meet the cost of using the rail network on a train-by-train basis, and are better suited to short-term flows or those which do not require the provision of new, additional terminal or wagon resources. In both cases, support payment is made to help bring the net cost of using rail down to the same level as that of road, leaving the customer to choose on the basis of non-cost issues. Around £25m of TAG was paid in 2002. The Scottish Executive and Welsh Assembly manage both grant schemes in their respective countries.

Whilst rail schemes which are fully justified commercially cannot attract grant, those failing to attract sufficient traffic do not generate enough social benefit to attract grant either. The grant mechanism is therefore targeted on the middle ground between these two extremes, and their logic may be understood as follows:

	Road profitable	Road not profitable
Road cost>rail cost	do rail scheme	do scheme if rail profitable
Rail cost>road cost	apply for grant	don't do rail scheme

Freight grants do not meet the full costs involved and are generally more than matched by investment or payment from private-sector players. The amount of grant awarded is carefully calculated on the basis of lorry miles saved by the use of rail; a monetary value is given to each lorry-mile, varying by type of road. The award is capped at the smallest of (i) the value of lorry journeys avoided, (ii) the difference between road and rail rates for the overall flow and (iii) the cost of the railway equipment. Awards are carefully audited to ensure probity and are subject to "claw-back" should expected traffic volumes and thus benefits fail to materialise. Freight operators must satisfy the SRA that their cost base is genuine and that lower rate quotations would be unviable. It must also be demonstrable that the customer faces a genuine choice between road and rail and is under no duress to use any one mode. The traffic flow need not be new to rail; it is sufficient that existing rail-borne freight would switch to road if investment in new equipment was not made.

For many freight flows, rail freight operators are able to quote competitive rates without any government assistance. However, in some markets, road rates are keen and profit margins slim, making it hard for rail to compete unaided. In 2001/02, the SRA made 23 offers of rail freight grants, worth £35 million and which would save 554 million lorry-kilometres. The SRA has recently updated the value of lorry journeys – expressed in so-called Sensitive Lorry Miles (SLMs). The benefit the SRA is prepared to support is higher for relieving lorry miles on some types of roads (e.g. urban single-carriageway) than others (e.g. rural dual-carriageway).

The SRA also plans to introduce a new rail freight grant, the "Company Neutral Grant" (CNG), specifically aimed at contributing to the cost of trans-shipping intermodal units such as ISO containers and swap-bodies so that they can use rail for part of their journey, rather than road throughout.

It also supports the railfreight industry further by strategic investment in the network, e.g. to ensure that the loading gauge on key routes will accept 9' 6" containers.

References

DETR (1998) 'A New Deal for Transport: Better for Everyone' (July)
DETR (1999) 'Sustainable Distribution: a Strategy' (March)
DETR (2000) 'PPG note 12, 'Development Plans' (January)
DETR (2000) 'Transport 2010: The Ten Year Plan' (July)
DETR (2000) 'PPG note 11, 'Regional Planning' (October)
DETR (2001) 'PPG note 13, 'Transport' (March)
DETR, then Strategic Rail Authority 'Rail Freight Grants' (various editions)

4 Demand Forecasting

Nigel G Harris, The Railway Consultancy Ltd

Many rail freight operations are planned when the amount of traffic to be carried is already known. Often, there is existing traffic currently travelling by road and a switch of mode is under investigation. However, sometimes facilities and services need to be planned from scratch, and forecasts of the likely demand are needed. Estimating the demand for rail freight services is quite different from the equivalent exercise for passenger services, because of the much smaller numbers of potential traffic flows and the greater level of commercial sensitivity surrounding them. So what can be done?

The key task of rail freight demand forecasting is in market sizing. Without this we cannot know whether the market is amenable at all to rail freight, or in what combination of train length and frequency a solution is likely to be found. This, in turn, has an impact on the cost of operations, since trainload, wagonload, mini-modal or road transport alternatives have significantly different cost characteristics. There are also impacts on shippers – for instance, less-frequent though larger deliveries have impacts on storage and terminal capacity, but avoid undue worry about failure to receive 'just-in-time' deliveries. Greater flexibility about arrival times may mean that freight operators can offer cheaper prices, from taking poorer-quality timetable slots and/or by fitting the traffic in with other flows.

4.1 Market Sizing

The rail freight planner first needs to know what quantity of goods travels between different regions. In some cases, specific flows may exist between specific industrial plants e.g. coal to power stations, or iron ore to steelworks. In other cases, however, smaller items of industrial output (e.g. white goods) or even parcels may be supplied to a conurbation, without a specific destination. Fortunately, in many developed countries, Government statistics can provide useful information about major trade flows at the regional level.

When the Channel Tunnel was being planned, regional trade statistics were a key data source about the potential for rail freight between Britain and Continental Europe. They provided information to support the intuitive suggestion that a connection to the Rhein-Ruhr industrial region was important, based on the quantity of goods being transported to and fro.

When Government statistics are not available, many industries will have available indicative sales by all suppliers of a particular product to a given region. However, potential railfreight consignors may have their own views on market potential and those planning rail solutions will have to make it clear that these solutions are dependent upon particular views of commodity demand.

4.2 Modelling the Demand for Rail Freight

For many years, planners have attempted to model freight flows in a bid to understand the flows likely to materialise. In 1971, Chisholm & O'Sullivan presented results of a gravity modelling exercise used to provide a forecasting capability. The gravity model of transport follows a formula of the form:

$$T_{ij} = \frac{k\ P_i.\ C_j}{d_{ij}^2}$$

where T_{ij} = the number of trips between i and j
P_i = the production of region i
C_j = the consumption of region j
d_{ij} = the distance between i and j, often raised to a power of ca. 2.
k = a calibrating parameter

Others have also tried to use this formulation, but its weakness is that it provides guidance on the expected overall level of interaction between regions, and not necessarily that of the rail share of that interaction.

Modelling Competitiveness
As with passenger demand forecasting, incorporating modal choice into a modelling framework is essential. Higginson et al. [1] were commissioned by the Central Railway Group to estimate the demand for accompanied trailers between England and France, with a view to sizing the capacity needed for their proposed new line. Complicating their work in assessing relative journey times and costs are details of the permitted working hours of lorry drivers, as these can make a significant difference to the competitiveness of the road option on particular routes.

For passenger traffic, demand is driven by generalised cost, which reflects the difficulty of making a journey across a range of criteria, including journey time, fare and the requirement to interchange. A similar conceptual approach can be considered for freight, with the relevant factors discussed in chapter 7, including transit time, cost and reliability.

The logic of this type of approach is that it fits the evidence of volumes of traffic increasing as journeys become easier. Many economists believe that stimulating trade increases wealth, but it is another issue whether this generates increased economic activity for the specific areas in question. For instance, Knoflacher [2] noted that, during periods of industrial unrest in Italy, traffic was generated on the rail "rolling motorway" through Austria as goods were moved to and from Germany for manufacture instead.

This approach has the benefit that it permits sensitivity testing, so that the variables of greatest impact can be identified – what really is critical in getting shippers to use rail?

Logit formulations are commonly used within models built to answer these questions, in order to provide a probabilistic estimate of demand rather than a deterministic one. In transport planning, they originate from the work of McFadden [3], and generate a distribution of outcomes as shown in Figure 4.1. Where the difficulty of option B substantially exceeds that of option A, option A is unanimously preferred. However, there is a band where the difficulty of the two options is relatively similar where the logit model predicts an even share of traffic.

For instance, even if rail is the 'best' solution for a problem, other ('unmodellable') factors may prevent this occurring – perhaps the availability of back-haul cargoes from another industry. On the other hand, environmental considerations may tip the balance in favour of rail where it is strictly not the 'best' solution. In that sense, application of the logit model reflects some of the non-quantifiable factors within a modelling approach.

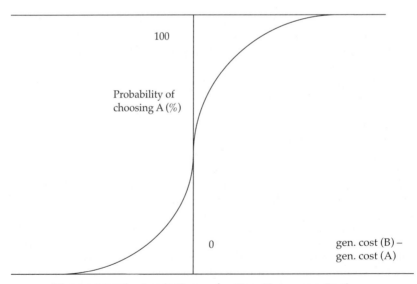

Figure 4.1. The Logit Curve for Two Transport Options

Stated Preference (SP)

A number of studies (e.g. Fowkes & Shinghal [4]) have tried to use SP techniques to isolate those more qualitative service aspects which can be as important as the more obvious physical ones. This technique involves offering respondents choices between sets of service characteristics and getting them to choose one in preference to another. Repeated choices give the researcher a good understanding of the real variables of interest and the way in which respondents are trading one off against another. By offering a number of variables together, it is relatively hard for respondents deliberately to bias the results.

Stated Preference can be incorporated within a generalised cost type of framework, with different valuations being placed on service attributes such as reliability and access to the network. Fowkes & Shinghal were also able to examine the extent of modal preferences – i.e. whether, even given all other attributes were the same, shippers would favour one mode (usually road) over another (e.g. rail). Unfortunately, results from such SP experiments are rarely transferable between different situations and would certainly vary between countries.

4.3 Incorporating Costs

Once it has been determined that a market for a particular commodity is x tonnes per week, it is then possible to provide more accurate costings, based on a choice of operating solutions, as suggested below:

Tonnes/week	*Likely Rail Solution(s)*
<10	Rail unlikely to be able to provide a reasonable alternative
10-100	Mini-modal; freight multiple unit; containers delivered from regional terminal
100-1000	Once/twice-weekly train; daily wagons delivered from regional yard
1000-10000	daily train
10000+	several daily trains, probably as part of a flow with dedicated resources

As will be seen in chapter 17, the economics of different solutions vary considerably. Full-length train operation weekly may incur considerable capital costs (e.g. in siding length), but the marginal cost of adding another weekly trip may be relatively small, if this can be achieved within the same level of resources. Smaller consignments are likely to require more frequent services and higher speeds, which have different cost implications. For instance, operation may not be viable unless flows are combined with other traffics. In addition, prices quoted for transport may vary considerably between operators,

31

depending on desired profit levels, whether or not the traffic requires dedicated resources, and on their need to recoup investment over a particular time-period.

The demand forecasting process therefore necessarily becomes iterative, with cost information being used to derive prices which themselves will form part of the package on offer, determining the level of likely demand. Demand forecasts are therefore firmly dependent upon both the likely volume and an assumed method of delivery.

References

1. Higginson, J, Hogan, T & Weil, M (1997) 'Evaluating the Demand for Supergauge Truck-on-Train Services in Western Europe', Eur. Jnl. Op. Res. 97 pp. 293–307.
2. Knoflacher, H (2001) 'Problems Caused by the Motorway/Railway Freight Share in the Tyrol', Jnl. Rail. & Rapid Transit. 215 pp 45–51.
3. McFadden, D (1973) 'Conditional Logit Analysis of Qualitative Choice Behaviour', in Zarembka, P (ed) 'Frontiers in Econometrics', Academic Press, New York.
4. Fowkes, T & Shinghal, N (2001) 'The Leeds Adaptive Stated Preference Metholodogy', Leeds University Institute for Transport Studies, Working Paper 558.

5 Network Strategy

Robert Goundry, Freightliner Group

Network strategy can mean a freight operator's strategy for defining the network of lines on which he plans to run his trains; it can also mean a strategy which provides a service to customers through the operation of a network of train services. This latter type of network contains interdependencies so that some or all of a customer's goods are carried by services which also convey another customer's freight, or the same customer's freight may be carried between points which do not amount to full train loads as individual flows, e.g. mail services.

5.1 Constraints

From the inception of the business sector concept in 1982, British Rail treated freight costs as marginal to passenger wherever the two ran on the same tracks and, in essence, this approach continues to be used. The final conclusions of the Rail Regulator's *Review of Freight Access Charges* published in 2001 took as an axiom that freight was only to be charged for the incremental costs of its operation. Freight operators continue to run their trains on the passenger network and are therefore implicitly willing to accept at least some of the constraints that this form of operation places on them – trains running outside the times of maximum passenger demand where there are, as in the London area, marked commuter peaks; poorer-quality[1] paths when passenger trains are running, and restrictions on weight and/or length when these may impinge on passenger operations. Difficult problems are created when the intensity or speed of passenger services increases, consuming timetable capacity used by freight trains, and when the amount of non-passenger weekday night time required for the maintenance of the line (usually to passenger standards) impinges into the time traditionally used for freight traffic. Resolution of these issues is currently difficult and uncertain, and may require public subsidy in some form, as may the upgrading of the network to carry the larger, longer, heavier and faster freight trains often required by emerging freight market forces.

In practical terms the British freight operator will want to run his trains on the passenger network, since no alternatives are readily available and the business does not in general generate sufficient margin to allow substantial infrastructure investment to take place. This means that freight operations

---

1 "Poorer-quality" usually means longer journey times as freight trains are recessed to allow priority to passenger trains

are planned on the basis of the known state, capability and capacity of the passenger network. Planners will seek to use that network to best advantage with routing and working practices which might appear sub-optimal if freight were to be the leading party. Thus, for instance, the additional fuel and maintenance costs of running trains at 75mph (120km/h) may not be justified by a commercial requirement for shorter transit times but may be the price paid to have viable paths on passenger routes. These costs may not be insignificant, as they may represent a 20% premium on normal costs, although this may partly be offset by better resource utilisation.

The parts of the passenger network to be used by freight trains must of course offer the characteristics required by the freight traffic seeking to run on them. Heavy bulk freight trains will require track and structures capable of carrying heavy axle loads, whilst containerised loads will require loading gauges appropriate to the profile of the containers being carried. In Britain, the legacy of the early days of railways means that loading gauges are particularly restrictive, so that only limited parts of the network are capable of carrying 8' 6" high ISO containers on conventional-height wagon platforms, whilst the network available to the wider European swap body is even more restricted. Also, the proportion of 9' 6" containers entering service continues to rise inexorably[2].

5.2 Strategy

In planning the type of service he wants to run on this passenger network, the freight operator will be aware that the natural unit of movement for a railway is a train load. In cases where high value or highly urgent consignments are able to attract premium rates, a train load may be quite small (and mail is light!). In general though, the operator's assets will produce the most favourable return when they are being used as near to the limit of their capabilities as is practicable. If the traffic on offer from origin to destination does not amount to a full train load (either financially or physically), the operator can:-

1. Charge sufficient to overcome the economies of scale he is not achieving, if the traffic will bear it.
2. Aggregate trainloads by exchanging portions between trains which are themselves fully loaded for the different legs of their journeys.
3. Aggregate trainloads by building up trains from smaller "trips" and breaking them down again into "trips" at the end of the trunk journey, but in the knowledge that trip working may not pay for the full costs of the resources it employs.

2 Wagon solutions to higher containers are, so far, uneconomic. Special wagons cost more, but are weight-restricted or have shorter available load platforms; this not only costs more per unit but also makes inefficient use of train and crane area length capacities.

4. Aggregate train loads by using road haulage for collection and delivery to/from rail heads.
5. Decline the business.

Options 1–4 are shown in Figure 5.1. Options 2 and 3 are crucially dependent on the volumes of business on offer, and the degree of certainty and variability in the traffic being forwarded. The economic effectiveness of locomotives, wagons and crews is governed by their ability to move revenue-earning loads. Once resources are allocated to a network carrying portions for different destinations or to trip working, the costs are effectively fixed until and unless the resources can be dispensed with or allocated to other revenue streams. If there is certainty that the portion trains or the trips will earn sufficient revenue to make a profit on their long-run costs then they are justified and will make a contribution to profit. However, it is tempting to regard trip workings as marginal to the full costs of the trunk services and ignore

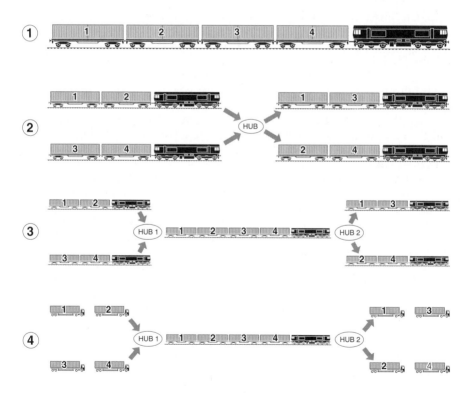

Figure 5.1 Options for Train Portion Working

the inescapable fact that the trip resources may well not properly cover their full costs, thus generating losses or imposing unacceptable cross-subsidy burdens on the trunk legs in question.

Even when portions or trips do generate worthwhile revenue, it is also clear that they generate a higher level of costs than those associated with well-planned trunk workings (see also chapter 17). Shunting manoeuvres call for additional infrastructure and staff and also impose additional safety risks which it will incur cost to mitigate. During the time spent shunting, main line locomotives and crews may be under-utilised or even idle and the shorter the journeys being made on trip or portion legs, the more challenging it becomes to produce effective resource diagrams. Even where there is constant and sufficient commercial demand for the services it will be difficult to balance demands throughout the various legs and there remains a constant risk of under-utilisation of expensive assets.

5.3 The Case of Freightliner

Particular illustrations come from operations conveying intercontinental containers, such as those carried out by Freightliner in Britain. The nature of transoceanic container shipping means that large ships are served by large ports and that there are generally high volumes of containers requiring inland transportation. Therefore, it is possible to meet some of the conditions described above; portion trains can be planned and, with keen commercial awareness and the use of intelligent pricing, it is possible to ensure that there is a high utilisation of planned capacity on a network of services. However, containers can easily be carried by road – after all, they have to go by road once they reach an inland rail terminal – and margins are therefore low and indifferent to the economic architecture of rail. The number of ports is smaller than the number of inland terminals and, whilst it should normally always be possible to fill trains to and from the ports, balancing this against the terminals will be more difficult. This makes the additional costs of planning, providing and operating portion trains measurably higher than direct point-to-point operations. Such portion services are always likely to be the weakest from an economic viewpoint. Whether the non-user and environmental benefits of carrying less-than-trainload volumes through such a network justify subsidy (or above average subsidy) is a political question but one which is currently being answered affirmatively. Where government or its agents want contestable subsidies related directly to the traffic moved, it is difficult to see how any operator can afford to run a network of trains when competitors can abstract the simplest block train traffic.

Train operating costs are made up of the traction costs (including fuel and crew), wagon costs and track access charges. Track access charges are determined by the Rail Regulator from his assessment of the network manager's costs, and set out in complex public tables as described in section 3.5. The

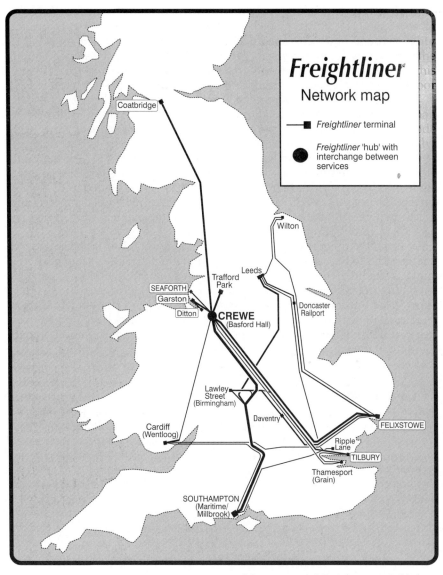

Map courtesy of Freightmaster Publishing

Figure 5.2 The Freightliner Network

other costs are private to the operator, and will depend on the utilisation he can achieve from his resources, which may be governed by such things as loading and turn round times, customer requirements and the physical characteristics of the routes. An operator's perception of these costs will also depend on his accounting systems and conventions and the way in which he treats financing costs, capital costs, overheads and so forth. Individual services may vary by as much as 20% or more from the average (both up and down), dependent on the factors outlined above. Once you know what your costs are, they can be compared with the revenue and profitability can be determined.

Networks are always complex, and understanding them (and their finances) is usually fraught with problems. Network strategy needs to keep the complexities to a minimum and provide as much clarity as possible so that operational performance can be robust and financial assessment can be secure. Unless this is done, freight networks can rapidly become unsustainable, and it can safely be said that operators should avoid them, if they can, unless they provide rewards commensurate with the risk.

As a result of this, in April 2002, Freightliner re-organised some of its services, in order to reduce the amount of shunting taking place at the hub of the network, Crewe. The hub-and-spoke nature of our network was changed, with more trains running directly from port to inland terminal, although in a number of cases they still run via Crewe, for purposes of changing traincrew. Worries that the new pattern would not suit all customers have proved to be largely unfounded and the success of the new policy demonstrates our understanding of the key issues as set out above.

5.4 Conclusions

Network strategy, therefore, has two components; obtaining the right lines and routes on which to run at affordable prices and running the combination of trains on that network which produces the best profit result. In the case of Freightliner, the best service pattern appears to be point-to-point. Simple, really!

6 Operational Approaches and Applied Technologies of Leading Heavy Haul Rail Freight Businesses

Arthur Durham (WS Atkins) with *Felix Schmid* (University of Sheffield)

6.1 Introduction

The providers of all modes of transport are developing their processes and skills as the demands of customers change. Competition is thus not static but evolving in both scope and scale. The search for the Holy Grail of profitable rail freight operations is becoming more and more difficult as railway businesses have to compete in the face of new logistics and transport solutions which are often more convenient and lower cost. Government interventions that focus on quick fixes and short-term gains have taken their toll on both state owned and private rail freight operations around the world.

However, there are pockets of excellence, particularly in highly specialised sectors where enhanced organisational approaches by privately owned operators and technical innovation have paved the way for business success despite competition from other modes. The authors of this chapter describe the challenges faced by heavy haul rail operators on three continents and outline the common strands of the operational approaches and technologies adopted by the leading heavy haul rail freight businesses.

A 2001 record for the then heaviest freight train run by any freight railway provides a good example of the progress achieved by the private operators: On 21 June 2001, BHP Iron Ore (see below) operated a train grossing 99,734t over a distance of 275km using 1 driver and 8 diesel locomotives distributed amongst the 682 ore wagons [1].

6.2 Ownership and Organisational Approaches

North America

In North America (i.e. Canada and the United States), private ownership and operation of vertically integrated railway systems have been the norm for over 170 years. This offers the management of the businesses a high level of control over the quality of the offer to the customer. Competition between major traffic centres ensures lower tariffs and continuous enhancements of the products. In some areas, railways without their own tracks to a particular freight hub have so-called trackage[(1)] rights on other railways to prevent anti-

---

[1] Trackage rights allow an operator without tracks to use the tracks of a competitor to reach a particular traffic generator, a major port, for example.

39

competitive behaviour. In recent times, similar arrangements have been adopted in Mexico, following the successful privatisation of the national railway. Thanks to the common standards for track gauge and loading gauge, adopted from the beginning of the railway age and developed continuously under the auspices of the American Association of Railroads (AAR), freight traffic now flows freely over a network of 380,000km of track without the need for transhipment. A standardised railway-owned fleet of wagons is complemented by shipper-owned fleets amounting to about 45% of the total of 1,500,000 rail freight wagons in North America in 2001 [2].

North American freight railways are profitable because they have developed relentlessly their asset base and operating methods, adapting to changing market needs and increasing productivity. Some examples of changes and improvements are:

- Elimination of most passenger services from interstate railroad networks, with the remaining services operated by AMTRAK (USA) and VIA-Rail (Canada) with government subsidies, essentially for tourism and to satisfy political demands;
- Wagon payloads have been increased from 18t in the 1800s to 100t in 1999, with purchasers in 2002 largely specifying 130t gross 4-axle vehicles;
- Axle loads of vehicles with traditional 2-axle, three-piece cast bogies have been successively raised from 25t to 32.5t over the last thirty years;
- Train configurations have changed from the typical 48 wagon and 724t payload freight train of the 1920s to today's heavy haul bulk commodity consists with between 4 and 6 3200kW (4400hp) locomotives hauling 120 to 150 wagons of 130t gross laden weight, with only two crew members.

The result of these developments is an integrated network of different types of railroads, including six very large national Class 1 operators, eight large Class 2 systems, thirty to forty moderate size regional systems and about 500 "short-line" operators, some combined into larger groups. Core rail freight in the United States has staged a remarkable recovery following the abolition of protected tariffs in 1980. The traditional railway organisations subscribing to the common carrier paradigm (see section 2.4) have effectively disappeared and the businesses have re-emerged as focused service providers, each with specific markets, appropriate cost bases and particular service capabilities. All this has been achieved at the cost of major job losses and the abandonment of services to many communities. Some communities and farmers' co-operatives now support seasonal freight services. The remaining jobs in the American freight sector are more secure today and the focused services are more reliable and relevant. Staff productivity has increased, particularly on the smaller systems, although the unions are still blocking some essential developments, e.g. the single manning of trains.

Operating speeds have generally been increased, even though many of the short-line operators have to operate their services at very low speeds due to the poor condition of the tracks [2], particularly because of the increased axle loads. In three distinct service segments, North American railways now operate rolling stock with 30t to 35t maximum axle-load capability at competitive speeds, namely:

- Relatively low speed general merchandise traffic (60–80km/h);
- Moderate speed bulk commodity trains, e.g., for iron ore and coal (80km/h);
- Higher speed inter-modal container, swap-body and piggy-back traffic (120-130km/h).

Haulage distances range from power-station coal flows of between 100 and 500km in the Powder River Basin area of Wyoming to transcontinental double-stack container flows, covering transits of 3000km and more. Many of the emerging freight operators in Asia, Europe and Africa emulate the North American practice of long and heavy trains hauled by several (diesel) locomotives, although most flows cover much shorter distances and often have to compete with passenger operations on the same tracks.

American interests joined forces with local businesses to take over most of Mexico's freight railway operations upon privatisation of the state railway company in 1997, as long-term concessions. In 2003, two of these operations merged with the Kansas City Southern system which had been instrumental in setting up the Mexican operations [3]. Other North American freight networks are also still being consolidated, with access to prime traffic generators and intermodal hubs at a premium. Both Chicago and Kansas City now constrain American rail freight because of yard capacity and limitations of the inter-company transfer operations, e.g. the Chicago Harbour Belt Railroad which is jointly owned by some Class 1 railroads. On the negative side, many American freight railroads are not in a position to maintain and renew their assets for the long term [4 and 5] since tariffs are too low.

Australia
There were three distinct reasons for the development of railway systems on this continent and three main construction periods. On the East Coast of Australia, in Queensland, a state owned and operated network was conceived back in 1863. 1067mm (3'6") gauge was adopted for cost reasons and to allow rapid construction, thanks to the smaller curve radii which eased the overcoming of topological obstacles to opening up the vast area of the colony. This network extended to 9600 route km by 2002 and further extensions are being built to tap new freight flows. In 2000, the network carried freight to the tune of 37,600Mtkm, on average 4Mtkm per km of route per year.

Outside the Brisbane area, the network is largely dedicated to freight flows, mostly coal but also some cattle movements. Coal is transported from large open-cast coal mines situated between 300 and 500km inland to the major ports for shipment to Europe and Asia. The track quality on the main electrified routes (25kV, 50Hz AC) allows high speed block train operation, interspersed with some limited long distance passenger services (Queenslander etc.), largely for social needs purposes. Very few freight flows move through Brisbane where there is an important suburban passenger network. A similar but much smaller network was constructed in Western Australia, around Perth, also using 1067mm gauge, to move agricultural produce and iron ore.

In the same time frame (i.e. between 1870 and 1900), networks were developed in New South Wales, South Australia and Victoria to carry agricultural products and coal for export and to supply the emerging major cities of Adelaide, Melbourne and Sydney. Some of these networks were constructed in broad gauge (1600mm) and others in standard gauge (1435mm). All of these experienced a severe downturn in the latter part of the 20th century, despite the construction of standard gauge links between the territories. Transhipment at the gauge break points created inefficiencies and slowed down transit times. In the 1990s though the fortunes of these networks started to revive, thanks to investment in modernisation, gauge conversion and the advent of private and open access operators. However, some new gauge breaks were created as a result of the continued development of the standard gauge interstate network and of state-initiated gauge conversions [6].

The mid 1960s, the second development period, saw the discovery of vast deposits of high grade hematite (iron) ore in the mountain ranges of Western Australia, the Pilbara. Coupled with the ever increasing international demand for steel, this led to the development of three private and fully vertically integrated mining, transportation and handling operations based on heavy haul railways, namely, BHP Iron Ore, Hamersley Iron Railway, owned by Rio Tinto, and the shorter Robe River system, as shown in Figure 6.2. All three systems were built to standard gauge [7]. In 2002, the Robe River and Hamersley Iron Railway systems agreed to build a link between the routes at the crossing point to allow shipment of ore from Robe River's West Angelas mine to Cape Lambert, by means of a 60km branch off the Hamersley Route.

The Hamersley Iron Railway system [8] opened in 1966 and operates 638 kilometres of track, carrying ore to the sea port of Dampier from three mines, located in the Hamersley Ranges, the most distant (Yandi) being 388 kilometres away. BHP Iron Ore, opened in 1969, currently operates 636 kilometres of route serving four mines and a staging yard located at Port Hedland, located some 428 kilometres from the furthest mine, Mount Newman. The BHP railway routes are formed of two joint ventures, Goldsworthy with 210 route km and Newman with 426 route km. Robe River operates a total of 265 route km and uses the tracks of Hamersley Iron Railway to reach its port at Cape Lambert. In 2003, Rio Tinto took over the Robe River operation and combined the Robe River Railway with the Hamersley Iron Railway to form Pilbara Railway Co.

Soon after the start of these operations it became apparent that the world's steel mills required significantly larger volumes of ore than the operations had been designed to supply originally. As the throughput increased, so did the pressure to operate longer and heavier trains, to limit capital expenditure, to contain operating expenditure and to maximise the single-track systems' capacities.

Until 2002, BHP and Hamersley each hauled between 50 and 60Mt net per year, equivalent to about 100Mt gross. Robe River hauled about half of this. In the case of Hamersley this translates into 23,000Mtkm or about 50Mtkm/route km, more than ten times the corresponding amount for Queensland Rail. Currently, BHP and Hamersley are probably the most productive freight railways in the world. In 2004, BHP and Pilbara Railway Co. are each expected to move 100 Mt net. Salient characteristics of the systems are:

- Trains have changed from typical configurations consisting of 144 four-axle wagons with 30t axle load and carrying 10,000t of ore to configurations with 240 wagons with up to 37t axle load carrying 26,000t ore while running at 40 to 75km/h [10];
- Trains of up to 37,000t gross are hauled using mid and rear locomotives controlled by radio from the cab in the front locomotive [7];

Picture courtesy of John Kirk

Figure 6.1 Heavy Haul in the Pilbara

43

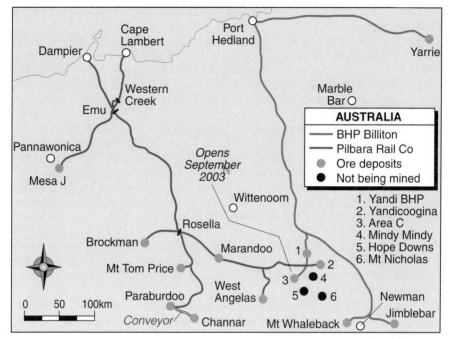

Map courtesy of Railway Gazette International

Figure 6.2 Map of the Pilbara Area

- All the lines have been built so that the ruling gradients favour loaded trains, apart from the Yandi branch of Hamersley Iron where the 29,000t gross trains have to climb 250m in 98km, an average gradient of 0.25% with the ruling gradient set at 0.6%. This requires the combined 13MW of power of 4 GE Dash 9-44CW locomotives, two at the front and two at the back, to travel at an average speed of 40km/h;
- Since operations started, axle loads have increased from 23 to 37t and are soon to rise to 40t. Much of this was achieved by increasing the predictability of ore car loading [10].

Throughout, the objective has been to reduce operating cost by minimising the number of trains and thus the number of drivers and by limiting the infrastructure requirement. The number of passing loops, for example, is a direct function of the number of trains in service. Providing longer passing loops involves laying more plain line track while additional passing loops require maintenance intensive point-work and more complex control sys-

44

tems. Only six to eight trains per day are needed in each direction to satisfy the shipping schedule.

The operators have carried out a great deal of research to improve track quality and to extend rail-life by buying in better rail qualities and using techniques such as grinding to maintain optimal profiles. In particular, they have adopted wheel and rail interface management at various level of sophistication:

- Choice of different rail profiles for tangent and curved track, single and two point wheel/rail contact based on an assessment of the effect of tractive effort on wheel/rail deterioration;
- Friction modification by lubrication and surface coating;
- Endeavours to provide route specific and compatible wheel and rail profiles.

The third phase of expansion of Australian rail freight started in late 2000 with the decision to build the line from Alice Springs to Darwin through the centre of Australia. This is essentially a freight railway designed to carry perishable food and mining products to the port of Darwin for shipment to the Pacific Rim countries [11]. The project is jointly financed by public authorities and private sector interests. Other new routes will be developed by the *Australian Rail Track Corporation* set up in 1997 to manage the 4400km interstate railway system. Open access will lead to further consolidation of Australia's rail freight operators.

South Africa
The South African rail freight industry is currently administered by Spoornet, a vertically integrated and state owned business division of Transnet Pty Ltd, a parastatal holding company which was created out of major parts of South African Railways (SAR). This 1067mm gauge[2] network, the most important railway in Africa, was developed largely in the 20th century to carry mining and agricultural products and to move large numbers of passengers in the major industrial conurbations. Three decades ago, SAR was not commercially driven and operated with medium axle loads (18.5t per axle), a level then common in Europe. Track was relatively light and there was little "know-how" about the nature of wheel and rail interaction or, for that matter, on the technical nature of vehicle steering. The accepted norm for rail life was of the order of 300Mt gross of traffic and wheel profile life was of the order of 20,000km, translating into a 100,000km total wheel life.

Ever since the de-regulation of the transport industry, brought about by the abolition of the road haulage permit system in the early 1980s and followed by the relaxation of road freight payload limits from 28t to 56t, the rail freight industry for general goods progressively lost market share. By the end

---

2 Also known as Cape gauge and used in Southern Africa, India and on the conventional network in Japan.

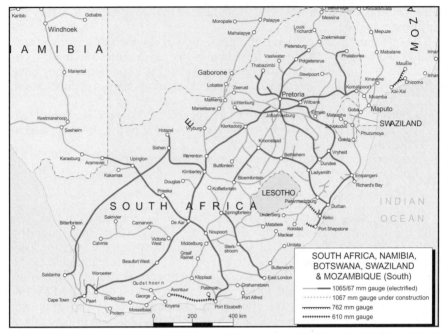

Map courtesy of Railway Gazette International

Figure 6.3 Map of South Africa

of 2000 only 22% of the 820Mt of goods transported within the South African borders were carried by rail.

The heavy haul industry in South Africa was born out of the need to transport efficiently iron ore and manganese over long distances to the ports from where these commodities could be shipped to the end user. Electrification of the main corridors took place in the 1960s with power supplied at 3000Vdc to eliminate steam traction, while minimising the need for imported diesel. In the main corridors to Durban etc, vacuum braked trains were operated initially, using 73t hopper wagons fitted with three piece bogies with plain bearings.

Train handling constraints due to technical limitations imposed by the rolling stock and difficult down gradients restricted the length of these trains to 35 wagons. Efficiency demanded longer and heavier trains. This led to the introduction of gondola wagons with improved load to tare mass, bogies fitted with roller bearings and AAR standard air brake systems. The first of these 50 wagon air brake trains were introduced in 1970. The train length was subsequently changed to 100 wagons, resulting in trains with a gross mass of 7400t, hauled by heavy electric locomotives, all on 1067mm track.

46

The need to export much greater volumes of iron ore and coal required that deep-water ports be constructed at Saldanha Bay and Richards Bay (see Figure 6.3). An 861 km single track line with passing loops was built to link the iron ore deposits at Sishen to the port of Saldanha Bay, initially as a private venture of the South African steel producer ISCOR and not connected to the national railway network. The Saldahna Bay line was electrified at 50kV 50Hz AC, a revolutionary choice at the time, and opened in 1976. The 5km long trains consist of 202 four-axle ore wagons of 100t gross laden mass and are hauled by three six-axle electric locomotives rated at 3780kW, assisted by a generally falling gradient from the mines to the port.

A 580 km heavy haul line was also built to link the coal mining area with the port of Richards Bay, becoming operational in 1976. The Richards Bay line evolved as two distinct operations, a 25kV AC trunk haul and a 3000V DC collection network joined at a marshalling yard located approximately 400 kilometres from the port. The 40 odd steam coal export mines, using a variety of wagon loading facilities, are serviced by short trains on a set of routes electrified at 3000V DC, which effectively forms part of the national network. On arrival at the marshalling yard, the short trains are reconfigured into 200 wagon trains before they undertake the last portion of their journey to the port on the new line.

Today, these Cape gauge heavy haul systems are commercially driven, operate trains with 26t axle loads and are experimenting with axle loads of up to 30t. Typical rail life of 1500Mt gross has been surpassed and re-railing programmes are extended to up to 2000Mt gross. A wheel profile life of 400,000km is being achieved regularly (1.6Mkm per wheel) [12], partly thanks to the introduction of radially steering bogies of the Scheffel type.

Most heavy haul railroads dedicated to the transport of iron ore and coal are driven by very competitive and demanding markets. The South African heavy haul railway industry is no exception. With premium rail costing $826/t (1999 prices) and Spoornet having to face the prospect of re-railing both their heavy haul lines within two decades, the increase in performance to up to five times the original norm has had a substantial impact on the profitability of these routes.

European Experience
Experience of heavy haul with high axle loads, above 22.5t per axle, is relatively limited in Europe, with many railways still restricting axle loads to 18t on parts of their networks. Even though British Rail had started successful operation at 25.5t for aggregate haulage in 1966, the practice was not adopted elsewhere. However, there are some established high axle load operations, most notably, the heavy haul system of RWE Rheinbraun in Germany and the Malmbanan in Sweden, formerly part of the Swedish State Railways (SJ).

The German energy company RWE Rheinbraun sources its fuel from a number of very large lignite (brown coal) opencast operations in the Cologne area. Since 1954[3], the company has operated an extensive, but little known railway network linking the mining sites of Garzweiler and Hambach to the four local RWE power stations with a combined output of 11,000MW$_e$ peak, in 2003. The mines and railway network also supply 3 refining operations, that is, briquette plants. The operation runs heavy haul trains on a network of 60km of double track main line, with a total track length of 320km of which 230 are electrified at 6000Vac 50Hz. Most of the rolling stock and all locomotives are designed to a loading gauge that prohibits their operation on the network of Deutsche Bahn.

The maximum axle load of the four-axle wagons for the lignite trains is 35t and that for the eight axle wagons (with 4 sub-bogies) of the overburden and back-fill trains is 30t. The modern Bo-Bo locomotives bought between 1998 and 2000 weigh in at 140t and have a rating of 2800kW. The heaviest coal trains consist of one locomotive and 21 wagons and are 270m long, with a total train mass of 3000t. Most coal trains though are limited to 14 wagons and are 185m long. Spoil trains are limited to one locomotive and 10 wagons and are 160m long, with a train mass of 2500t. Based on a tare weight of the coal wagons of 33t, the most heavily used section between the North-South railway and the Hambach mine carries 65Mt per year for the coal transport alone. Added to this is a substantial level of spoil, ash and overburden haulage.

Track maintenance on the RWE Rheinbraun railway is necessarily of a very high standard and is undertaken by the company's own staff using modern machinery and equipment. Track is of the ballasted type with heavy concrete sleepers and UIC60 rail. All the point-work in the main tracks is of the swing-nose crossing type to minimise wear and impact loads on both wheels and rails. This is essential since all the trains operate at the relatively high speed of 60km/h. Overall, the traffic carried in 2002 amounted to 1420Mtkm.

In Northern Sweden, the iron ore operation of the mining company LKAB requires transport of its output from the Kiruna area to the ports of Narvik and Luleå. Transport forms a substantial part of the cost of the operations. Between 1993 and 2000, 520km of this single-track electrified route (15kVac, 50Hz) were upgraded for axle loads of 30t instead of 25t. In 1996, progress was accelerated thanks to the formation of MTAB as the railway operator, with LKAB as the majority partner. Operations with new, heavier trains started between Malmberget and Luleå on 7 March 2001 [13]. Co-Co+Co-Co locomotives rated at 10,800kW now haul 68 high capacity ore wagons over this part of the route. The remainder of the route is due to be upgraded by 2004. Based on their experience, MTAB have concluded that they could lower transport cost by one third, thanks to the move from 25 to 30t axle-load, see Table 6.1, adapted from [14].

---

3 This is the opening year of the North-South railway, the main trunk route serving all the power stations.

Axle-loads	25t	30t		25t	30t
No. locomotives	17	9	Total weight of train	5200	6800
No. wagons	936	650	Loaded trains per 24h	19	12
Payload per wagon	80t	100t	Loaded trains per year	6910	4230
Train length	470m	740m	Annual loco fleet usage	2.4Mkm	1.4Mkm
Wagons per train	52t	68	Annual wagon fleet usage	120Mkm	96Mk
Payload per train	4100t	6700t			

Table 6.1 Comparison of operating requirements for 25 and 30t axle-loads, based on [14]

6.3 Commonalities

In a modern economy, a freight railway must have a certain critical traffic density to be viable. The haulage charges levied must offer a return on the original capital invested and must cover the cost of operation, maintenance and renewal. Whilst justifiably proud of the tonnages handled, Queensland Rail's operation is marginal in revenue terms but essential to the profitable coal mining industry and extensions to the network are thus added regularly as new mines are being opened.

Development and Ownership

In many instances, it was the major shipper who initially built a heavy haul route to open up the resources of a particular area. This was the case for the line from Sishen to Saldahna and is still true for the lines in the Pilbara area of Australia. In such situations, the economics of the railway tend to be tied into the success of the main shipper and thus are not exposed to true market forces. A key example of such an arrangement can be found in the Western Sahara where the railway from Tazadid to Nouadhibou (704km) forms part of the now state-owned phosphate mining operation. Rheinbraun of Germany has operated a company internal heavy haul network on a similar basis for many years.

More recently, the iron ore producers at Kiruna established Malmbanan (see above), a joint venture of the mining company LKAB with Sweden's Banverket, for the operation of the electrified heavy haul line between Narvik and Luleå. The line had been operated in a vertically integrated manner by SJ before the separation between infrastructure and operations in Sweden, in 1988. The key objective of this joint venture was to establish a form of virtual vertical integration to ensure better and more cost-effective use of an asset essential to the mining industry.

Vertical Integration
The main benefits of operating a vertically integrated system with dedicated resources and a long term business perspective may be summarised as follows:

- Sound understanding of all business processes and their inter-relationships;
- Substantial degree of control over the asset base;
- Opportunity to create goal-focussed organisational structures with short chains of command and agile, multi-skilled work forces;
- Potential for early identification and analysis of deviations from the steady state;
- Opportunity to adopt an integrated economic life cycle cost strategy for all asset maintenance, renewal, re-engineering or replacement programmes.
- Scope for broad based commercial and operational risk management programmes;
- System optimisation of all wear-fatigue and impact interfaces.

By their very nature, heavy haul freight operations involve the management of many critical interfaces, often requiring difficult trade-off decisions, ideally based on whole life cost considerations:

- Wheel wear vs. rail wear and train capacity vs. track maintenance;
- Vehicle first cost vs. infrastructure attrition (speed & load related dynamic forces);
- Pantograph/catenary interactions;
- Gradient vs. speed vs. power supply or prime mover capacity;
- Traction or braking forces vs. speed and journey time;
- Autonomous power[4] vs. electrification;
- Operational optimisation of cycle time = loading time + train formation time + train inspection time + train travelling time +offloading time + train standing time.

Today's heavy axle load rail operations thus demand optimisation at the wheel-rail interface and in many other areas. A good example is the adoption of swing-nose crossings for the point-work on both Queensland Rail's

---

4 Train with a prime mover and on-board energy storage. Today largely the domain of the diesel engine.

and Rheinbraun's heavy haul operations. While the first cost is much higher than that of fixed cast crossings, there are much greater long term savings in maintenance[5] and in the avoidance of unnecessary disruption to services. Organisational separation at the wheel-rail interface may work against this type of optimisation [15]. However, there are encouraging signs that new contractual arrangements and better monitoring systems may facilitate the management of disaggregated railways' operations.

Separating infrastructure management from the management of operations above the rail has the effect of disengaging infrastructure investment decisions from rolling stock and other operations investments. Disengaging these investment decisions from each other, even partially, is like to have the ultimate effect of sub-optimising the cost structure and of impeding the process of network rationalisation.

"No transport mode involves as synergistic a relationship as the steel wheel/steel rail combination or, as we speak of it today, vehicle-track dynamics"[8].

Applied Technologies
The International Heavy Haul Association (IHHA) was founded in the late 1970s by American, Australian, Canadian and South African Heavy Haul operators. The association has subsequently expanded to include Chinese, Russian and Swedish Heavy Haul operators. The original criterion for membership was the operation of a commercially viable and vertically integrated rail freight business operating with at least 26t axle-loads. The members of the association meet every two years and, by way of workshops and seminars, share their technical experiences.

The ever-increasing requirement to compete with road hauliers, coastal shipping and barge traffic by lowering rail freight costs have lead to many leading edge technologies being conceived, tested, refined and transferred among the members. Such technologies include:

- The realisation of 30t plus axle loads;
- The successful operation of freight trains with more than 200 wagons;
- The control of locomotives in the middle and at the end of trains from the cab of the leading locomotive;
- The realisation of a rail life of more than 1,500Mt gross on curved track;
- Steady state wheel life of wagons in excess of 1.6Mkm;
- Optimised maintenance and life cycle models for fixed and movable assets;
- Vehicle behaviour models and derailment risk assessments.

---

5 QR reported in 1999 that it had been necessary on some routes to surface weld conventional crossings at intervals of 2 weeks or less whereas swing-nose crossings were virtually maintenance free.

BHP-Iron Ore provides a good example of progress in operations management: From 1972 to 2002 train length increased from 131 to 240 wagons and train cycle time reduced from 40h to 28h, yielding much lower cost. Scientific investigation has also shown that axle-load increases are possible without risking major maintenance cost increases. Nielsen and Stensson [16], for example, have shown that axle loads can be increased by 20% from 25t to 30t at the same time as increasing speed by 20% while only incurring an increase in track wear of 3%.

Engineering Skills
Heavy haul operations challenge engineering skills as much as, if not more than high speed railways. Happily, engineers are at their best when they are confronted with problems and incipient failure!

Firstly, once a decision has been made to increase axle loads, engineers will have to find solutions to the problems arising from this change. Herbert Scheffel took up just such a challenge of high wheel wear following the introduction of higher axle loads. He overcame the then limitations of bogie construction and created a cross-braced self-steering bogie that increased wheel life, not just incrementally, but by orders of magnitude.

Secondly, engineers from different disciplines need to talk to each other. The leaders in the Heavy Haul railway industry have a multidisciplinary approach to all infrastructure interface management and research.

Thirdly, there is and must be investment in the training of engineers. Within the IHHA engineers are encouraged to rub shoulders with the best in their field and are made aware of the latest benchmarks and are challenged to improve on them.

6.4 Heavy Axle Load Case Study

Allan M. Zarembski and Jim Blaze, ZETA-TECH Associates, Inc., for Railway Age, edited by F. Schmid

Introduction
The present case study on the economic implications of raising axle loads from 30t to the current US limit of 32.5t (286,000lb) has been adapted from an article in Railway Age, with material from a paper presented at the UIC/ERRI Heavy Axle Load Conference on 11 March 2003. The kind permissions of the authors and the publishers are gratefully acknowledged herewith. All numerical values in the case study have been translated into metric tonnes [t], with US short ton values in brackets. HAL stands for Heavy Axle Load operations.

By increasing the weight or capacity of freight wagons, it is possible to increase train capacity by 10% to 25%. The consequential reduction in the number of wagons required to carry a fixed amount of goods results in a

Axle Load		Gross Mass	Net/Tare	Status
t (tonne)	US tons	kg		
22	24	88,000	n.a.	Old European Limit
25	27.5	100,000	2.7	UK and Select European limit
30	33	120,000	3.1	North American free interchange limit Banverket limit on Malmbanan
32.5	36	130,000	3.5	Current standard HAL weight for North American Class 1 RR
35.5	39	142,000	3.7	In use in Australia Used on some routes in US

Table 6.2 Gross Mass and Net/Tare ratio as a function of standard axle loads

measurable decrease in the capital costs associated with wagon acquisition as well as in reductions in equipment maintenance costs, thanks to the reduced number of wagons. This is shown for a range of typical axle load values in Table 6.2.

In addition, there is a corresponding reduction in the number of trains required to carry the same fixed quantity of goods with resulting savings in fuel, crew, and (in many cases) locomotive costs. This may also result in more capacity on the route for other services.

This trend to heavier wagons has been accompanied by considerable research into the costs and benefits of larger wagons and heavier trains. This includes both the issues of increasing wagon size, through the introduction of new equipment, and of increasing the loading of existing wagons. Whilst there are many benefits from a train operations point of view, there are also clear drawbacks from the point of view infrastructure maintenance. Studies in both Australia [18] and the United States [19-24] have examined the issues. These studies have been augmented by a multi-year testing programme at the Facility for Accelerated Service Testing in the US. The tests focused on the impact of heavy (36 tonne) axle load equipment [25]. ZETA-TECH developed its own economic cost/benefit system-wide assessment method based on its accumulated experience since the mid 1980s as shown in Table 6.3.

Component	Damage Exponent n	Damage per Axle*	Damage per MGt*
Rail Wear	1.0	+9%	0%
Rail Fatigue (internal)	3.0	+29%	+19%
Rail Fatigue (surface)	1.8	+16%	+7%
Rail Joints	3.33	+32%	+21%
Sleepers	1.5	+13%	+4%
Good Ballast	1.0	+9%	0%
Poor Ballast	5.6	+60%	+47%
Turnouts	3.0	+29%	+19%
*Damage per axle and MGt are based on the introduction of 130t wagons.			

Table 6.3 Heavy axle load (HAL) damage factors and their impact

The ZETA-TECH Assessment Method
The primary analysis approach for the effect of HAL traffic on the track structure and its key components is the damage exponent heavy axle load analysis approach [19, 20, 22]. This approach was publicly introduced in the late 1980s and has been validated, calibrated, upgraded and refined in several recent studies [24, 26]. It is based on a detailed evaluation of component deterioration and their replacement over time, calculated as a cost per axle passing over the section of track under study.

This damage exponent analysis approach uses the damage factor equation:

Damage Factor (per component) = $[P/P_0]^n$

Where P = new axle load (32.5t)
P_0 = old axle load (30t)
n = damage exponent

This damage factor equation determines the per axle damage effect. By adjusting this damage to account for the difference in net to tare ratios between wagons (and thus the different commodity capacity per wagon), the damage per MGt can be calculated likewise. The individual damage exponents are presented in Table 6.3 by component and component failure mechanism since these factors vary for different failure mechanisms [19]. Table 6.3 also presents the component based damage effects on a per-axle and a per-MGt basis. Again note that the per-MGt results have been adjusted to account for the reduced number of axles needed to carry the same level of commodity movement.

It should be noted that these damage factors and the associated damage mechanisms were developed based on extensive research in the area of track component degradation and the factors were subsequently calibrated against the heavy axle load test results obtained from the Facility for Accelerated Service Testing (FAST) [19, 20, 26]. The damage impacts are then applied to the actual railway's permanent way maintenance costs, by component area (e.g. rail, sleepers, ballast, and turnout), to determine the corresponding increase in total maintenance expenditure.

The Short-Line[6] Case Study

ZETA-TECH conducted a heavy axle load (HAL) study on a midwestern U.S. regional railroad with approximately 230km (143miles) of track maintained to FRA Class 3 standards[7], with a 50km/h (30mph) operating speed. Annual traffic volumes averaged 2.7MGt (or 3MGT – 3 million gross tons) over recent years and was moved predominantly in 30 tonne axle load wagons. No HAL traffic was permitted at the time of the study. The traffic was primarily grain (53%), coal (8%) and sugar (13%). The railway's route topography is flat, with gradients generally less than 0.5% (1 in 200) and curve radii greater than 880m (less than two degrees). Overall track condition was excellent for FRA Class 3. Rail was predominantly 115-pound RE jointed rail and sleepers (ties) and ballast were in generally good condition.

HAL cars represent an increase in axle load from 30t (32.9tons) to 32.5t (35.8tons), or about 8.5 %. This results in an increase in the net load carried of 9.1t (10tons). Depending upon car design, this results in an 8–10% increase in load utilisation per car, per trip. This is one of the secrets of achieving a net financial return: the increased costs associated with permanent way maintenance are offset in part by the number of axles needed to carry the same amount of commodity.

Using ZETA-TECH's HAL analysis models, potential damage effects were determined for this low traffic density short-line railroad. The following track maintenance cost increases were determined, based on an initial assumption that 100% of all existing traffic would be converted to HAL wagons with 32.5t axle-loads:

- Increase in rail and turnout maintenance costs[8]:   27.5%
- Increase in sleeper costs: 12.0%

6 Short lines are small railway operations which are often spin-off organisations set up to run branch lines formerly owned and operated by Class 1 US freight railroads.
7 The US Federal Railroad Administration (FRA) sets safety classes of track with associated maximum speeds within each FRA Class of Track
8 Including capital costs associated with rail and turnout replacement

- Increase in surfacing costs: 23.0%
- Overall increase in maintenance costs 17.0%

However, these increased track maintenance costs were shown to be offset by the operating costs savings with an overall cost benefit of 6.6%.

The particular traffic pattern and available rolling stock on the railroad allowed only a transfer of 50% of the grain traffic to HAL operation. The study results were therefore refined and showed that an increase in maintenance costs of 4.7% could accommodate half of the grain traffic (27% of total traffic) in HAL freight cars, again more than outweighed by the reduced operating cost.

From these two variable market-based assumptions, even the short-line railroads can anticipate that the expense of shifting customer traffic to HAL equipment is line-specific and traffic-density-specific. The financial benefits from lower operating costs and lower equipment capital costs have to be factored in, as do financial gains from certain marketing advantages. Per-car revenue will change, based on rates and agreements between all parties involved in a particular flow. After the costs and benefits are calculated, a railroad must examine its business situation and prepare the resulting pro forma implications before proceeding.

Normally, however, the much larger Class 1 railroads are the first to migrate towards offering customers a share of the net economic benefits of heavy axle-loads. The big railroads can achieve net savings over huge distances (e.g. 1000 miles), resulting in fewer axle passes (including when empty).

The need for an action plan

On the basis of the cost benefit assessment for the study case, ZETA-TECH developed the following action plan to be carried out before starting HAL operations on railways of this type: Complete ultrasonic rail test of the track in question, including rails, joints, and turnouts; spot replacement of defects; a bridge rating examination with improvements as needed; and a detailed inspection of sleepers and fasteners, particularly in all curves, with replacement as required. After start-up of HAL operations, small railroads should undertake the following maintenance programmes:

- Rail testing on older track with lighter rail weight due to increased rail fatigue and fracture risk associated with HAL traffic.
- Quality improvements to crossties used near rail joints to a minimum-standard Number 4 hardwood.
- Periodic track geometry inspections performed, at minimum, every other year. More frequent inspections may be necessary for higher density lines.
- Use of high quality ballast for all surfacing and ballast applications to reduce the rate of degradation, fouling, and loss of surface, alignment, and cross-level.
- Weld repairs of rail joints with proper grinding and slotting. This is of

particular importance on jointed rail, where HAL traffic will increase the rate of surface batter at the joints.

- Inspection of switch points and frogs on an ongoing basis, with a particular emphasis on surface condition (e.g. frog and switch point batter) geometry, and fracture of key components.
- Lubrication of all curves with radii smaller than 900m to reduce rail wear, which inevitably increases with HAL traffic.

A detailed damage factor assessment should still be carried out before contemplating the introduction of HAL traffic, regardless of the introduction of a maintenance programme as shown above.

6.5 Operational Lessons and Challenges of Heavy Haul Railways

In most countries traditional freight carriers still tend to adopt a line-of-business management structure in which sector teams focus on specific commodities and customers, with broad responsibility for the pricing, service design and revenue as well as profit results for their particular product line. Effectively, there are several internal organisations competing for network access, sometimes even involving passenger businesses, as in Britain and Switzerland. As traffic levels and congestion mount, however, so do the problems of joint use. Freight traffic is often just as service sensitive as passenger traffic. Rail freight operators are therefore no longer willing to share tracks with other services since, in so doing, they risk losing demanding customers.

Today's challenge to handle freight at a speed in line with the requirements of the customer, on-time and at the lowest possible cost, can only be addressed if track capacity is allocated without compromise to a service, in notable cases, to serve just one master. Track standards, capacity and maintenance levels can then be targeted to the specific needs of the specific customer using the line.

The main trade-off in the heavy haul freight business relates to the cost reductions on the operations side by increasing axle load and the unavoidable increase in track maintenance cost. Moving up the efficiency curve requires the right balance. This is hard enough with players in the same team; if different teams are involved, each with their own agendas, it is nigh impossible to get it right.

6.6 Conclusions

A long standing and eminent member of the International Heavy Haul Association recently put forward the hypothesis that freight railways can only survive in the information age when they obtain full benefit from exploiting available heavy haul technologies to maximum advantage. At present this appears viable only in high-volume, dedicated, bulk commodity and double-stack container traffic.

"In a globalised, informationalised environment, freight railways can only survive in niches where permissible speed and axle loads are sufficient to give them an invincible advantage over road hauliers"[17].

The prognosis looks bleak for railways that do not exploit heavy haul technologies to the full to reduce costs, and that effectively cling to traditional practices.

References

1. Editorial, 'BHP breaks its own 'heaviest train' record', Railway Gazette International, vol.157, no.8, p.508, August 2001.
2. Burns, D., 'Heavy Wagons Finally Prove Their Worth', pp. 40–41, International Journal, August 1997.
3. Editorial, 'KCS and TFM to merge', Railway Gazette International, vol.159, no.5, p.244, May 2003.
4. Burns, D., 'In Search of the Profitable Railway', Railway Business Report, Railway Gazette International, pp.24–26, 1997.
5. Burns, D., 'The cost of being profitable', Railway Gazette International, vol.158, no.8, p.417, August 2002.
6. Editorial, 'Victoria to deal with gauge frontiers', Railway Gazette International, vol.157, no.6, p367, June 2001.
7. Editorial, 'Pilbara ore lines ride out Far East recession', Railway Gazette International, vol.155, no.6, p.366, June 1999.
8. Editorial, 'Pilbara peace deal will take tracks to West Angelas', Railway Gazette International, vol.157, no.8, p.509, August 2001.
9. Vanselow, R.G (1989), 'Productivity Improvement in Heavy Haul Railway Operations - The Hamersley Experience', 4th International Heavy Haul Railway Conference, 11–15 September 1989, Brisbane.
10. Moynan, M, A. Cowin, G. Offereins and G. Tew, 'Benefits justify higher BHP axleloads', Railway Gazette International, vol.155, pp377–381, June 1999.
11. Editorial, 'Australian Dream is close to take-off', Railway Gazette International, vol.157, p.386, June 2001.
12. Le Roux A.S (1999), 'Definition of the Wheel and Rail interaction problem', Wheel/Rail Interface, STS Conference, International Heavy Haul Association 14–17 June 1999, Moscow.
13. Kalay, S. and C. Martland, 'Five phases of HAL research bring billion dollar savings', Railway Gazette International, vol.157, no.6, pp407–411, June 2001.
14. Editorial, 'Europe tiptoes towards higher axleloads', Railway Gazette International, vol. 159, no. 4, p193, April 2003.
15. Reoch, J.A. (1997) 'Railway Privatization – The CN experience', 6th International Heavy Haul Railway Conference, 6–10 April 1997, Cape Town.
16. Nielsen, J.C.O. and A. Stensson, 'Enhancing freight railways for 30 tonne axle loads', Journal of Rail and Rapid Transit, Proceedings of the Institution of Mechanical Engineers, Part F, vol.213, no.F4, pp255–263, 1999.
17. van der Meulen, R.D. (1997) 'Industrial age meets information age: Heavy Haul as a survival strategy for freight railways', 6th International Heavy Haul Railway Conference 6–10 April 1997, Cape Town.

18. Marich and U. Mass, 'Higher Axle Loads are Feasible – Economics and Technology Agree', Fourth International Heavy Haul Railways Conference, Vancouver, BC, 1986.
19. Newman, R. R., Zarembski, A. M., Resor, R., 'Burlington Northern's Economic Assessment of High Capacity/Heavy Axle Load Cars', Bulletin of the American Railway Engineering Association, Bulletin 726, Vol. 91, May 1990
20. Newman, R. R., Zarembski, A. M., Resor, R., 'The Effect of Increased Axle Loads on Maintenance of Way and Train Operations on the Burlington Northern Railroad', International Heavy Haul Railways Association/Transportation Research Board Workshop, Vancouver BC June 1991.
21. Hargrove, M., 'Economics of Heavy Axle Loads', Proceedings of the Workshop on Heavy Axle Loads, Pueblo, CO, October 1990.
22. Newman, R. R., Zarembski, A. M., Resor, R., 'Economic Implications of Heavy Axle Loads on Equipment Design, Operations, and Maintenance', American Society of Mechanical Engineers, WAM RTD-Volume 4, Rail Transportation, December 1991.
23. Zarembski, A. M., 'The Economics of Increasing Axle Loads', European Railway Review, June 1998
24. Zarembski, Allan M., 'The Implications of Heavy Axle Load Operations for Track Maintenance on Short Lines', American Railway Engineering and Maintenance of Way Association Annual Technical Conference, September 2000.
25. 'FAST/HAL Test Summaries', 1st Annual AAR Research Review, November 1995.
26. Zarembski A. M. and Paulsson, Bjorn, 'Introduction of Heavy Axle Loads in Europe: Economics of 30 Tonne Axle Load Operations on the Malmbanan', European Railway Review 1998.

Other Reading

1. McClellan J.W (1997) 'Restructuring the Rail Industry: The U.S. Experience', 6th International Heavy Haul Railway Conference 6–10 April 1997, Cape Town.
2. Bock Brian (1999) Which "Horse" for your "Course"? Wheel/Rail Interface, STS Conference, International Heavy Haul Association 14–17 June 1999, Moscow.
3. Tournay Harry M (1999) 'Rail/Wheel Interaction from a Track and Vehicle Design Perspective', Wheel/Rail Interface, STS Conference, International Heavy Haul Association 14–17 June 1999, Moscow.
4. Marich S et al (1999) 'Assessment of Wheel/Rail Interaction and vehicle dynamics at BPH Iron Ore', Wheel/Rail Interface, STS Conference, International Heavy Haul Association 14–17 June 1999, Moscow
5. Allen Roy A. et al (1999) 'North American Heavy Haul Facts, Fiction and Conventional Wisdom', Wheel/Rail Interface, STS Conference, International Heavy Haul Association 14–17 June 1999, Moscow
6. Nibloe I.M. (1989) 'The Evolution of a Heavy Haul Railway', 4th International Heavy Haul Railway Conference, 11–15 September 1989, Brisbane
7. Schofeld D. 'The Development and Testing of Improved Wheel Profiles for Queensland Railways', 4th International Heavy Haul Railway Conference, 11–15 September 1989, Brisbane

7 Logistics Operations and Railways

Charles Watson and Felix Schmid, University of Sheffield

7.1 Introduction

Logistics is defined as "the art of moving, lodging and supplying troops and equipment" [1]. However, current use of the term relates mostly to the manufacturing and retail industries, and the Council of Logistics Management thus defines logistics as that part of the supply chain process that plans, implements, and controls the timely, efficient, effective forward and reverse flows of goods between origin(s) and point(s) of use, as well as the associated storage, services and the exchange of related information, in order to meet the requirements of all parties of a supply chain. In most cases, more than one movement of materials and information will be involved in the logistics activity. The supply-chain as a whole can be described as a set of activities leading from the sourcing of raw materials or raw data to finished goods and services, in line with specifications, and to performance levels which satisfy the ultimate customer. It can include procurement, manufacture, distribution and final disposal, together with associated transport, storage and information technology.

This chapter covers the subject of logistics from a general perspective, briefly covering the history of logistics to the present day and some relevant aspects of the history of rail freight. The aims of logistics are examined next, again in general terms. Rail's role in modern logistics is then explored in some detail, with an analysis of where rail went wrong in the past, how it is recovering and what the future might hold for the rail mode.

7.2 History of Logistics

Stone-age people were hunter-gatherers, and did not need much transport. However, when the Egyptians built the pyramids, they required good organisation to supply raw materials to the work sites and food to the workers. This was possibly the first example of large-scale logistics. The Phoenicians also developed long distance transport of goods in order to supply raw materials not available locally, to meet demand for goods not produced locally and to provide relief of shortages in times of crisis. Here, society was reorganised through the introduction of shipping. There then followed the development of trade around the coast of the Mediterranean and further afield. As mentioned in chapter 2, substantial land transport was not feasible before the Romans constructed their long-distance network of roads which allowed them to balance supply & demand between parts of the Empire. The Roman Empire was indeed only possible thanks to the excellent logistics operation for the supply of troops and civil servants.

Following the hiatus of Mediaeval times and the reliance on local sustainability, the discovery of the Americas and renewed trade links with the Far East and Africa, transport of raw materials and luxury goods resumed over long distances, some on land via the Silk Road and using river shipping, but mostly by sea. There was still the difficulty of moving goods from the ports to inland consumers but this was partly solved by the development of toll roads and canal networks, slow as they were. The canals also allowed the shipment of low value commodities, such as coal, at an economic cost.

The canals, roads and railways could be built thanks to the emergence of a mobile workforce of people made redundant by agricultural reform, the disappearance of small-scale rural textile production and the availability of substantial surpluses in food production. Changes in transport technology and operations were thus both stimulus and consequence of advances in the production of perishable and durable goods. The most notable change was that from craft based production in small workshops to mass production in factories.

7.3 Development of Large Scale Manufacturing and Need for Transport

The main characteristic of craft-based manufacturing is the allocation of most steps in the production of an item to an individual with the skills and know-how to perform all necessary operations to an acceptable standard. Both quality and productivity tend to be variable over time and depend greatly on the competence of the worker. Until the early years of the industrial revolution, craft-type production had dominated most types of manufacturing, from the forging of ploughshares to the making of handguns. It minimised logistics efforts and thus the requirement for transport. Generally, the end user was in direct contact with the producer. Today, this type of manufacturing is limited to certain luxury goods and bespoke items, e.g. clothing.

The factory system of industrial production, characterised by the highly organised mass production of standard products, did not appear overnight. It developed slowly as business people discovered that specialisation of workers could reduce unit costs. Well before the middle ages, some goods had been produced in industrial processes e.g. bricks and mining, where production on an individual or domestic basis had always been uneconomic.

Evolution of the Factory System

The early factory system relied on the allocation of specialist tasks[1] in the manufacture of a product to dispersed independent workshops where

---

[1] The division of labour describes the segmentation of activities involved in making a product into smaller tasks involving a restricted range of skills and thus requires a minimum of instruction of staff.

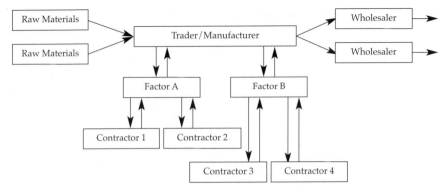

Figure 7.1 Early Division of Labour and Transport Flows

families and small groups of workers would carry out one or several steps of the process (see Figure 7.1). This type of arrangement was typical for the watch and lace industries in Switzerland in the 19th and early 20th centuries, for example. A factor[2] managed the subcontractors and the logistics of supplying them with raw materials or semi-finished goods and of collecting their output. At the time, it was an efficient way of manufacturing because risk was distributed throughout the chain of production and because competition forced each contractor to minimise labour cost and to maximise labour productivity. Decisions about the further (sub)-division of labour though were left to the subcontractor.

The system shown in Figure 7.1 generated some demand for transport, but only for relatively small-scale short-distance flows, because the contractors tended to live and work close to the base of the factor. However, the system with independent contractors managed by a factor was not really suitable for large-scale production and the large markets emerging during the period of the industrial revolution and associated mechanisation of factories. The workshop-based system was therefore superseded by the factory system.

In 1776, Adam Smith [2] compared craft-type production and the factory system and observed that the latter resulted in very substantial economies. Charles Babbage [3] extended this to an analysis of production by machine rather than by hand[3]. The better quality and consistency of products resulting from specialisation, the associated collective experience and the use of

---

[2] Hence the term factory, the place where final assembly, finishing and packaging took place.
[3] Babbage begins his critical chapter 19, "On the Division of Labour," by asserting that "Perhaps the most important principle on which the economy of a manufacture depends, is the *division of labour* [Babbage's italics] amongst the persons who perform the work". . . . his analysis of the division of labour constitutes an advance upon the classic treatment of the subject of much greater dimensions than has yet been recognized.

appropriate machines offered the financial incentive to invest in larger facilities, the factories.

The Railways and the Factory System

The coming of the railways supported and accelerated all of these processes. The relatively fast transportation provided by rail (>50km/h) allowed industrial growth on a scale never witnessed before as economies of scale were achieved in the large factories of the late 18th and of the 19th centuries. All steps of production could now be undertaken in one place or even under one roof, with most supplies, and in some cases labour, brought in by rail reliably and cheaply. For more than 100 years, the focus was on co-locating all production facilities to ensure full control over cost and quality. A few major manufacturers continued until the mid 1900s to produce in-house even minor components, such as bolts and nuts, purely for this reason of control.

Rail served as the backbone to this type of production and benefited greatly from the associated traffic from company siding to company siding. Limited to movements within national borders until the late 19th century, international rail freight started to be available thanks to the OTIF rules for wagon exchange. Suppliers anywhere in Europe could now compete for the supply of components, as long as production costs were low enough to allow for the cost of transport. Transport costs dropped thanks to the use of longer and faster trains equipped with airbrakes. The internationalisation of trade was encouraged by the establishment of standards for engineered products and for weights and measures.

Footnote 3 continued

As Babbage reminds his readers, Smith attributed the increased productivity flowing from the division of labour to "three different circumstances: first, to the increase of dexterity in every particular workman; secondly, to the saving of time, which is commonly lost in passing from one species of work to another; and, lastly, to the invention of a great number of machines which facilitate and abridge labour, and enable one man to do the work of many" (p. 175). Babbage goes on to assert that Smith had overlooked a key advantage that flows from the analysis of the *Wealth of Nations,* and that the analysis is therefore seriously incomplete.

When there is only a limited division of labour, he argued that each worker is required to perform a number of tasks, involving a variety of skills and physical capabilities. The supply of such skills and capabilities varies considerably, for reasons having to do with length of training, previous experience, and natural differences in physical endowment. . . . Thus, with a limited division of labour the employer is required, in effect, to purchase "bundles" of labour. Consequently, a workman who is capable of performing highly skilled work will need to receive a wage appropriate to these high skill levels, even though he will spend much, perhaps most, of his time performing work of lower skill, and pay, levels.

Seen from this perspective, the great virtue of the division of labour is that it permits an "unbundling" of labor skills, and allows the employer to pay for each separate labour process no more than the market value of the lower capabilities commensurate with such work. Under an extensive division of labour, the employer is no longer confronted with the necessity of purchasing labour corresponding to higher skill levels than those required for the specific project at hand. [quoted from [4]].

As the 19th century came to a close, railways had displaced canals as the main mode of inland transport and the network reached virtually all areas of industrial activity, often penetrating into factories for internal transport. The railways were moving freight in a number of different ways in response to the logistics needs of their customers. Bulk raw materials for industry, such as coal and iron ore, were moved in trains that carried only a single commodity. Agricultural products and manufactured goods were transported in wagonloads, where a train normally would be made up of a number of different suppliers' wagons. Time sensitive cargo, such as newspapers and perishable food, was transported in express vans that could be marshalled in passenger trains.

From the Factory System to Modern Supply Chains
The trend to concentrate production in ever-larger integrated facilities persisted until the early 1960s when diseconomies of scale started to appear. These were associated with relatively low flexibility in responding to market demands and the cost of managing very large facilities and complex production systems, as well as the labour problems stemming from low quality manual jobs and poor working environments. The desire to control all aspects of production was replaced by a need to reduce overhead costs and inventory, and to enhance flexibility and return on investment.

In the 20th century, the development of the internal combustion engine and an expanding good quality road network gave businesses without easy access to the rail network economical links to their markets. Standardisation of basic components (e.g. fasteners and common sections) enhanced both quality and efficiency, since some companies could now focus on just a few simple products, distributed to many OEMs[4] via stockholders and wholesalers or supplied directly, as shown in Figure 7.2. By the 1970s, most European manufacturing had therefore moved to this type of operation.

The state funded expansion of the transport network in the 1960s, with motorways and lower cost air-transport, changed further the face of manufacturing. Transport between manufacturing stages was no longer perceived as a problem. Cheap, reliable and fast transport allowed the development of new manufacturing paradigms where major manufacturers would develop close relationships with suppliers, allowing batch size reduction and just-in-time (JIT) production, thus saving on work-in-progress. The resulting distribution of component and subassembly production and concentration of final assembly and consumer packaging lead to further flexibility increases in manufacturing while allowing the retention of core-skills in the lead-company.

---

[4] Own Equipment Manufacturer, a producer of finished goods for which the company provides a full warranty even though it may be using components from many sources.

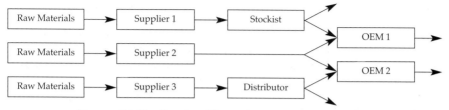

Figure 7.2 Production Flows in 1970s Manufacturing

7.4 Just-in-Time, Outsourcing and the Increasing Importance of Logistics

The introduction of Just-in-Time (JIT) and Kanban based production did much to change the logistics function from the low level management of transport activities into the modern supply chain management system that it is today. With JIT and Kanban, frequent small consignments of raw materials, components, subsystems and intermediate products replaced the infrequent large movements of raw materials and finished goods which had been suited to rail transport. These small shipments have to be scheduled very accurately to ensure that materials arrive at the production line when needed since there is no longer storage space available to hold a stock of supplies. As shown in section 4.3, it is difficult for rail to be competitive where consignments are small, even if there is a high frequency of shipments.

At the same time, many businesses closed or relocated their manufacturing overseas (to access cheaper labour), with remaining operations moved to green-field sites, generally without rail access but close to the rapidly developing motorway network. Almost overnight, due to JIT and relocation, rail lost very secure traffic flows between sidings, at a time when competition between road and rail had already reduced transport cost and thus revenue. Interestingly, the reduced cost of transport also led to the strange situation where it has become worthwhile to transport batches of semi-finished goods several times between specialised manufacturing plants where particular operations may be cheaper or where quality is better.

The 1990s were characterised by the next stage in the development of manufacturing with the emergence of outsourcing and multi-sourcing, where even core activities are bought-in from major suppliers. This leads to skill concentration in supplying companies. Communications and decentralised production are used to bring greater efficiencies. Today, for example, branded food products can be produced at multiple sites or a single site to the same standards with no discernable difference between the products. Most major newspapers are today produced at a number of satellite plants. The automotive industry has adopted contract manufacturing, where suppliers both provide the components and the labour force to fit them to the vehicle on the production line, again reducing the potential for large volumes in transport.

The abolition of many artificial barriers to trade (e.g. import duties on manufactured goods) is leading to worldwide competition for parts of supply chains. Modern logistics thus has become a core-skill of organisations and a vital part of the supply chain.

7.5 Rail Freight in the New Environment

The early 20th century brought a number of enhancements to rail freight operations. Longer, heavier and faster freight trains improved the use of railway capacity and reduced transit times. Automation in loading and unloading for major flows was also developed to improve efficiency and major marshalling yards were constructed to improve services for wagonload customers. However, the utilisation of freight wagons tended to be low where customers had their own sidings, since they usually expected to load and unload the trains or wagonloads themselves, at their convenience. Effectively, the railways' assets were used as 'free' warehousing facilities.

More and more consignments were transported to and from the railway at each end of the journey by road haulage where customers did not have private sidings, adding manual loading and unloading and associated time and cost. This was no longer in tune with market requirements. Basic intermodal services were therefore developed to cope with increasing competition from roads (see chapter 10). However, customers started to value fully road-based solutions, not just because of the speed and cost, but also because of the much closer control over the timing and quality of service. Transport by means of in-house resources (lorries and staff) did not have latest loading times and was not left in sidings to allow higher priority trains to overtake.

Initially, the major developments in manufacturing industry and in retailing, in particular, the just-in-time and small batch production revolutions, were not recognised as threats by the railways. They happened at a time when the railways were cutting back their networks to the "profitable core" and when relatively small consignments were not seen as attractive for rail. The rail managers' mantra was that trainload traffic was the only way in which rail could compete. Traffic with maritime type containers had just started and appeared to offer the solution to rail's conundrum of whether to be involved in logistics or not.

7.6 Logistics in the 21st Century

Today, logistics managers are expected to source inputs for processes at lowest cost, to provide cost effective, efficient and timely movement of goods between processing locations and to hold goods until they are needed, whether by the end consumer or a subsequent step in the manufacturing process. No longer is the transport of goods seen as a necessary evil that adds cost; instead, it is viewed as a part of logistics and is now expected to add value to the supply chain. The key tasks in the management of logistics operations relate to the following objectives:

1. Source raw materials, components and semi-finished goods on best terms;
2. Maintain control of the goods at all times (reliability);
3. Satisfy stringent collection and delivery times and competitive journey times (punctuality);
4. Efficient and careful handling throughout the journey (dependability).

The logistics function manages the resources and their deployment, maintains communication with all the partners in the supply chain and ensures the tracking of consignments. As stated in the previous section, most goods today travel many times between processes and may be stored in several places before ultimate delivery. Figure 7.3 offers an example of the role that the discipline of logistics plays in typical food manufacturing and retail situations today. Here, the most important function of logistics is continuity of supply of all product ranges, combined with maximum flexibility of supplier choice to ensure low prices.

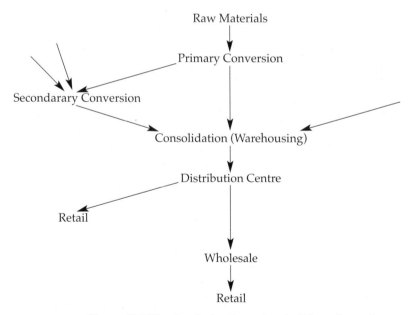

Figure 7.3 The Logistics Function in Manufacturing

As shown in Figure 7.3, logistics consists of the management of the flows (as shown by arrows) between the various stages of production and the warehousing functions required throughout the process. In addition to these physical stages, there are also data exchanges between the various links in the chain to manage the various functions.

There are also several other subsidiary aims of logistics, in addition to those listed under 1 to 4 above:

- Maximise flexibility of labour distribution and minimise labour costs;
- Maximise stability of production systems, spreading work over a number of factories anywhere in the world;
- Minimise risk of shortages in the supply of goods and services while using the lowest cost supplier;
- Minimise real cost to the environment, as is required by law, by using the most efficient transport modes available;
- Minimise the quality risk by reducing the number of modal transfers during a journey.

It is clear that there are many opportunities for particular modes of transport to become involved in the process but, in order to be successful, the mode has to contribute positively to the process.

Capabilities Required in Modern Logistics

Logistics requirements for different markets are very different. The needs of automotive, perishables and general food, supermarket logistics, power station coal and steel vary in both the quantities shipped and the way that they need to be supplied. Automotive manufacturers operating Just-in-Time processes require regular deliveries of small quantities of fault-free components of the correct type for the model currently being produced. In some cases, an individual shipment may cover as little as half a day's production, which must be delivered reliably, sometimes with delivery windows as short as 15 minutes. Some suppliers to the automotive industry are building their factories even closer to the car plant in order to reduce the distance, and hence the time, between the two. An example of just how close a supplier can be to the customer is at the Chrysler plant in Campo Largo in Brazil where suppliers have built factories adjacent to the plant.

Perishable foods and other goods need to be delivered from farms to factories to distribution warehouses to supermarkets in a very short time (see the case study below). This requires a high degree of reliability in the logistics process, with the quantities and product mixes changing at each step of the supply chain. Perishables need to be delivered to supermarkets nearly every day, while grocery items can be warehoused for longer. However, supermarkets do not generally have sufficient warehouse space to store more than a few days' supply of the most popular items.

Power stations still consume vast quantities of coal in order to meet the growing demand for electric power. Modern logistics has enabled electricity generators to reduce the amount of coal held at the power station, so deliveries are required several times a day, even though more and more coal is sourced from overseas and needs to be transhipped at ports.

In modern logistics, the responsibility for different aspects of the function (e.g. stock holding, transport and management) also needs to be allocated. A specialist logistics contractor may take on the whole process or may share it with the client, such as Marks and Spencer. The latter approach may offer the business more control over the logistics function but runs counter to the business model of separating core skills and activities from functions to be supplied by the market. Distributors, warehousing companies and transport companies can combine forces to provide a complete logistics service to a company, but this requires complicated alliancing agreements if it is to be successful. Logistics contractors, such as Exel or Lowfields, provide logistics for a large and diverse number of companies, from supplying supermarkets to just in time supply to automotive manufacturers.

7.7 Negative Aspects of all Transport Activities

Many risks must be managed by logistics suppliers: Unreliable delivery times caused by congestion or poor information flow between supplier and customer can disrupt production by late arrival, and can cause warehousing problems if goods arrive too early. Goods can be damaged in transit, which also disrupts production and leads to additional transport of goods being returned. The time spent in transit is costly as there is a discounted cash flow penalty, especially when transit times are long, such as in deep-sea shipping. All transport also uses scarce resources, which is more prevalent when transport networks are operating at or near capacity. There is also the issue of the land take required for links, storage and waiting. The relatively low cost of the transport component of logistics may encourage organisational inefficiency.

7.8 Rail's Role in Modern Logistics

Rail can still have a vital role to play in modern logistics but it must keep up with the ever-evolving structure of industry. The globalisation of production has resulted in smaller numbers of larger and more distant facilities, and regionalisation of distribution centres means that there are now longer inland trunk hauls. Deep sea containerised trade continues to grow throughout Europe, with the ports of Rotterdam, Antwerp, Southampton and Felixstowe handling vast quantities of containers. Globalisation of supply, regionalisation of distribution and deep sea connection are all areas where rail can make an impact.

Rail has many advantages that can attract shippers to use the mode. Trains can move large volumes more efficiently than lorries, both in terms of manpower (because one driver and traction unit can move the equivalent of 100 lorry loads), and in terms of environmental impact (because the low rolling resistance[5] makes moving a given load more energy efficient by rail than on the road). The main factors though which affect the choice of mode for a particular logistics activity are reliability, price, time, flexibility and control. In a survey of 1500 logistics users, reliability was the most important factor in deciding which mode to use [5]. Although some progress has been made, rail still has room for improvement in all these areas, especially in reliability and journey time. However, there are some trade-offs between these variables and, as with passenger rail planning, the overall service offered may be measured in a 'generalised cost' manner [6]. In this concept, the key variables (weighted to reflect the issues of importance to the shipper) are added together to form an index of the ease of transport.

In theory, Just in Time (JIT) production does not work in rail's favour because its aim is to reduce costs by reducing the amount of stock held and the elimination of the associated warehousing. Moreover, JIT can lead to increased shipping costs, because transport costs are inversely related to the quantity shipped [7]. Rail though may benefit from the move to JIT, ultimately, if it can offer timed and unitised deliveries linked into manufacturers' and retailers' MRP[6] systems.

As traffic on the rail network is highly regulated, it is possible to timetable movements down to the minute. Additionally, rail has direct access to the heart of towns and cities, which is becoming increasingly difficult for road in the light of lorry bans and restrictive access hours. Rail is also viewed as environmentally friendly, especially where electric traction is used. Speeds can also be higher than road for some types of freight; 144km/h inter-modal trains are currently being trialled on the East Coast Main Line by EWS.

In 2003, rail has suffered some significant setbacks in its involvement in logistics, largely due to the changing structure of some industries. Steelmaking is reducing in Great Britain and major steel users (such as car manufacturers) have transferred their activities elsewhere or have lost market share to imported products. The electronic revolution allowed satellite printing of newspapers from the 1980s, eliminating a major time critical flow for rail logistics. The UK's Royal Mail reviewed its rail operations in 2003 and may be switching to road for all its logistics in March 2004 despite a £150 million investment in new terminals and equipment. This will increase the total number of road journeys by around 160,000, covering 30.5 million miles, and will also increase road congestion even further [8]. The Royal Mail has also abandoned their dedicated 2-foot gauge rail network located beneath London [9]. However, the emergence of transnational parcels services (e.g. Federal

5 Thanks to the stiff interface between the wheel and the rail.
6 Manufacturing Resource Planning (MRP) has evolved into a sophisticated tool with the ability to predict logistics requirements.

Express, UPS) with major air freight hubs in Paris, Brussels and Cologne, presents new opportunities for rail freight as a connector.

Intermodal traffic is also difficult to move by rail in Britain because the restrictive loading gauge means that containers can only be moved on certain routes, and piggy back movements of road trailers requires a specially designed trailer, unlike on many continental European networks.

Nevertheless, the future for rail-based logistics is promising. Increasing road congestion has reduced the average HGV speed on motorways from 60 km/h in 1990 to 52 km/h in 2000 [10], while the average journey length has increased from 80 to 98km over the same period. Infrastructure upgrades will mean that trains will be able to get both longer and heavier than at present, while new vehicles and locomotives will permit higher operating speeds. The European Interoperability Directives will encourage longer journeys into Eastern Europe and Asia. Both smaller and larger terminals will act as local drop points and major international trade centres respectively. Self propelled freight multiple units (see chapter 8), and cargo trams will allow the movement of smaller quantities of goods more profitably and give better access to city centres [11]. The emergence of mini-modal, where goods are carried in small containers measuring 2250mm square and 2535mm high which can be carried on standard low platform wagons, will improve rail's ability to transport smaller quantities profitably. This is enhanced by the ability to load mini-modal containers onto rail or road vehicles using a standard fork lift truck, thus eliminating the need to provide specialist handling equipment in dedicated terminals [12].

7.9 Case Study: Supermarket Stock Delivery

Paul Cosgrove, University of Sheffield

Introduction
Efficient product distribution is critical to the profitable operation of modern supermarkets. Supplying hundreds of stores nationwide with thousands of tonnes of stock per week, UK supermarket operations represent 29% of the two billion tonnes of freight currently transported around the UK each year [13]. Supermarkets therefore require logistics solutions that can cope with the pressures from government, the public, competitors and customers and from the supply chain itself. At present, such distribution solutions are almost entirely dependent on road transport.

The road transport system in the UK is, however, becoming increasingly problematic. Costly environmental protection measures and worsening congestion problems[(7,8)] are expected to compromise road haulage activities

---

[7] According to the Commission for Integrated Transport, road congestion is forecast to grow 15% overall by 2010, inclusive of a 28% congestion increase on inter-urban trunk roads [14].
[8] Congestion costs UK companies an estimated £20 billion a year [15].

seriously. As a result, road transport will become considerably more expensive, more time consuming and less attractive than it is now.

In light of these foreseen problems, UK stores are beginning to assess the alternatives. One option that logistics managers are looking to increasingly is the integration of rail freight services into supply chain solutions. Although a relatively unknown concept to British businesses, a typical freight train can move up to two thousand tonnes of product, equivalent to 100 HGVs [16]. Providing significant road congestion relief, the diversion of freight from road to rail as part of an inter-modal transport chain can potentially provide a more efficient, responsive and sustainable approach to supermarket deliveries.

In order to assess the market for future integration of rail freight in the supermarket supply chain, an understanding is required as to the nature of the existing road operations of the major players.

Overview of Supermarket Stock Supply
The Regional Distribution Centre (RDC) lies at the heart of the supermarket stock distribution system, with leading stores currently using as many as twenty centres nationwide. Products are received from suppliers – *primary distribution* – for onward transit by road to stores within the service area of each RDC – secondary distribution. On average, one RDC will supply 40 stores sited over 3 UK regions, although RDCs holding non-food products will often supply an entire store portfolio across the UK [17].

In order to maximise the sales area of a store, holding-stock levels and thus in-house storage volumes are kept to an absolute minimum. Guaranteed daily deliveries throughout the week are therefore critical to the effectiveness of a store's supply capability, particularly in relation to short-life products. Typically, each supermarket will receive daily consignment deliveries according to four individual categories – chilled, ambient, frozen and non-food items. Within each category, stock is sourced from a dedicated RDC, although a number of RDCs are multi-functional, supplying for example, chilled and ambient goods.

Deliveries are completed using articulated heavy goods vehicles (HGVs) capable of carrying a twenty tonne load equivalent to 24 palettes of stock, or 48 cubic metres[9]. Utilising fleets of up to 800 HGVs, leading stores can distribute around 10 million cases of product per week nationwide, equivalent to 10,000 separate HGV deliveries transporting a total of 200,000 tonnes of freight [18]. Whilst select supermarkets own and operate their entire fleets, many are now opting for a hybrid service reliant on third party distributors.

In addition to RDC-based deliveries, stores will also receive daily deliveries from a number of independent suppliers. Covering products such as bread, milk, newspapers, magazines and cigarettes these deliveries are supplied

---

[9] A typical pallet of stock represents a delivery volume of 2 cubic metres.

from independent distribution centres or the production source, with loads ranging from one pallet to a complete HGV load for cigarettes and dairy deliveries respectively.

In planned response to weekly deliveries, backhauling of empty pallets, salvage stock and packaging is carried out using either vehicles returning to the RDCs or a dedicated returns vehicle, depending on weekly requirements. In a joint effort with suppliers, a number of stores are also beginning to integrate the collection and delivery of primary stock from the production source as part of their backhauling operations. By reducing the number of empty vehicles returning to RDCs, such initiatives serve to provide savings in terms of both operational and environmental costs.

Supermarket Delivery Patterns
Outlined below are the daily delivery patterns for three leading UK supermarkets located in the Sheffield area of South Yorkshire. For each store analysed in detail, the number and type of daily HGV deliveries are presented in the associated table. Data was sourced from store and distribution managers representing each company.

Case 1: Sainsbury's

Location: Archer Road, Sheffield

Store Size: 2000 m^2

No. Stores Within 5km Radius: 3

	No. Per Day	Origin	Dist. (Kms)	Time
Chilled 1	1	Rotherham	15	24:00 - 02:00
Chilled 2	½	Haydock	100	04:00 - 06:00
Ambient	½	Warndon	190	12:00 - 13:00
Frozen	½	Stone	100	16:00 - 17:00
Beer & Wine	½	Stoke-on-Trent	80	09:00 - 15:00
Non-Food	¼	Hayes	280	09:00 - 15:00
TOTAL	3 ¼			

Figure 7.4 RDC Sources – Sainsbury's, Sheffield

Case 2: Safeway

Location: Ecclesall Road, Sheffield

Store Size: 3000 m^2

No. Stores Within 5km Radius: 3

	No. Per Day	Origin	Dist. (Kms)	Time
Chilled	2	Warrington	95	24:00 - 07:00
Ambient 1	1	Tamworth	100	09:00 - 10:00
Ambient 2	1	Stockton-on-Tees	190	09:00 - 10:00
Frozen	1	Warrington	100	12:00 - 17:00
Beer & Wine	¼	Delivery Merged with Dry Goods		
Non-Food	¼	Delivery Merged with Dry Goods		
TOTAL	5 ½			

Figure 7.5 RDC Sources – Safeway, Sheffield

Case 3: Tesco (24 Hours)

Location: Abbeydale Road, Sheffield

Store Size: 6000 m^2

No. Stores Within 5km Radius: 3

	No. Per Day	Origin	Dist. (Kms)	Time
Chilled	4	Doncaster	35	18:00 - 07:00
Ambient	4	Middlewich	100	19:00 - 24:00
Frozen	2	Doncaster	35	18:00 - 07:00
Non-Food	1	Middleton	70	12:00 - 17:00
TOTAL	11			

Figure 7.6 RDC Sources – Tesco, Sheffield

74

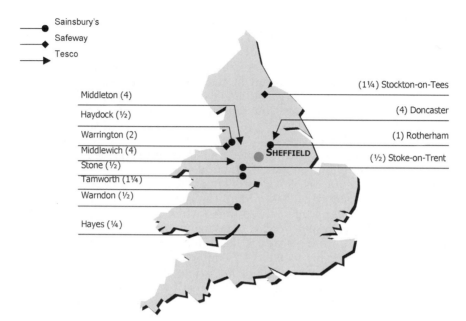

Figure 7.7 RDC Sources for all stores analysed

RDC Location Overview
Figure 7.7 displays all RDC locations for the three stores analysed. The total numbers of HGV deliveries received from each centre per day are shown in brackets.

Delivery Pattern Analysis
With the exception of Sainsbury's non-food supply, all stock consignments are sourced from RDCs lying within a 200km range of each store. Based on an average haulage speed of 87km/hr (54mph) this represents a maximum road journey time of 2.5 hours between source and destination [14]. The distribution of Sainsbury's non-food products from Hayes, 280km from the store, highlights the strategy of using one RDC to supply all stores across the UK.

Clearly as the size of a store increases, the total volume of daily deliveries increases accordingly. Per week, the numbers of HGV deliveries are 22, 38.5 and 77 for the three stores, equivalent to weekly freight loads of 444, 770 and 1540 tonnes. As is apparent from Cases 1 and 2, fractions of HGV deliveries arise due to a strategy of supplying a number of neighbouring stores from one HGV.

In order to maintain a Just-in-Time delivery strategy, all fresh produce is delivered in the early hours of the day (before 07:30am), thus ensuring store the necessary replenishment for the day's trading. This pattern indicates a general trend evident from UK road haulage studies, notably that the activities of chilled and ambient product distribution are at a peak level between the hours of 24:00am and 7.30am [19]. Typically, ambient and frozen foods and non-food products are delivered during store opening hours, between 09:00am and 17:00pm. This trend is largely due to the longer 'shelf-life' of such items, allowing greater flexibility for store replenishment throughout the day.

Existing Rail Initiatives
Since March 1999 Safeway has operated a six-day a week rail delivery service in Scotland. Using inter-modal swap bodies, a range of ambient, chilled, frozen and fresh produce is hauled by rail from the Bellshill RDC near Glasgow to Inverness (a distance of 300km) and Georgemas Junction (500km) (see Figure 7.8). The compartmentalised units, which allow for a mixed cargo, are then loaded by crane onto road vehicles for onward delivery to stores in the North of Scotland. Carrying nearly 50,000 tonnes of stock per year, the system has enabled the company to avoid 1.75 million kilometres of road haul per year, equivalent to the removal of 3000 lorry loads from the main A9 road route. Reflecting the environmental benefits of reducing lorry traffic, the

Picture courtesy of EWS

Figure 7.8 Safeway Intermodal Train

76

Scottish Government Office has, in conjunction with the Strategic Rail Authority, provided Safeway with a Freight Facilities Grant of £680,000 towards the investment costs in new inter-modal equipment, certainly a positive incentive for others to follow.

Sainsbury's has also begun to integrate rail freight into its distribution system. Currently transporting loads between Colchester, Essex and East Kilbride near Edinburgh, Sainsbury's transfers 200,000 km each year from road to rail and carries more products per trip. In addition, a new distribution centre in North Warwickshire will also include an integrated rail link, thus providing the infrastructure for future rail freight operations to service the Midlands region of the UK.

The Future

In consideration of the number of nationwide outlets per store, this study highlights the significant volumes of supermarket produce that are currently transported around the UK. With reference to an average supermarket such as that outlined in Case 2, up to 40,000 tonnes of produce will be received via the road network over a one-year period. Multiplied over a chain of 250 stores this equates to approximately 10 million tonnes of freight annually, all of which is distributed by road.

Clearly, the nation's road network is the critical factor in the successful operation of such distribution operations and thus for the profitability of any national supermarket chain. In light of the difficulties associated with road freight (in terms of its ability to cope with mounting pressures, and the success of existing multi-modal operations), it is inevitable that rail must be given serious consideration within this industry as an alternative method of transport.

In response to future market growth and sustained efforts to increase operational efficiency and lower costs, the supermarkets require a choice of adaptable distribution methods in order to maintain effective transport solutions. Utilising both rail-connected RDCs and intermediate road-rail exchange terminals, a future shift to rail freight can provide significant economic advantages even when assigned to small distances under 150kms [8]. As such, rail has the potential capability of providing an increasingly competitive alternative to serve the industry's needs.

Crucially, UK Government policy is strongly in favour of a modal shift from road to rail and, as part of its ten-year transport plan has committed to investing £4billion to develop existing infrastructure for an integrated system [21]. Encouraging more freight to be moved by rail, the Government and the Strategic Rail Authority (SRA) are working closely with the rail freight industry, in a joint effort to meet a projected 80% increase in rail freight over the next ten years. In addition, the Highways Agency and the SRA are currently undertaking assessments intended to identify traffic flows large enough to support development of new inter-modal freight facilities. Aimed at diverting further proportions of traffic from road to rail, such efforts represent a clear response to the increasing interest for a modal shift.

In terms of the logistics required and associated costs for adapting existing distribution operations, in addition to the available funding incentives from Government as negotiated by Safeway, other major stores such as Sainsbury's are currently in the process of downsizing their RDC network in favour of larger 'fulfilment factories.' Providing a more concentrated distribution of supply centres, such progressions present the ideal opportunity for the integration of rail links and would considerably reduce the cost and logistics of a multi-modal system.

7.10 Conclusions

This chapter has examined the role that logistics plays in the supply chain, and how it has evolved from the supply of materials for major construction works and armies into a vital function of industry. Railfreight displaced canals as the main form of inland transport in the 19th Century, was itself overtaken by road in the mid 20th Century, but is now starting to make a comeback mainly due to increasing congestion on the roads. The aims of logistics have been shown to be the efficient transport and storage of goods between subsequent steps of the manufacturing and distribution processes through a supply chain process. Within this, rail can be competitive in the modern environment by exploiting its natural characteristics. The future of rail freight is bright, given the level of innovation being applied to the industry, but rail has to improve its performance in the following areas:

- Collecting and delivering goods with the highest levels of reliability and punctuality;
- Offering short transit times where required by the client;
- Responding rapidly to demands for new links and for change in capacity on a route;
- Developing efficient and controllable means of moving wagon load and less than wagon load shipments;
- Ensuring that rail's services can be integrated into the information technology systems of all clients whether suppliers, manufacturers, distributors or retailers;
- Working more closely with non rail logistics companies.

References

1. Fowler, F. G., and H. W. Fowler Eds., 'The Oxford Handy Dictionary' 6th Ed. Oxford University Press, 1991.
2. Smith, A., 'The Wealth of Nations', 1776, Methuen, London, 1904.
3. Babbage, C., 'On the Economy of Machinery and Manufactures', fourth edition, 1835; reprinted by Frank Cass & Co., London, 1963.

4. Rosenberg, N., 'Exploring the Black Box: Technology, economics and history', pp. 27-28, Cambridge University Press, Cambridge, U.K. 1994.
5. Gallop, N (2000) 'Seamless Service: the Holy Grail of Railfreight', Rail 383 pp. 32 ff.
6. Harris, N G (1992) 'Introduction', ch. 1 in Harris, N G & Godward, E W, eds. 'Planning Passenger Railways', TPC, Glossop.
7. Jackson, G. C., J. J. Stoltman and A. Taylor, 'Moving Beyond Trade-offs', International Journal of Physical Distribution & Logistics Management, Vol. 24 No. 1, 1994, pp. 4-10, MCB University Press, 1994.
8. EWS, Press Release NR2003037, 6 June 2003
9. Holley M., 'Mail Rail ends after 76 years under London', Rail, June 11 – June 24 2003, p. 14, EMAP Active Ltd., Peterborough. 2003.
10. Department for Transport, 'DfT (2001), Transport Statistics Great Britain: 2001 Edition', HMSO, 2001.
11. Layfield, E., 'Minimodal Freight Train', Railwatch, No. 94, Nov. 2002, p. 4, Railway Development Society, 2002.
12. Rien, W. and M. Roggenkamp, 'Can trams carry cargo? New logistics for urban areas', World Transport Policy & Practice, Vol. 1 No. 1, pp. 32-36, MCB University Press Limited, 1995.
13. *Transport of Goods by Road in Great Britain 2000*, Department of the Environment, Transport and the Regions: London May 2001.
14. *Rail Freight: Delivering on Growth*, Commission for Integrated Transport, March 2002.
15. *Getting Goods On Track: A Guide for Councillors and Planners on Promoting Rail Freight*, Freight on Rail 2000
16. *Incentives for Rail Freight Growth*, Commission for Integrated Transport, April 2001.
17. *Asda Supply Chain Strategy*, IGD Retail Analysis 2003 (http://www.igd.com/analysis/)
18. *The Long Haul*, Charlie Pye-Smith, International Institute for Environment and Development July 2002
19. *Analysis of Transport Efficiency in UK Food Supply Chain*, Logistics Research Centre, Herriott Watt University, April 2003.
20. *Rail Freight: Dispelling the Most Commonly Held Myths About Rail Freight*, Commission for Integrated Transport, June 2002.
21. *Transport 2010: The 10 Year Plan*, Department of the Environment, transport and the Regions, July 2000.

8 The Freight Multiple Unit

Simon Colbourne, Railfreightonline Project Manager, Exel Logistics

8.1 Introduction

Much of the movement of freight in Western Europe is in the hands of a limited number of logistics companies, such as Exel and TNT. These companies move huge quantities of freight in full load format, and are experts in supply chain management. Road haulage dominates traffic flows, either through the management of customer dedicated fleets or via transport planning systems that commission third parties to undertake deliveries on our behalf.

When the logistics companies look at how they design sustainable solutions for their customers, however, they are increasingly aware of the challenges that face road haulage. In planning for the future they have identified a number of factors which have the potential to disrupt existing supply chains and increase costs.

Congestion: large sections of the European road network are becoming increasingly congested. The state of traffic at given times of the day on the M25, M6 and M1 is well-known, whilst major routes in and out of continental ports such as Rotterdam are also becoming difficult to manage.

Tolls and taxation: decisions are being taken across Europe about road tolls and taxes. French and Swiss motorway charges could well be replicated elsewhere and the potential for technology to enable roadside tolls to be deployed in major cities will add costs to current road freight services.

Centralisation and Globalisation: across Europe the trend in manufacturing over the past decade has moved from regional production planning to successive programmes of rationalisation, as described in chapter 7. There are now fewer manufacturing sites in Europe producing more, with goods therefore having to travel further to reach consumers, within ever-shorter timeframes.

Environmental: through a combination of international, national and regional legislation and good practice, companies are growing ever more aware of their environmental responsibilities. Increasingly, freight transport is seen as a target area for the reduction of carbon based emissions and, whilst road vehicle emission levels are reducing helped by the latest engine designs, increasingly performance improvements are measured in decimal points. The reality is that, unless a major fuel cell breakthrough can be delivered, tangible improvements in commercial vehicle emissions are unlikely.

8.2 Targeting the Fast Moving Consumer Goods (FMCG) Market

The third party logistics (3PL) sector in the UK is very highly developed. The majority of retailers and manufacturers now use 3PLs for some or all of their transport services and warehousing. It is now estimated that the 3PLs control in the region of 50% of all movements of retail consumer goods between manufacturer and distribution centre (DC) and DC to retail outlet. Decisions being taken today about production and DC locations need to ensure that the pressures that will face the road network are reflected. To what extent rail forms a part of those structures is as yet uncertain.

The existing rail freight operators have failed to capture the imagination of FMCG manufacturers and retailers to any great extent. The Freight Operating Companies (FOCs) are seen as traditional service providers and their service offering has been some way from the levels of flexibility and cost transparency that the UK road freight business expects from third party suppliers.

To address these problems, the Strategic Rail Authority sponsored a competition for "Innovation in Rail Based Logistics" in 2000, which resulted in three awards being made to successful applicants [1]:

- The Blue Circle/ Babcock rail development of new piggyback technology in both wagon and road unit design for cement movements;
- The Minimodal Project developing and building new small Intermodal equipment capable of being handled by forklift trucks; and
- The Exel/Amec Rail/Isotrak development and trial of a UK based freight multiple unit (FMU).

The first two of these are described briefly below, whilst the remainder of this chapter sets out in some detail the development programme for the FMU.

Blue Circle/Babcock Piggyback: £2.9 million was awarded to the consortium by the SRA, from which development work continued until approval in 2002 [1]. The aim has been to allow the piggyback transport of Blue Circle (now Lafarge) cement products, reducing substantially the costs of distribution terminals, and providing greater flexibility of operation. Unfortunately, the vehicles have a lower payload than conventional cement wagons (32t, as opposed to perhaps 60t in a normal vehicle of similar length). Two types of wagons have been developed – a top-loading non-tipping tanker, and a curtain-sided trailer (for bagged cement). However, commercial trials are currently taking place on the relatively-short haul (50 miles) between Westbury and Southampton.

Minimodal: The SRA awarded £1 million to a consortium including Direct Rail Services and TDG, to develop a smaller box suitable for carriage by both road and rail; after consultation, this was finalised at 2.55m square, since five of these can be carried on a standard road trailer, and six on a standard rail wagon. Various trials have already occurred, including by EWS between Warrington and Mossend (near Glasgow), and by DRS, using two locomotives in push-pull mode on the Settle-Carlisle line. This latter approach also reflects the desire for rail freight to get into the traffic of a wider range of products over shorter distances.

8.3 Development and Trial of a Freight Multiple Unit (FMU)

Gathering customer input

Prior to the final submission, the project team undertook a series of customer interviews looking at the rail freight experience to date. The interviews addressed current perceptions and sought to identify what purchasers were seeking from rail. Their needs were identified as:

- Reliability and speed (in that order);
- Cost Transparency;
- Good asset utilisation;
- Good staff utilisation;
- Flexible (in type of freight that could be handled);
- Modern technology (especially track and trace);
- Able to use both open access and dedicated sites.

Taking this feedback and the overall market pressures being faced by road, the project team were keen to understand whether a FMU could be developed to provide a vehicle for the UK rail network that would meet many of the requirements set out by customers.

Project Objectives

The project objectives were as follows.

1. To design, configure and run a freight multiple unit in the UK;
2. To generate a specification for a UK FMU;
3. To design build and run new command and control technology capable of providing services akin to those available to the road haulage sector;
4. To engage as many customers as possible in the design, specification and operational competency of the trials;
5. To engage all parties, whether designers, rail engineers, operators, politicians, network providers or operators, in understanding the project and the market potential;
6. To share information on the project and rail sites though a project website;
7. To run a series of demonstrations of the train at showcase events;
8. To run full-scale commercial trials of the train for a selection of customers in an environment that sought to match closely existing or future state supply chains, which may currently be provided by road haulage; and
9. To communicate the successes and failures of the project both throughout the life of the project and by providing a final report for the SRA.

Amec and the European Freight Multiple Units (FMUs)

The project team were aware of the development of two projects looking at FMUs in Europe. Deutsche Bahn had commissioned the design and build of

Figure 8.1 Windhoff/Amec FMU

two designs of FMU in Germany by Windhoff AG and Bombardier, with the designation Cargosprinters. In addition, during the preparation of the submission, a demonstration of how a UK FMU might look and work was undertaken by Trucktrain Developments.

Amec Rail had a strong relationship with Windhoff through the development of the Multi Purpose Vehicle (MPV) for Railtrack. This unit was based on the Deutsche Bahn prototypes and had sufficient similarities to provide an excellent vehicle for the provision of a demonstration unit in the UK.

Railtrack uses the MPV for light maintenance duties such as leaf blowing Sandite[1] application and weed spraying. The unit comprises a master and slave and operates within UK gauge restrictions. The project team saw this as an ideal vehicle for adaptation to an FMU by taking two MPVs, discarding the slave units and configuring two master units to work in tandem, thereby providing power levels much closer to those provided by the German Cargosprinters.

The Amec team were confident that the units could be demonstrated as an FMU and support from Railtrack for the lease of the necessary units was received. They therefore constructed the units, at a cost of around £1.5m, during 2001; the dimensions of the vehicles are as set out below.

Their weight characteristics give them access to a larger proportion of the rail network than conventional freight trains, opening up possibilities for rail freight on rural branch lines, for instance. The costs mean, however, that any business case for using them is going to have to be constructed carefully. Shuttle-type operations achieving high levels of vehicle utilisation are likely to be promising.

---

[1] This is a gel applied to rails to increase adhesion during icy conditions and the leaf-fall season

> **FMU Technical Details (Tranche 2 MPVs)**
>
> Length 40m
>
> 4x 265kW diesel motors through a 5-speed gearbox
>
> Max speed 75mph (although timed to 60mph in trials)
>
> Gauge W6a
>
> Wagon codes FKA
>
> Weight of goods carried (tonnes):
>
> | MPV 1 | car 1 | car 2 | car 3 | car 4 | MPV2 | Total |
> |-------|-------|-------|-------|-------|------|-------|
> | 23.06 | 28.6 | 28.6 | 29.56 | 29.56 | 23.06 | 162.44 |
>
> source: AMEC SPIE Rail (UK)

Figure 8.2 Freight Multiple Unit Technical Details

Isotrak and Command and Control Technology
Exel and Isotrak have a strong relationship. Much of the Isotrak technology was developed together and Exel remain Isotrak's largest customer. Isotrak's contribution to the Railfreightonline (RFOL) project was primarily to apply new technology in the rail freight environment, based on the experience and capabilities gained in the road fleets. The application of the technology in the rail environment superficially has parallels with road fleet operations. However, it was acknowledged from the outset of the trial that there would be considerable modification and enhancements required of the Isotrak Fleet Management System to meet the operational requirements of a rail freight operation.

Although Isotrak had extensive experience in the implementation of the system in road fleets and, especially, in multi-depot retail environments, the needs of the RFOL project required some innovative development. The constraints for the method of operation, fitment in the cab of the Freight Multiple Unit (FMU), the safety case and VAB (Vehicle Acceptance Board) approval required extensive research and subsequent development of:

- A new In Cab Unit with a large colour display, processor, aerials, power management and housing case;
- New applications to operate in a browser environment;
- Bespoke applications to manage the allocation of tasks to FMU units;
- Assessment for the operating environment for compatibility (environmental and electromagnetic) of the equipment.

8.4 Phase One Trials

The MPV units were hired and configured for technical trials in July and August 2001. The objectives of these trials were to:

1. Configure and test the train and its component software modules;
2. Install V1 Isotrak hardware and control systems;
3. Run the train with varied tonnages;
4. Run the train with both all fours engines and with only three engines;
5. Run three showcase events to demonstrate the concept and engage potential customers for full scale trials in 2002;
6. Gather performance and technical information to ensure efficient commercial trials in 2002.

Bulmers (the Hereford-based cider manufacturers) provided loads for this phase of the project and trains ran between Hereford and Willesden for deliveries of both keg and bottled product into their London depot.

The MPV units themselves are not very amenable to carrying freight, having a deck height higher than the intermediate rail wagons. In these trials the MPV water modules were retained on the units to provide ballast and traction.

The train performed well ahead of expectations. Given this was the first time the unit had been configured in this way and given the new technology deployed there were some tangible results.

8.5 Phase Two Trials

The second round of trials built upon the success of the first and were designed for a number of clients who engaged the Railfreightonline team during the original trials. There were a large number of interested parties who discussed how the new train might work for them and the following customers agreed to undertake commercial trials in spring of 2002.

- Bulmers;
- Amylum;
- Comet;
- Goodyear;
- Marks and Spencer.

The selection process involved ensured that the train carried differing types of freight in both primary and secondary flows. A pre-requisite was the need for the train to mirror as closely as possible the existing supply chain demands for departure and arrival times, loading techniques and delivery patterns.

Three routes were selected to demonstrate diversity around the type of distance where the Cargosprinter could be best deployed (i.e. not long distance trunking). The flows selected demonstrated a number of characteristics.

DATE	MPV 1	CAR 1	CAR 2	CAR 3	CAR 4	MPV 2	Total Payload
30/07/2001	23.06	28.60	28.60	29.56	29.56	23.06	162.44
01/08/2001	23.06	27.48	27.39	29.56	29.56	23.06	160.11
03/08/2001	23.06	24.88	29.30	29.46	4.60	23.06	134.36
06/08/2001	23.06	29.56	29.10	4.60	4.60	23.06	113.98
08/08/2001	23.06	29.70	16.66	4.60	4.60	23.06	101.68
10/08/2001	23.06	27.78	4.60	4.60	4.60	23.06	87.70

Note:
Water modules carried 19,000 litres of water. Each module is 4.06 tare and GESeaco curtain side swap bodies are 4.6 tonnes tare

Table 8.1 FMU Payloads for Bulmers trial

- Imported product from port to inland hub;
- Raw material from factory to manufacturer;
- Retail goods from Distribution Centre to Regional Distribution Centre;
- Retail goods from Distribution Centre to Store.

Goods included liquid glucose, tyres, clothing and electrical goods.

Intermodal equipment used included:

- 20' ISO tanks, both laden and unladen
- 45' containers 9' high
- 45' swap bodies

Technical specification
The train set was broadly the same as the first trials with two sets of FKA wagons sitting between the traction units. Low height container units containing aggregate rather than the MPV water tanks provided ballast this time. The train control software provided was a new updated version that had been re-written following lessons learned from the initial trials.

Isotrak equipment had also evolved from the first trial and, following customer feedback, included improved hardware and software facilitating improved Internet access, improved mapping and operational functionality.

Trial 1: Goodyear/Dunlop and Geest Lines
Tyres between Tilbury and Hams Hall (W Midlands), May 6th to 15th 2002
Goodyear/Dunlop tyre production plants are spread across Europe. Both import and export flows move between sites in the Birmingham area and central and Eastern Europe. Geest Lines perform most of the unitised movements for Goodyear/Dunlop on these routes and supply a short sea feeder service between Rotterdam and Tilbury. Onward delivery is normally undertaken by road. This trial offered both the customer and the shipper an opportunity to understand how rail might provide a dedicated service between the port and the Midlands. With Goodyear moving into a new central DC at Fort Dunlop, a rail connected site, in 2002 this was an ideal opportunity for both parties to assess their supply chain plans for the future.

The freight multiple unit performed faultlessly during the two weeks of the Goodyear/Dunlop Tyres/Geest trial. Import/Export vehicle tyres were conveyed in 45' long x 9' high Geest shipping containers, shipped to and from Germany through the port of Tilbury. The adjacent Victa Railfreight terminal handled these at their Riverside terminal, whilst Mid-Kent Freight of Maidstone undertook the local distribution between port and terminal.

ABP Connect undertook train reception and release at their Hams Hall terminal, whilst Geest carried out local road distribution to the customer's West Midlands distribution centres at Hams Hall, Aldridge, Marchington and Wolverhampton.

Key Performance Indicators (KPIs) for this trip were set at arrival on terminal within 20 minutes of schedule. There was only one serious delay during this trial, due to a crew change problem at Wembley; however, all customer deliveries were made on time.

Trial 2: Bulmers and Amylum
Liquid Glucose from Greenwich to Hereford, May 20th to May 31st 2002
Bulmers receive liquid glucose from a number of UK suppliers. Amylum based in Greenwich was keen to support Bulmers in looking at the route by rail connecting through the Tilbury rail terminal. Bulmers receives around 12 loads per week from Amylum so the train ran into Bulmers three times a week for each of the two weeks. This service would reflect closely how Bulmers would use this type of train. The unit could be used for London collections twice a week (two trips of six tanks) and twice a week for collections from their other main supplier based in Trafford Park.

The freight multiple unit performed faultlessly during the two weeks of the Tilbury to Hereford trial, carrying bulk glucose in 26,000-litre ISO tanks supplied by Exsif Worldwide. Product was moved from the Amylum production plant at Greenwich. Exel (Tankfreight) undertook the road distribution between Greenwich and the Victa Railfreight terminal at Tilbury Riverside.

It is noteworthy to point out that, with a total payload in excess of 160 tonnes, plus intermediate railcar tare weight totalling 97.2 tonnes, the two

Figure 8.3 FMU Entering Bulmers siding at Hereford

master-master MPVs topped Llanvihangel Summit at 40 mph from a standing start at Abergavenny, following a signal check on the first trip out to Hereford. The key performance indicator for the trial was to arrive on site at Hereford for inbound movements within 15 minutes of schedule, which was achieved on all but the last run. This delay was caused by awaiting access from Railtrack to proceed along the Moorfields Branch to Bulmers' private siding, across a manually operated level crossing. Similarly the return leg met the standard on all occasions. Operational issues have been discussed in more detail elsewhere [2].

The ISO tanks were handled within the H P Bulmers private siding/factory by a Containerlift vehicle having a lift capacity in excess of 32 tonnes. The average off-loading time of a full tank and transfer to a road skeletal trailer took in the region of 20 to 30 minutes. The ideal solution would be to pump the product directly from the railcar-mounted ISO tanks, however, the location of the glucose storage vessels within the Bulmers factory currently prevents such a streamlined operation from taking place. The ISOs were subsequently transferred between rail siding and product discharge point by Exel Tankfreight vehicles and pumped off with a land-based pump in a time of between 50 and 60 minutes.

All product discharge was undertaken within the expected time constraints and there were no issues with product integrity.

Trial 3: Marks and Spencer/JRL and Comet
Widnes to Glasgow, June 4th to 12th 2002
This was always going to be the largest challenge for the project: two large blue-chip retailers offering flows of store goods from distribution centres in the

Manchester area into Scotland. This is an ideal flow for either client, both of whom have regular traffic on this route. The project team worked closely with both parties designing a flow that suited their order processing and delivery lead times for this time sensitive route and the path was scheduled to mirror the current road-based solution.

The FMU performed faultlessly during this two-week trial. During the outbound journey on 11 June, the oil pressure light for engine number one was displaying. The unit was temporarily 'looped' at Wigan, where the oil levels were found to be normal. As a precaution this specific engine was isolated and the unit continued its journey to Mossend and return to Widnes on three engines only. No significant loss of performance was evident, although the payload was not exceptional on this occasion. Fuel consumption was very much as if the unit had been running with all four motive units in synchronisation.

Despite all our best-laid plans the first outbound trip suffered a departure delay from the AHC Warehousing terminal due to train release documentation difficulties between the terminal operator and EWS. This is the kind of problem that we had sought to prevent by ensuring good communications between all parties and is one that would hopefully not be repeated in a normal working environment. Subsequent network congestion in the Oxenholme/Penrith area forced the FMU to be further delayed, arriving at Mossend some 162 minutes late. The delivery into the customer's Cumbernauld RDC was resultantly 50 minutes late. This was the only customer delay throughout the six weeks of trials.

AHC Warehousing undertook the NW area road distribution. Electrical retail goods on behalf of Comet were moved between their RDC in the Warrington area and the Widnes terminal, whilst retail clothing on behalf of Marks and Spencer was moved in 45' shipping containers from their Middleton RDC. EWS Mossend Euroterminal handled train reception and release in Scotland, whilst W H Malcolm performed the road distribution for M&S to the GIST RDC at Westfield and the Comet Outlet at Possil Park, Glasgow.

Summary of Trials

The train performed remarkably well for a prototype configuration. The work undertaken in the phase one trials was time well spent and ensured that performance standards were achieved.

The logistics of implementing door-to-door services that fully integrate seamlessly is not easy. To undertake them for one off trials is even harder. If we total all parties supplying information, services and goods for these trials they number 27. This is a major logistical operation that stretched all parties. The real success was that, with the exception of the problem encountered regarding train release on 4th June, this would have been an exemplary result.

The really outstanding performance of the train was taking 160 tonnes over the Llanvihangel Summit from a standing start. Whilst the team were always confident that the power to weight ratio was sufficient to achieve this, there had been some press speculation that the unit would not be able to meet this type of task.

8.6 Use of Isotrak Command and Control Technology for Rail Freight

The decision to include Isotrak as partners in the project was taken well before the initial submission and is seen as a major success of the project in delivering tangible services which are now being developed further within the rail industry

From the users' perspective, the Isotrak system started as an interesting source of additional information and moved to being a major aide in evaluating train performance and enhancing the transparency of service by keeping all parties informed in real time of the trains' status. In the Phase two trials, where the control hub was placed in an Exel traffic office (rather then the Railfreightonline project office), communications between the train and the hub were considerably enhanced by 24-hour cover.

Text messages from the train to the hub, when queried about delays, were very useful and in most cases the hub operatives were able to advise the operator, EWS, of problems before they knew themselves. The system automatically updated project team members through text messages to mobile phones of key events. This was particularly useful on the Scottish trials where no project team member was based at either Widnes or Glasgow.

The Victa rail terminal team at Tilbury received text messages when the Bulmers train passed through Gospel Oak in North London, enabling them to remain tucked up in bed until they were needed at the terminal.

The development of Isotrak in the RFOL project was a great success, despite the number of obstacles and difficulties that were encountered at various times throughout the trial. The Isotrak system was adapted and developed for rail operations and the use of the system has been extended to a passenger Train Operation Company in partnership with Exel and Amey. This has now seen a fully fledged product called RailTime launched into the rail passenger and freight markets.

8.7 Moving Forward

The interest from within the industry was high. In many cases companies sought to add value to our proposals and supplied information to support us technically. The project saw:

- 79 rail service providers and engineers
- 23 press publications and TV and Radio

- 24 representatives of industry bodies and academia participated in the project at some time or another.

Two on-going projects are worthy of note:

HSBC Rail have commenced work on how an FMU might be adapted for the urban environment. Their partnership with Exel, the University of Westminster, Amec, Bluebird Electric Vehicles and Transport for London (TfL), has recently received funding from TfL for a feasibility study into rail freight in an urban environment.

Inbis Rail has been working alongside Amec Rail in the design of an FMU for the UK timber industry. The two organisations have shared data and specifications and have undertaken trials in Wales during 2002. This project is a likely applicant for 'Innovation' funding from the SRA in 2003.

There are, then, considerable opportunities for developing the FMU concept into regular and sustained use.

References

1. Cordner, K (2003) 'The SRA's Innovation Awards', Modern Rlys. 60. no 658 pp. 49–50, July.
2. Dunn, P (2002) 'Can Rail Really Take on the Road Hauliers?', Rail 438 pp. 36–43.

9 Higher Speed Freight

Alan Williams

With the increasing number of new high speed lines being completed across Europe and the accompanying general increase in maximum line speeds on existing routes, the potential for the fast, timed movement of freight by rail both within and between major countries of Europe has never been greater.

9.1 The Rise and Fall of the Mail Train

The earliest example of the use of rail for higher-speed goods was for the movement of mail. In Britain, railways were used for the conveyance of mail from 1837 and, as the rail networks of both Britain and Europe grew, so did their use by the respective postal authorities for the fast, often overnight, movement of letters and parcels in trains running to scheduled timetables at passenger train speeds. In several countries, these trains also regularly carried staff to sort mail in transit, so they were also equipped with lighting, heating and toilets. In some countries, similar trains were provided for the overnight carriage and sorting of newspapers. Likewise, growers and processors of fruit and vegetables and fish soon spotted the potential of railways for getting their products to market, and these trains, too, were operated at near-express passenger train speeds to a regular timetable. In France, for example, such trains were used for the rapid movement of produce from the far South West of the country to Parisian markets, while in Britain the London and North Eastern Railway established regular, fast freight trains to carry freshly-caught fish from the ports of North East Scotland over the 600 miles (960 km) to the markets of London and the South East of England.

However, the advent of motorways and autoroutes from the 1960s brought higher road speeds and permitted larger, heavier road vehicles, allowing road transport to begin to match rail in terms of both speed and price. The rail administrations of Europe responded by first raising maximum speed limits on conventional lines, and then, led by France, building new high speed lines. However, these were almost entirely optimised for fast passenger train use, with steep gradients and relatively low maximum axle-loading, making them unsuitable for heavier freight trains. The now-extensive French Ligne a Grande Vitesse high speed rail network remains banned to all freight use with the sole exception of four specially-built postal TGV units. Likewise, the Cologne-Frankfurt Neubaustrecke high speed line, opened in 2002, has been built specifically for passenger use, with tunnels and other structures to suit, and gradients as steep as 1 in 25, compared to 1 in 35 on

Picture courtesy of La Vie du Rail

Figure 9.1 Postal TGV Being Loaded

the French high speed network and on the Channel Tunnel Rail Link (CTRL), now under construction in South East England between the Channel Tunnel and London.

This is in contrast to the earlier German north-south Hannover-Würzburg and Mannheim-Stuttgart high speed lines, both opened in 1991, which were built for use by both passenger and freight trains and involved heavy engineering work and therefore higher cost to provide the gentler gradients necessary for freight trains. Similar criteria have been applied in the construction of high speed lines in Italy and Spain. In Britain, with the exception of the CTRL, the emphasis has continued to be focussed on the improvement of existing lines with a maximum speed of 125 mph (200km/h) rather than the construction of specially-designed high speed lines. These lines have remained available for the high speed transit of freight although, in practice, there have been problems in providing suitable paths on the congested network and there has been little development beyond the traditional letters and parcels traffic. Even if special rolling stock were to be available for high speed, time-sensitive freight, much of it needs to travel overnight. Unfortunately, one of the great disadvantages of the high speed lines – and, increasingly, conventional lines in Britain – is that they are often closed for maintenance at night. Transit times are therefore extended and, worse, unreliable.

For this reason, even the traditional high speed, time sensitive traffics have begun to slip away. No daily newspapers are now carried by train in Britain. Very few European postal authorities now use rail for the overnight transmission of urgent letters and parcels, and some do not use rail at all. With the rapid increase in the number and size of competing courier companies, almost all of which use road or air services rather than rail, postal authorities have followed suit.

La Poste, the French Post Office, once used rail extensively for the movement of mail including Travelling Post Offices. Now, the only use of rail is for the four specially designed Postal Trains a Grande Vitesse (TGV), built for the opening of the first French high speed line between Paris and Lyons in 1981, and now extended to Marseilles. No further trains have been built for the subsequent Atlantique and Nord high speed lines and none are proposed for the new Est line to Strasbourg. Although operationally identical to the passenger carrying TGVs and able to run at the same maximum 300km/h line speed, they are unable to put this to advantage at nights, when most needed, because of line closures for maintenance.

This has also been the problem in Britain. Even though, in contrast to most other European postal authorities, the British Post Office invested in a fleet of

Picture courtesy of Milepost 92½

Figure 9.2 Mail-Carrying Class 325 Electric Multiple Unit in Britain.

16 new 100 mph (160 km/h) four-coach electric trains and five purpose built mail-handling stations in the mid-1990s, it has suffered continuing reliability problems, particularly in more recent years. Although performance is better than almost all passenger services in Britain, Royal Mail, which is itself under pressure to cut costs and improve its overnight mail service in the face of competition, announced in 2002 that all 17 of its overnight Travelling Post Office trains would be withdrawn by the beginning of 2004, and that the remainder of the rail postal services were under review, including the option of switching all postal traffic to air or road. The general expectation, however, was that some core traffic will remain on rail, actually carrying more mail but using fewer trains and running mainly during the day for less time critical mail.

9.2 The Impact of New Lines

So why, when there are now more high speed lines available than ever before, when the talk is all about interoperability, roads are becoming ever more congested and when airfreight is increasingly subject to delays as a result of increased security checks, is there still so little truly high speed freight on the world's railways?

For this is not just a European phenomenon. In Japan, where the high speed train era started in the 1960s with the 'bullet' train, the now widespread 'Shinkansen' network is still used by passenger trains only and there is no high speed freight network. And in the USA, apart from the passenger-only Boston-New York -Washington north east corridor, all rail routes are limited to just 79 mph (128 km/h).

Some of the reasons have been outlined above – high speed lines optimised for passenger trains, reluctance to provide additional express paths on classic lines during the day, and insistence on closing lines for repair at night, the very time when roads are least congested and aircraft are cheapest to hire.

One of the major disadvantages of rail transport is that, unlike road and air transport, its network does not readily lend itself to the 'hub and spoke' method of distribution. This approach is increasingly in use today, especially for high speed, time sensitive products and services. Unless rail networks can effectively provide either the inward or outward or, ideally, both spokes of such operations, they will be disadvantaged. In Britain, in an attempt to provide such a service, an experimental overnight high speed 'piggyback' service of specially-adapted road trailers was run between London and Glasgow for the Parcelforce subsidiary of Royal Mail. But the advantages of the fast end-to-end transit on the West Coast Main Line were often negated, not so much by the delay in re-configuring the vehicles from road to rail use and then vice-versa at the other end (this was achieved remarkably quickly) but by the need to change from electric to diesel traction to shunt the trains into sidings at each end of the line.

9.3 Successes and Constraints

Capacity constraints are a problem, too. Where volume rather than weight defines how much freight can be carried in a single vehicle, more and more road trailers are being double-decked, so that one road vehicle can carry as much as two conventional rail vehicles. Loading gauge constraints, particularly in Britain, have so far constrained the development of double-deck rail vehicles, other than for car-carrying. But national railway administrations and their Governments, too, have been slow to realise that high speed transits are only part of the attraction for potential customers. Rapid, reliable handling at terminals at each end is vital to compete with road end-to-end timings, as is freedom from the threat of industrial action, still too prevalent on many of the railway systems of Europe.

But there have been some recent successes. English, Welsh and Scottish Railways, who operate mail trains for the Royal Mail in Britain, have begun running timed, overnight parcels trains for private couriers between the Midlands and Scotland at speeds of up to 110mph (176 km/h), while for a time recently, fast, overnight conveyance was provided for Unilever by attaching freight vehicles to the nightly Amsterdam – Milan sleeping car train.

In Britain, the high speed Channel Tunnel Rail Link (CTRL) has been built with passing loops to hold freight trains while Eurostar trains pass at 300 km/h. But interest among freight operators in taking advantage of this faster line has been slow to develop, even though it also enables larger European Continental gauge vehicles to reach London. This is largely because of the history of disruption by asylum seekers at the French Frethun terminal and the apparent inability of both the French and British Governments to take effective action to prevent it.

Eurotunnel, operator of the Channel Tunnel itself, has been alarmed at the lower than predicted growth of international freight traffic through the tunnel, and will start to lose money when current agreements expire in 2006. It has proposed a high speed, frequent freight shuttle from Lille in Northern France through the tunnel to an appropriate terminal in South East England using continental gauge vehicles.

Generally, railway administrations have been reluctant to back speculative investment in special rolling stock and terminal facilities for the movement of freight at higher speeds. In marked contrast to investment in passenger rolling stock, which has almost always been to replace or further enhance existing services with assured revenue streams, the development of trains for timed, high speed freight transit remains in its infancy. But a major spur to new development could be the open access regulations which came into force across the railways of Europe in March 2003. For the first time, private operators will be able to own and operate their own freight trains, running them across borders independent of the major rail administrations. As the various requirements for harmonisation and interoperability between countries come into force, fast, long distance freight transits free from traditional and time consuming locomotive and crew changes at national borders will become possible. As Kuhla has noted, there are a number of proposals for rail freight terminals at airports, complementing the air hub with some rail 'spokes'.

It remains to be seen whether there will be sufficient interest and, perhaps even more importantly, confidence from within the private sector to invest in the necessary new rolling stock and other facilities to provide networks of high speed freight trains. There are opportunities – but will they be taken?

Reference

Kuhla, E (2003) 'Seeking a High-Speed Freight Market', Railway Gazette Intnl. pp. 210–211.

Editors' note:

In June 2003, Royal Mail announced its intention to cease using trains for the carriage of mail by end of March 2004 because it had been unable to agree a new contract with its supplier, EWS. It stressed that this was a straightforward commercial rather than a political decision, and that ideally it would prefer to retain a rail element in its transport mix. It has therefore not ruled out a return to rail at some time in the future.

10 Intermodal Transport by Rail

Ties van Ark, Railway Consultancy Ltd

10.1 Introduction

Intermodal transport is the movement of goods using more than one transport mode. It deals with cargo transfer by using specially designed load carrying and protecting units that can be swapped easily between several modes of transport. This avoids unloading and reloading of individual items but results in a lower overall payload, due to the duplicated load-bearing elements of the rail vehicle and the load carrying units. As a transport system, intermodal business tries to combine specific advantages of otherwise competing transport modes to achieve an overall gain for all partners involved. The options to complete an intermodal journey include a selection of the road, water, air or rail modes to carry the consignment from origin to destination. Intermodal transport by rail is the carriage of goods for at least one section of that journey by rail.

If this book has a separate chapter about intermodal transport by rail, the first question that arises is, what is the difference? What is the difference between intermodal transport and conventional transport? What from, a railway perspective, is the difference between an "intermodal train" and a conventional train? The answer is simple: nothing. The intermodal train travels from origin

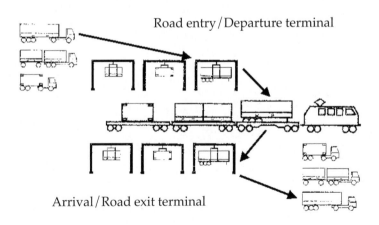

Road entry/Departure terminal

Arrival/Road exit terminal

Fig. 10.1 Intermodal operation chain

98

to destination, will be hauled by the same engine, by the same skilled driver over the same two pieces of steel. To haul an intermodal train is just as easy (or difficult?) as hauling a conventional train. So why another chapter, why "Intermodal Transport by Rail"? The answer to this question lies in the customer. The intermodal customer is different, the intermodal customer has an immediate choice for every consignment, thereby the intermodal customer has forced and is forcing the Railways to change and will continue to lead the way in today's changing railway world.

10.2 The Intermodal Customer

So who is this customer with a difference, why is he so important, why is this customer so different, why is this customer so demanding and why can this customer enforce change? To this question there is no single answer, so we need to try to develop an image of the intermodal customer:

- The intermodal customer lacks 200 years of railway heritage in his veins. Many arguments and especially incidents affecting performance with which railway staff and conventional clients have grown up and understand as legitimate, are not understood and are being challenged.
- The intermodal customer has not made considerable investments in railway infrastructure. This gives the intermodal customer far more flexibility towards his mode choice. For every consignment a customer can make a new choice whether to use rail or opt for road or water transport.
- The intermodal customer operates under continuous pressure from his clients to improve performance and to lower prices in a very competitive market. Especially in a period where transport demand is low, road transport will often offer very competitive prices to keep the trucks rolling. Where low road rates result in road haulage firms going out of business, this does not lead to loss of transport capacity and thereby an upwards pressure on prices. Equipment becomes available on the second hand market at reduced costs.
- The intermodal customer interacts continuously with the changing world outside the railways. Thereby the customer is operating in a far less sheltered environment than the traditional European Rail Freight companies and their staff, resulting in a more customer orientated attitude towards his clients and greater focus to meet customer demands.

This image paints a customer that is exactly right for the railways. For the freight railways and the rail system to continue its revival and to increase its market share in freight transport, it needs external pressures to fuel the internal drive to create efficient and effective organisations that are able to supply services tailored to their customers needs. The intermodal customers have proven to be able to demand change and will continue to do so.

Picture courtesy of National Railway Museum

Figure 10.2. Early Intermodal Operations in Britain

To serve this customer the railway needs to be dedicated, focussed, very efficient, effective and innovative, always aiming to cut its costs a little bit more, always aiming to increase margins to reach or maintain profitability. These railway organisations need to be capable of delivering a high quality transport operation, day-in, day-out, and that to a customer who doesn't want to understand the traditional sorrows and excuses so often accompanied by using the railways (either as a passenger or a freight customer).

Having created the image of the Intermodal Customer, the question arises, who is this customer? The first revelation is that there is always more than one and, unfortunately, the answer will never be complete. Examples of the intermodal railway operator's customers are:

- The shipping lines, often the decision maker, with always a ship about to depart;
- The agent, who has hired train capacity and is trying to sell his train, with just one more container to catch the train;

100

- The terminal manager, who has got the lorry driver waiting at the gate and a train to load;
- The end user, who is awaiting delivery of his goods;
- The sender, who made the decision to send his consignment the intermodal way;
- The road haulier who has arranged to deliver the cargo at 0800 hours.

This short list of customers and also often partners in the transport chain, again highlights a difference with more conventional railway traffic: the number of parties involved in an intermodal train is far larger than with more conventional rail transport. A comparison with the parcels business is justified. Although all parties are part of the transport chain, each participant has to pursue their own interests and profitability. Each participant has to fight to maintain its profitability. Occasionally this will result in a party choosing to pursue its own short term interests in preference to the chain's long term interests, for the moment conveniently forgetting that all involved are riding the same train.

10.3 The Container

Without any doubt the most visible format of intermodal traffic is the ISO container. The ISO container that fits on a train, transfers to the road, sails on a boat and, in one form or another, can accommodate nearly every type of good to be transported. It is the most widely seen "packaging" in intermodal transport by rail. From a railway perspective, it is slightly unfortunate that containers come in many sorts and sizes, 40 feet, 45 feet, 30 feet, 20 feet, tanks, flats, high, refrigerated, empty as well as full. All of these can be transported by rail. However, more dedicated rail/road systems have also been developed to accommodate particular flows of traffic, for instance:

- The road trailer (adapted for transport by rail) combined with a well-type wagon;
- ACTS, a system where the equipment on the truck is used to transfer special containers direct to and from dedicated rail wagons often found for refuse transport, although having far greater capabilities.

To transport this variety of "packaging", many different designs of rail wagons are in operation, with varieties in wagon length, number of axles, loading capacity and height of the wagon. The combination of wagons available aims to provide the optimal mix for the different container types in a train. The combination of wagons must provide a flexible and efficient loading capacity, so that the train can accommodate varying types and weights of containers and that no loading capacity is lost. Unfortunately, the available mix of containers is not the only reason for this variety of wagons. The dif-

Figure 10.3. Container During Lift

ferences between the loading gauges and weight restrictions of the different rail networks make additional requirements for more adapted wagons. For instance, the UK wagons able to carry High Cube containers have to be lower than wagons for high cubes on the continental networks, because of the smaller loading gauge (see chapter 12).

10.4 Containers on the Track?

With the introduction of the "container", the traditional European railway companies saw a strong decline in conventional traffic to and from the European ports. The "brown closed wagon", departing and arriving from warehouses and sidings gradually became an inefficient relic of the past. Warehouses and quays themselves became just as redundant and large areas of formerly busy harbours were vacated. In general, harbours moved seawards to accommodate the ever increasing container volume in ever larger vessels. To maintain market share and to follow the trend, the railway companies felt forced to find and offer solutions for transporting containers to and from the European harbours. This culminated in the formation of "Intercontainer" for the trans-European transport of port related container traffic. Intercontainer's main role was to market and sell rail as a mode for container transport. Within countries, the traditional railway companies provided transport, either directly or via subsidiary companies, in addition to national traffic and continental traffic. However, nothing much changed: the traditional companies transported wagons with containers in much the same way as they always transport harbour traffic: from terminal, small siding to shunting yard, in dedicated or mixed trains to the next shunting yard, to a border station, where the neighbouring railway company supplied its own engine and its own driver to continue the pattern till the destination station was reached, the now empty wagon would then often follow a longer only part-loaded return journey to its "owning" railway company. The result was that the railways acquired an often loss making share of the container market, waiting, hoping and "pricing" for the growth in numbers to return the companies to good fortunes.

Although many efforts and improvements were made, often the intermodal market stayed a loss-producing sector of the railway business, especially for companies who covered a short distance and were either origin or destination of the consignments, like the Netherlands. Continuing competitive pressure to reduce prices and demands to improve transport quality, with a need / political pressure to keep the train rolling, led to increasing losses, while the total volume of containers on the move kept growing and the environmental and congestion problems required a greater role of rail. The traditional railway companies were forced to reduce losses and improve results.

Many of the traditional European railway companies significantly increased utilisation of their hardware and staff by increasing the number of productive hours of engines and staff, enabling substantial reductions in the numbers of these resources. In many cases this resulted in removing the slack that kept the European rail machine running. With the reduced operating costs the ability to deliver some quality evaporated. This resulted in ever increasing delays of international trains, more unfulfilled expectations and more dissatisfied customers. In a political climate of privatisation and open access the traditional railways helped to create the need for new and different Railway Operators to enter the market. The price paid by Europe's once mighty railway companies for their limited ability and often refusal to change and modernise their ways is significant loss of market share and the establishment of new internationally operating railway companies, like ERS. Intermodal transport is on the track and is there to stay.

10.5 Service Industry

Although transport of freight by rail has elements of the process of manufacturing products, a better understanding is achieved when transport is viewed as a service industry. The characteristic of a "service" is that it is consumed while being produced. If the service view is applied to rail transport, it is easier to understand that an incident during "production" is likely to have an impact on the end performance of the rail section (delayed arrival), as well as the transport chain's total performance (delayed consignments). To view rail transport as a service notes that with every mile travelled, time has passed and the train comes nearer to its destination. When viewed as a service it also becomes clear that, once a train has departed, there is very little that can be done to ensure that it will travel according to its intended timetable. Disruptions will occur often due to outside influences and, once an incident has occurred, the operator can only try to minimise its impact. The image of transport as a service is further strengthened by real time tracking and tracing, where delays become visible for the customer almost immediately.

In order to deliver a high performing service, the key to a good performance lies very much on "preparation". The only way to reduce the risks of incidents and disruptions lies in the design of the service and the preventative maintenance of equipment.

10.6 A Robust Production Plan

A proven way to achieve a well prepared intermodal train service is to produce a "production" plan. The production plan should describe tasks and responsibilities in the chain, as well as more typical railway issues like a timetable. The plan requires input from all participants in the chain and within the railway operator. The plan should result in each participant knowing what and when to do. The plan is not a law, the plan is a tool to achieve high performance. The danger of the well communicated and agreed plan is that it becomes inflexible, while it is essential that all parties maintain the flexibility to make changes to improve performance.

The production plan for an intermodal train should consist of:

- The transport chain parties involved and their responsibilities;
- Arrangements with the terminals;
- A train timetable, including engines and driver arrangements;
- Communication arrangements;
- Rail document and customs arrangements;
- Wagon arrangements;
- Tracking and Tracing arrangements;
- Quality assurance.

The natural tendency of a railway organisation appears to be that, in the development of a plan, the emphasis is strongly on the train planners. Although they are an important contributor, the input of the operational staff is just as important. The operational staff have to make it work and their experience and input is invaluable in ensuring a robust and executable plan. In putting the plan together, it is essential that railway staff feels and is motivated and challenged to investigate what is needed to achieve a robust service, rather than merely identifying all sleepers that might block the track.

A further important consideration before embarking on the plan is that it has to work in a 7 x 24 hour industry, spread over many participating locations.

Communication in a 7 x 24 hours environment is notoriously difficult, far more difficult than communication in the (head) office environment. You can't call a meeting with all participants together and issue new instructions. If all involved need to be addressed it might require 3 to 4 meetings to bring the message across. The consequence of this is that, if the plan has to work night and day, day in day out it is essential that procedures and arrangements are as simple and understandable as possible.

Terminal arrangements
Terminals come in all sorts and sizes (and costs), in much varying levels of activity. There are terminals served by only 1 train a day, and terminals where arrivals and departures are an almost continuing process through the day and night. The first terminals will not very often cause a problem for the railway operator as there is an abundance of capacity to load/unload the train The second terminal has evidently a far more dynamic process and both internal processes and external imported causes can cause delays. One of the external causes for delays is, unfortunately, the railway operator himself when trains arrive late for loading or unloading. With my feet firmly in the railways, I am restricted to observations about terminal processes and the essentials of what needs to be agreed between railway and terminal operator.

The terminal process is not something that starts when the train arrives; large parts of it are completed before the train's arrival. The busy terminals tend to work with slots booked for particular trains. Well before the train arrives, the terminal has started to organise its response: locations for arriving boxes have been identified and boxes to be loaded are transferred to the train loading point. This operation, which might start many hours before the train's actual (planned) arrival results in terminal capacity being "occupied" and flexibility in the terminal processes being lost. The rail operator has to be prepared for the delays in terminal processes that occur, including (to name just a few) high winds, dense fog, crane failures, staff shortages, incorrectly loaded boxes, dangerous goods incidents and, last but not least, late arrival of incoming trains. All these are issues that will arise and upset terminal operations and loading/unloading of trains. So, while terminal managers are inclined to use all their creativity to plan a slot for the next new train service required to start, thereby increasing their business, both terminal and rail operator(s) have to be devil's advocates and ensure that the terminal plan remains robust and executable. An allocated slot needs to be of sufficient capacity to load/unload the train and, with a slighter wider perspective, the terminal plan itself should never exceed its capacity and thereby become the cause of delays before the train is ready to start rolling.

To the gain of both parties it is necessary to find creative solutions for the terminal-rail interface. The terminal needs operational advance information about wagon composition of the train to be able to make a train-load/unload plan. The rail operator requires information about wagon/container combinations, like weights and presence of dangerous goods. In seeking efficient and practical solutions it is possible to increase efficiency. Double entry of data can be eliminated and an opportunity to reduce production costs might occur. In a similar way it is possible to implement solutions where railway staff assist in terminal operations or terminal staff execute rail tasks to increase chain efficiency. Leaving the traditional divides between tasks opens opportunities to improve the efficiency of the transport chain. These issues rise above the details required for the operational plan and show that a good interaction benefits the transport chain. With regard to the production plan, issues that need to be included are:

- Loading cut off time, train available for rail operator;
- Train available for terminal operator;
- Administrative procedures and deadlines;
- Delay train messages.

When problems have arisen and delays are occurring it is essential to have established procedures to minimise their impact and to resume normal operations as quickly as possible. It may be better to have one train seriously delayed than all trains slightly delayed. Decisions about which actions to take are painful, but one has to be aware that not taking a decision has usually the worst impact on overall performance. Agreeing with terminal and customers in advance the priority of the service might reduce the customer's willingness to buy the service but creates clarity for all involved.

It is often easy to come to some sort of understanding with a "local" terminal, however, with international trains the other terminal might be far away, have its own habits and find it difficult to communicate in a common language. It is essential that the arrangements with the "other terminal" are of similar quality and precision to prevent problems starting at the "other end". An option to be considered is to appoint an "agent" to facilitate communications and arrange operational details, with both terminal and possibly other rail partners involved in the transport chain. The man on the ground can often achieve more than the man on the phone.

The rail operator
Before we start this section, let us just remind ourselves of the position of the railway operator in the intermodal chain: "The railway operator has to transport within the corset of the intermodal transport chain, the straightjacket of the railways and the strop of the banks round his neck". The combination of these three leaves very little room for errors and every problem identified and solved during the planning process of the train service decreases the occurrence of problems during "production". In the planning process of a new train-service, one encounters a dilemma of the railway industry-service: We are all used to working according to plans (like the timetable), resulting in

organisations where the planners play the first and last violins and the voice of the staff working "on the line" seldom reaches the "Ivory Tower". This has led to rail planning becoming an "Art". Other staff can say what they like or do not like, but the plan stands above all. An anecdote of the "Art of Planning" is a short distance service requiring two electric engines and three diesel engines to travel from origin to destination, about 200 miles. The plan was very efficient, often filling gaps in rosters of engines, but the journey was slow, every change of engine requiring additional time. The planning department was very proud of this achievement. The train's customers were invited to travel in the cab to experience "their" Intermodal journey, resulting in a "never again" verdict. The then customers are now railway operators using heavy diesels in international traffic to cross the borders.

The rail operator should not try to sell what cannot be produced. The rail operator should aim to make the customer aware that, although paying the price of a taxi, he will never receive more than a bus. The planners should not be forced to develop plans which require a daily degree of luck to be executable. Planners need to be in touch with the day-to-day operations; they need to listen to feedback. Most importantly, planners should aim to reduce situations where interdependencies between trains are created, even if it is all a little less efficient and looks a bit more expensive to do so. Planners should aim to change drivers at hubs, rather than in the middle of nowhere, or not at all; a driver going home will use the train to get there. Planners should aim not to squeeze a train into a "virtual" path. A "virtual" path is a path that only exists on the planner's graphs but, in reality, disappears due to daily occurring disturbances.

Planners should know that, especially in international traffic such as Rail4chem's (see Figure 10.4), a train needs to arrive on time at a border crossing to have any chance of a timely arrival at its destination. By minimising the number of interdependencies the planner helps to keep the train service controllable. This minimises the effect of the daily disruptions and, above all, the need for additional drivers and engine resources is reduced. The addition of somewhat extended stops at the hubs creates some flexibility in the timetable, while a time gap between arrival and the start of terminal operations ensures that the rail service becomes more reliable. Creating a plan as a tool is not rocket science but, hopefully, the planners are able to see it as a more interesting challenge.

The timetable, rosters and engine changes are essential parts of the production plan. The limitations on train length, axle weight, available routes and loading gauges are a necessary though often somewhat unwelcome part of train reality.

Communication
Communication is difficult and, in the railways, very difficult. Every reader will have asked a question to platform staff in a disrupted situation and received

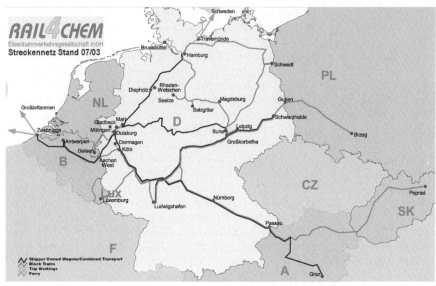

Map courtesy of Rail4chem

Figure 10.4 Rail4chem's International Network

an evasive answer. The man/woman can't say what he/she doesn't know. Formalising communication and issues to be communicated help to improve reliability. In international traffic, communication in a different language to a different culture, with different values and above all to staff with their own set of priorities (domestic traffic!) is a challenge. To ensure communication, multi-lingual staff, messages or the "man on the ground" might prove a necessity.

A location where customer/terminal operator can reach the rail operator 24 hours a day can be a costly but essential part of operations. Knowledgeable, customer orientated, multi-lingual staff, available to monitor performance and to assist and solve problems can be a great help to ensure best performance and customer care. In addition, the concentration of staff involved in short term planning (extra trains, bank holidays, strikes etc), wagon control and maintenance planning, quality control etc. will greatly facilitate communications.

Documentation and Customs
An often-neglected area of transport by rail is documents and customs, the problem being that without these the train is still able to roll, but not allowed to depart. A particular problem of the intermodal train is that the administrative efforts are often larger than for a conventional train. There are more

boxes than wagons and often a larger variety of cargo. Detailed attention in the operational plan to the requirement for consignment notes, custom documents and goods banned from the train will help to ensure that paperwork and customs do not become an obstacle to performance. If transport is completed under CIM conditions, the customer needs to be aware of his obligations and his minimal rights.

Wagons
The mix of wagons in a train aims to provide the most efficient transport capacity for a yet unknown mix of containers. When trains follow a shuttle concept, a helpful tool to control wagons sets is a graph showing the expected location of the sets during the week. It is a valuable tool to assess quickly the opportunities to correct serious disruptions.

Intermodal wagons in a shuttle are used far more intensively than the normal freight wagon in wagon load systems and, unfortunately, a number of incidents have proven that to maintain reliability, additional preventative maintenance has to be considered to prevent "stress injuries". Trains going backwards and forwards in the same direction are likely to cause excessive wear and tear. By additional preventative maintenance it is possible largely to prevent serious defects, which might require wagons to be removed from the train at some obscure location far away. It can prove a nightmare, first to locate a wagon that has been labelled "red" and, consequently, to ensure a solution is found for further transportation of the cargo or repair of the wagon. The most embarrassing situation occurs when the customer informs the railway operator that a wagon is missing from the train. An effective way to ensure the wagon and its cargo resume their journey is forwarding the next train one wagon short and agreeing with the intermediate station that the repaired wagon is to be added to the next train, even if an additional stop is required. This is often a solution far preferable to wagon and cargo joining the wagonload system before eventually arriving at their destination.

10.7 Tracking and Tracing

Tracking and tracing of trains is a fairly standard requirement of customers and also necessary to measure the rail operator's internal performance. Based on GPS and mobile phones, solutions appear to be available to monitor independently the position of the train. It becomes slightly more challenging if the information has to be combined with information from operational systems of other networks, if these are the only source of information. Networks can be very restrictive in allowing access to their internal systems showing train location and delays. Internationally implemented messages based on train operators' production administration seem to suffer from indifferent reliability. Although the aim is to use information actively to encourage foreign networks to keep the train rolling or give expected arrival times after delays, it is even more challenging to find officials willing to assist and sometimes divert resources.

The new international train operators are in a far stronger position to provide accurate tracking and tracing facilities with through trains/engines and their own staff on board. A situation comparable to the road haulier can be achieved. Staff can be reached by mobile telephones and staff can take the initiative to contact the operations centre to report problems and delays and can also encourage traffic control to allow the train to proceed on its journey.

10.8 Quality Control

To be able to investigate problems and improve the production plan it is necessary that data is collected and processed. The aim of collecting data should be two-fold: it enables the rail operator to show the customer and partners his performance, whilst it is also the starting point for investigations into problems and improvements in the production plan. Traditional railways found the collection of data and the investigation of causes often a very challenging task as little informed forums existed to do so. Communication between the railways was at timetable and commercial levels, although both might be necessary to solve problems where a structure to improve performance did not exist. This was not being helped by the fact that, formally, the customer had a contract with each individual railway company participating in the train. Outside the railway industry collection of data and investigation of causes is often more rooted and shows evidence that a well organised system can be an essential tool to help improve performance.

10.9 Conclusions

Intermodal transport by rail is here and is here to stay and, with the dynamics of open access, old players will disappear and new operators will appear. The introduction of new operators will ensure that remaining old players change their ways and that innovation will continue into the future. Further innovation is necessary if the demand on the "Railways" to increase production and contribute to solving environmental and congestion problems is to be met, with Intermodal transport one of the promising concepts to do so. Still, in the highly competitive business environment, it will be difficult to achieve this and to provide the quality and performance that customers demand for an acceptable price. The above-mentioned production plan only briefly shows some signs of the intense commercial (and political) pressures on the railway operators in the intermodal chain. By this pressure, compromises in quality and price are being forced, sometimes to the point where production plans become ideals and everyone in the transport chain struggles to maintain some sort of quality. The internationally operating open access operators will have some of the answers towards providing a higher quality service at a lower cost, thereby ensuring continuing innovation.

11 Freight Rolling Stock

Felix Schmid (University of Sheffield) *and David McIntosh*
(The Railway Consultancy)

11.1 Introduction

In the past, freight vehicles often received scant attention because they were seen, essentially, as either cheaply produced commodities or highly specialised equipment for freight flows which can only be handled by rail since it is a very high integrity means of transport. This includes, for example, the transport over public land of nuclear waste from power stations or molten steel between smelter and mill. However, freight markets in general and logistics operations in particular have become much more sophisticated over the last 15 years, demanding better service if the market share of railways is to remain constant or increase.

The authors of this chapter discuss the state of the art and also propose applications for novel materials and approaches to freight systems, making best use of existing and new technologies and management methods. Following a general discussion of rail freight systems and wagon elements they advocate four guiding principles for the design of freight vehicles, namely, economy, intelligence, quality and ecology.

11.2 History and Background to Freight Rolling Stock

Although primitive, the early rail freight vehicles used on the Liverpool and Manchester railway and elsewhere in the 1820s had many of the features we expect to see in today's rolling stock, including a basic suspension, couplers and even all over advertising. In general, they were of composite construction, using iron or steel under-frame components, wood planking, iron reinforcing straps and substantial helpings of tar, both to keep down costs and to minimise empty vehicle (tare) mass.

A diversity of freight vehicle designs proliferated in the 19th century, partly due to the general carrier obligation placed on both private and state-owned railways by the national governments (see section 2). Suffice to say that there were wine barrel wagons, glass containers for acids and absurdities like racing pigeon carriers. Such specialist vehicles resulted in uneconomic empty stock movements.

From the early 1900s, freight wagons were being used more and more to handle cross-border traffic in Europe, frequently spending long periods away from the owning network. Standardisation of vehicle types and components therefore became essential so that rolling stock could be used freely under international arrangements, such as RIV. The European railways thus developed a range of mass-produced standard freight vehicles, suited to the carriage of most general cargo and of bulk commodities. The main standard types of rolling stock were the open truck or wagon, the boxcar, the flat wagon and the tank wagon. Most wagons built in Europe until the 1960s were of two axle[1] design because many administrations did not like the complexity and extra cost of bogies. In the Americas though, four-axle bogie rolling stock, suited to the relatively poorly laid track, had started to dominate the scene in the late 1800s.

In Britain, early standardisation by the Railway Clearing House[2] went too far: While the un-braked 17'6" long freight vehicles with a 10' wheel base were certainly cheap to build, their operation became uneconomic in the 1940s and 1950s due to the limited payload, high cost of handling cargo and excessive maintenance requirements. Their small size led to the situation where the British Transport Commission (later British Railways) had to take on its books 1,270,000 freight vehicles at the time of nationalisation in 1948, one for every 40 inhabitants of the British Isles. Impact damage to cargoes was a particular problem with this type of wagon because trains were loose coupled and all but the most experienced drivers could not avoid longitudinal oscillations during acceleration and braking.

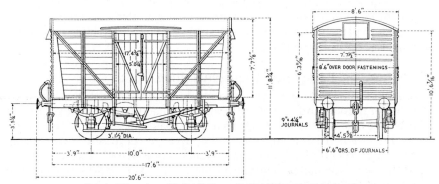

Principal dimensions of British Railways standard 12-ton covered goods wagon

Picture courtesy of National Railway Museum

Figure 11.1 Standard 12-ton British Railways Covered Goods Wagon

---

1 Three axle freight railway stock was relatively common in the 19th and early 20th century. However, the poor ride quality, the complexity of the laterally adjusting centre axle and the increasing capability of the infrastructure (higher axle loads) soon resulted in their demise.

2 The organisation tasked with managing the attribution of fares and tariffs to the (private) railways involved in the carriage of freight and passengers originating or termination outside their own network.

112

The 1980s and 1990s saw the re-emergence of more specialised wagons, such as different types of inter-modal vehicles, three level car transporters and steel coil carriers. Some railways also still own vehicles for the carriage of out-size load, such as Deutsche Bahn's Uaai 836 with 20 axles and a payload of up to 317t. If new and high value traffic is to be captured for the railways then it is essential that freight services and, by implication, freight vehicles are optimised for their particular duties. Better design, more efficient manufacture and appropriate use of freight vehicles can result in lower first cost as well as fuel and maintenance savings, while offering the customer better performance.

11.3 Limiting Parameters for Rail Freight Vehicles

The absolute limiting parameters in the design of a rail freight vehicle are (i) the most restrictive loading gauge applicable to any route where it is to be used and (ii) the smallest radius curve to be encountered. Table 11.1 exemplifies limits imposed on the carrying capacity of inter-modal vehicles in Britain by the former constraint. The gauge capability on Britain's main line railways is indicated by the letter "W" followed by a number. The latter rule presents particular difficulties in the case of two-axle designs.

Unit Type	Container*		Swap Body#					
Unit Width	8ft		2500mm		2550mm		2600mm	
Wagon Type	IFA	IKA	IFA	IKA	IFA	IKA	IFA	IKA
Maximum Unit Height	Feet, Inches		All dimensions in mm					
W6	8'	8'6"	2448	2565	2421	2535	2393	N/A
W7	8'	8'6"	2448	2568	2448	2565	N/A	N/A
W8	8'6"	9'	2665	2795	2665	2705	N/A	N/A
W9	9'	9'6"	2775	2895	2775	2875	2755	N/A
W12	9'6"	9'6"	2955	3075	2955	3075	2905	3025

Table 11.1 Loading Gauges Applicable to the British Railway Network[3] (Source: Network Rail, 2002)

[3] Explanation of Terminology: IFA = "Multifret" wagon with a deck height of 945mm above rail level, IKA = "Megafret" wagon with a deck height of 825mm above rail level, N/A = cannot be carried. Other wagon types are available with lower deck heights, but are unable to carry certain units. * ISO standard heights / widths shown, taller heights may be possible for non-standard containers. # Maximum heights assume flat-top swap body, heights may differ for "tent-topped" swap bodies

The allowable mass per axle, commonly referred to as the axle load, is a further important constraint. In most cases though, this last constraint can be overcome by reducing the payload when using a particularly restrictive route. In Britain, the maximum allowable axle load is now generally 25.5t and the axle load capability of railway routes is classified in terms of Route Availability (RA) with the following main ranges:

• RA 1-6 up to 20.3 tonnes per axle;
• RA 7-9 up to 24.1 tonnes per axle;
• RA 10 up to 25.4 tonnes per axle.

Throughout most of Europe, wagons were still being built in the 1970s for axle-loads of 18.5t when fully laden. All the same, lightweight construction allowed reasonable payload to tare ratios. By the 1990s though allowable axle loads on many major routes had risen to 22.5t, thus offering some economies in the operation of freight services. Many vehicles passing between Britain and the rest of Europe thus have to be loaded to limits below their maximum design capacity for such journeys.

Throughout this section we will frequently refer to the gross loaded weight (glw) or capacity of individual vehicle designs. This is made up of the tare weight and the payload. Maximising the payload per length of train is one of the major objectives of operators and designers. In North America and on specialised heavy haul lines worldwide, axle loads are often 32.5t or more (see chapter 6). The North American standard bogie car is now 130t glw (286,000lbs). Today, European railways also favour bogie vehicles over 4-wheel (2-axle) wagons as they are generally more track-friendly and offer greater payload within the same overall train length.

11.4 Standard Freight Flows and Vehicle Types

The types of freight rolling stock can be defined by their physical characteristics, the traffic flows and the goods for which they are designed. As mentioned in section 11.2, there are several widely used standard types, such as box wagons, but there are also many specialised types for particular goods or environments. Even relatively specialised types though may carry a variety of goods at different times in their lives. However, the bogie tank cars developed by the Central Railway of Peru for carrying liquid fuel over a 4500m high pass to the mines of the Andes probably took versatility to its practical limits since they returned to the coast loaded with ingots.

Clearly, there is a wide variety of freight flows, from bulk liquids to high value sundries, from inert substances to highly corrosive and flammable goods. They can be handled in general purpose wagons or may require dedicated and specialist rolling stock. Very often, handling and management are specific to the particular flow of freight and may result in the need for special transhipment facilities, e.g. retention systems for oil spillage etc. Quality parameters, such as permitted acceleration, temperature range and humidity, differ between bulk commodities, such as grain and coal, and high value white goods and new cars. An overview of typical freight vehicle types, their key features and areas of application is provided in Table 11.2.

Bulk Commodities

The *open box wagon* or gondola (US) is probably the oldest and most basic freight vehicle. Until the 1970s, the restricted size of both loading and discharge locations had held the UK fleet down to 12/16t capacity 4-wheelers with a 10ft wheelbase. These were largely displaced by the 45t glw, 32t capacity 'Merry-go-Round' (MGR) hopper. The modern open box is still very popular, as it requires no sophisticated terminal discharge facilities beyond a simple grab crane. In the UK there are both 4-wheel (MEA) and bogie (JNA) variants. In North America, the gondola is the most significant vehicle type, with many featuring a rotating centre-coupler, allowing rapid discharge through a rotary dumper facility. Similar vehicles are used in the UK by Corus for the iron ore flow between Immingham docks and the Scunthorpe steel making complex.

The most popular bulk commodity wagons are *open hopper* wagons because of their capacity for rapid unloading where the necessary discharge facilities are provided. The provision of door gear and a sloping body profile tends to mean that hoppers have a slightly higher tare weight than the equivalent open box but the shorter turn-round times and thus higher productivity balance this loss of capacity. The traditional MGR 4-wheel coal hopper has recently been displaced in the UK by 102t glw bogie hopper wagons on most routes, although 4-wheel hoppers are still exclusively used for the West Country china clay traffic, fitted with moveable hoods to protect the load. Roadstone, limestone and other aggregates tend to be typical traffics moved in open hoppers, although increasing environmental concerns over dust pollution have made the provision of hoods a modern requirement.

The *closed hopper* is a common variant where protection of the load from the elements is required or where light or powdery traffic is involved. Again, there are 4-wheel and bogie variants. The former have traditionally been used for traffics such as grain, lime, alumina, china clay, soda ash and petroleum coke. The bogie variants are increasing in popularity as the availability of more track-friendly bogies and the drive for ever-higher productivity takes effect. In North America, the grain hopper features prominently, often owned by governments, states or shippers' cooperatives. Where the commodity is a light powder, the gradient of a wagon side is insufficient to permit rapid and complete discharge by gravity alone. In these circumstances, it may be necessary to turn the wagon body into a pressure vessel to allow the load to be blown out. For such a *pressure-discharge hopper*, a tank is the most economical design. As this makes the vehicle more expensive, it is only resorted to when essential. Some traffics, such as gypsum and fly-ash, used pressure discharge

Picture courtesy of EWS

Figure 11.2 New 102t Bogie Hopper Wagons for British Coal Traffic

in the past until more sophisticated hopper designs permitted gravity discharge to become fully effective. Sometimes the borderline between pressure-
discharge hoppers and tank wagons is largely a cosmetic detail of design.

The *tank wagon* has gone through many changes over time but it is now
clear that the bogie tank offers the optimum balance between whole-life cost
and capacity, where infrastructure and terminals are able to accommodate it.
Pipelines may be a more economical option for very large volumes of light
products but the bogie tank car offers greater flexibility for smaller volumes and
the denser liquid products. Tank cars are used for a wide variety of bulk liquid
products such as crude oil and other petroleum products, molasses, milk,
water, acids and other chemicals and liquid gasses as well as pressure-dis-
charged powders such as cement, soda ash, and sulphur. Particular cleaning
procedures must be adopted depending on their use.

General Merchandise Flows
The *box car* or *covered van* still features prominently in the fleets of most railways
for traffics vulnerable to environmental damage. Until the 1960s, bulk commodities were often carried inefficiently in such vans in very small units, e.g.
bagged grain, fertiliser and coal, requiring manual handling. This major design

flaw of inefficient and expensive loading and discharge through small doors has largely been overcome as railways have adopted the best available technology. Easy access for palletised traffics is now generally possible with 100% side access available through two or three wide doors, curtain-side or sliding wall type arrangements.

Within Europe the ubiquitous bogie 'Cargowagon' or 'Transwagon' type offers a payload of up to 62 tonnes, or more than twice that of its nearest competing road vehicle, all accessible to fork-lift truck for loading and discharge of rows of up to 54 'Euro' size pallets or 42 industrial pallets on 60 square metres of floor area[4]. The drive for ever-greater tare/payload balance has seen widespread adoption within Europe of the close-coupled twin-set van, avoiding the need for heavy bogies. For the bulkier traffics these typically offer 26% more floor area for 17% extra overall length, with less than 1 tonne extra tare, when compared with the equivalent bogie van.

Flat wagons are most useful for heavy or long loads not requiring protection from the elements, typically steel or timber. They are built in two-axle variants and bogie designs with four and in some cases six axles. The most common British 4-axle flat wagons are designed for steel plates, coils of steel wire or both military or commercial small road vehicles and agricultural machinery being delivered to customers. For container carrying flats see the section on 'multimodal' equipment below.

When fitted with bolsters or stanchions, typical loads are steel girders, billets, reinforcing rods, telegraph poles, timber or other long loads. Some of the more specialised flat wagons have a depressed 'well' between the bogies to allow the carriage of large loads, such as otherwise 'out-of-gauge' road vehicles or tanks, ships' propellers and transformers or, supported by a trestle, large steel plates.

In the era of the 'common carrier' obligation, railways often provided very specialised vehicles for the conveyance of *'out-of-gauge' loads*. Because of their generally poor utilisation and limited earning capability, most types are now extinct, except where special reasons exist for their continued use, such as nuclear flask wagons.

Wagons for Inter-Modal Operations
Multi-modal equipment comes in many forms, largely dependent on the available loading gauge. In North America, most types of ISO containers are carried in special well wagons allowing 'double-stack' loading on many major routes (see Figure 11.3). In Britain, normal container flat wagons can only accommodate 8'6" high containers. The newer 9' high ISO containers require special low floor vehicles and are restricted to specially enhanced routes. The larger loading gauge in mainland Europe permits up to 9'6" high ISO containers to

---

[4] From the beginning of 2003, road hauliers have started to operate bi-level trailers accommodating up to 52 pallets. Railways must respond to this threat.

Vehicle Type	Typical UK Vehicles			
	Description		Length	Volumetric Capacity
Open Wagon	Open AB Mega Box 4-Wheel Box	OB/OCA JNA MEA	10.1m 13.9m 10.1m	57.3m³
Covered Van (Box Car)	COV AB Cargowaggon Twin	VDA/VGA IWB/PIA PIA	10.1m 20m 27m	46 Euro Pallets 72 Euro Pallets
Temperature Controlled	Interfrigo			
Flatbed Wagon	Early Freightliner Later Freightliner Megafret twin Tiphook Pocket Lowliner Tiphook Flat Thrall Tilt	FFA/FGA FSA/FTA IKA KQA FLA KFA FAA	20m 20.7m 36.6m 20.7m 15.2m 21.3m 20.7m	60' platform 60' platform 2x45' 9'6" Box 40' 9'6" Box, W9 40' 9'6" Box, W8 60' platform 40' 9'6" Box W8
Hopper	MGR Hopper Polybulk 2-axle Hopper Bogie Coal	HDA PIA/PBA PHA HTA	8.2m 14.8m 7.9m 18m	71m³ 32m³
Tank Wagon	102t Tank 2-axle Tank	TEA PCA	17/18m 8.3m	100m³ 38.5m³
Steel Wagon	Bogie Steel Hooded Coil	BAA/BBA BIA	15.5m 16.2m	
Specialised Wagon	Flask Wagon Car Carrier	FNA IPA		
Road-Railer		FHA		
Skeletal and Well Wagons	Double Stack Carriers etc.			

Table 11.2 Typical Types of Rail Freight Vehicles

Load Capacity	Speed (mph)	Additional Comments		
		Freight Flow	Unitisation	Requirements
24t 78t 32t	75 60 60	wood logs, farm produce (sugar beet)	loose, stacked	crane or other mechanised loading kit
24t 53.3t 62t	75 62 62	fertiliser, bulk foodstuffs (sugar, grain), animals	sacks, bags	cheap labour force, good cleaning
		packaged foods, general cargo loose components	pallets pallet boxes	large access doors, mechanised loading
		perishable foods	crates, pallets, boxes	reliability, careful handling
52t 61.2t 87t 67t 35t 61t 34t	75 75 75 75 75 75 75	any containerised goods, waste flows	container (standard, tank, refrigerated etc.) swap-bodies (standard and low height)	specialist lifting and handling gear
32.5t 57.3t 38t 76t	60 60 60 75	foodstuffs (grain), coal and chemicals in bulk, aggregates	wagon-load	discharge conveyors, loading chutes
75.5t 38.5t	60 60	fuel, liquid gas, chemicals	wagon-load	secure storage and no spillage
77.5t 74t	60 60			heavy cranage
		nuclear fuel, new cars, molten steel	as appropriate	Integrity logistics arrangements
		brown & white goods, mail, parcels, high val.	application specific	very basic trans-shipment points
		high value (brown and white goods)	combined transport	specialist handling areas

Figure 11.3 'Double-Stack' Container Wagons

be carried on standard flat wagons. Thus, the specialised ISO container carrying wagons are less common than in Britain.

'Swap-body' (road trailer bodies, modified for road/rail use) equipment is widespread within Europe although it has yet to achieve much market penetration in the UK, except for Channel Tunnel freight. The more generous loading gauge available outside Britain makes the carriage of road vehicle trailers or complete tractor-trailer combinations a common solution for special circumstances, e.g. the provision of 'rail-bridge' traffic through environmentally sensitive areas. In North America the Trailer on Flat Car or (TOFC) train has been a common sight for many years, as is the European Rollende Landstrasse (RoLa) or 'piggyback' train, transporting complete lorries (and sometimes also their drivers) across Austria, Switzerland, Germany and France as well as transiting the major Alpine rail tunnels (see also chapter 10). The Channel Tunnel *'Shuttle'* piggyback trains are another good example of what can be achieved when a generous loading gauge is available.

The 'Road-Railer' concept of a road trailer, which can be fitted with railway running gear, has only gained limited commercial success in North America, where both Amtrak (for US Post Office traffic) and BNSF ('Triple Crown') have made significant use of the concept. However, both operators also still make extensive use of conventional boxcars (Amtrak) and TOFC (BNSF) for high rate mail and express business.

11.5 Specialised Freight Flows and Vehicle Types

Motor Vehicle Transport

Movement of new vehicles from assembly plant to dealer forms a substantial traffic for many railways and the design of dedicated rail vehicles has progressed rapidly from the 'Carflats', converted former passenger vehicle under-frames, with which British Rail began services in the 1960s. Modern sophisticated designs now offer full protection for the load in high capacity rail vehicles of which the North American *'AutoRack'* is probably the best-known, but see also Figure 11.4 for a British example. Using the benefits of the generous loading gauge, new vehicles are transported on three levels in covered vans, as block train loads between assembly plant and final distributor. Traffic is often routed via a dedicated intermediate marshalling centre, where loads from various origins and manufacturers are sorted to form complete blocks for a single destination.

The more restricted European loading gauge still permits double-deck rail vehicles for the carriage of all but the largest SUVs and commercial vehicles. In Britain, Freightliner entered 2003 with a new contract to haul vehicles for Ford using a new design of *'Autoflat'* covered rail wagon.

Picture courtesy of Charles Watson

**Figure 11.4 Fully-Enclosed Double-Deck Car Carrier Wagons
(note articulated design)**

Forest Products
A common vehicle on North American railroads is the specialised forest products wagon, composed of a heavy underframe and light body, designed for conveying over 90t loads of packaged timber for use in the construction industry. In Europe, raw timber tends to be moved on flat cars with side stanchions, and wood chips in open gondolas. The 'high-cube' 120t glw box car is still favourite for paper products.

Insulated/Refrigerated Traffics
Insulated rail vehicles for the carriage of perishable goods have existed for many years. Most railways now tend to use inter-modal equipment where highly perishable traffic is to be carried, in order to eliminate intermediate handling and to make use of easily available road trailer technology. Road trailers with integral refrigeration plant are standard equipment in the supermarket trade. It is this type of kit which Safeway uses in Scotland for its rail based trunk hauls. US railroads now cater for monitoring and refuelling of the trailers' refrigeration plant on long transcontinental hauls of fruit and vegetables.

Self-Discharging Trains
Obviously, gravity discharge wagons are 'self-discharging' but this category of train is meant to refer to more specialised systems such as the Redland

Picture courtesy of Lafarge

Figure 11.5 Redland Self Discharging Train

'self-discharging' train used for aggregates traffic from Mountsorrel quarry in Leicestershire (see Figure 11.5). The end vehicle has an adjustable-arm conveyor discharge facility, fed by conveyors running the length of the train. No terminal facilities other than some hard-standing are required if this train is used, a considerable advantage when short-term traffic flows are involved (see also section 12).

11.6 Wagon Design and Technical Development

Recent developments indicate that even basic vehicles must be designed for a long service life, while offering a good quality transport environment: in the USA for example, freight wagons built after 1974 have recently been given the all-clear to be in use beyond the former 40 year limit for interchange between railway companies. There are moves to extend this concession to wagons built between 1964 and 1974, a fleet of 435,000 cars currently still in operation [1]. Although, at first sight, this might appear to be bad news for the freight wagon manufacturers, it makes investment in freight vehicles more attractive and also increases the opportunities for re-manufacturing. In essence, freight car design has become important; it is no longer a straightforward task left to the trainee.

In the following section, the authors address some of the issues which should be considered when ordering and designing new rail vehicles.

Vehicle Elements
Standard and special purpose freight vehicles, with the exception of Road-Railer type vehicles, always consist of at least the following elements:

- Running gear (axle, guidance, bogie and primary suspension), an example of a low track force bogie being shown in Figure 11.6;
- Braking equipment, usually distributed between bogies and underframe;
- Secondary suspension, where applicable, either between bogie and underframe or using a sub-frame in the case of single axle arrangements;
- Under-frame or integral structure and associated hardware;
- Couplings (manual or automatic) or draw-gear and buffers;
- Control gear (currently only on sophisticated vehicles or those allowed to run in passenger trains);
- Specialist elements (refrigeration equipment, etc.).

Normally, a freight vehicle will also require a body, either fixed or, in the case of inter-modal and container freight, removable. A fixed superstructure can act as a structural or main load bearing element, e.g. in the case of tank wagons for liquids and powders.

In most of the regulatory environments components are highly standardised,

Picture courtesy of Powell Duffryn Rail Ltd.

Figure 11.6 Low Track Force Bogie

based on the work of organisations such as AAR, ISO, UIC and OSSH[5]. There are also a number of interface standards for freight vehicles, e.g. the UIC norms or 'fiches' for loading gauge and draw-gear, ISO norms for containers and their fixing, AAR norms for vehicle identification and the auto-coupler standards of the railways of the former Soviet Union. Such standards are very important for interoperability but restrict innovation if they are too narrowly formulated.

Materials Selection for Rail Freight Vehicles
Carruthers et al. [2] discuss some of the key requirements for passenger rail vehicles from a composite materials perspective. Freight vehicles, unlike passenger rolling stock, do not necessarily have to satisfy very exacting aesthetic standards. However, materials for freight vehicles must satisfy several similar qualifying criteria, namely, high standards of corrosion resistance, impact

---

5 AAR: Association of American Railroads, ISO: International Standards Organisation, UIC: Union Internationale des Chemins de Fer (Europe), OSSH: the organisation of the railways of the former Eastern Block.

resistance, crashworthiness, fire resistance, high strength for a given mass and, importantly, maintainability. Freight operations are a demanding environment where rolling stock is subjected to impacts and abrasion. Depending on the type of cargo to be carried in the vehicle, one, two or all the factors will be significant. An interesting set of requirements was that applying to the tourist and lorry shuttles built for the Channel Tunnel between England and France.

The most stringent requirements are placed on containers for highly flammable liquids and pressure vessels, such as those for LPG. It is important to note that, in a freight incident, the effects can be far more damaging both to people and the natural environment than in a passenger accident. In the context of the present chapter it is impossible to provide more than an outline of the key characteristics of materials:

- Carbon steel offers excellent performance in terms of crashworthiness, fire resistance and reparability but requires regular surface treatments to prevent corrosion. Manufacturing complexity is limited, with efficient methods available for both small and large batches;
- Stainless steel is similar in performance to carbon steel but has poorer crashworthiness characteristics. It is inherently corrosion resistant and does not require regular surface treatments. However, it will only ever be appropriate for a limited part of a structure due to cost. Manufacturing techniques are broadly similar to those for mild steel although casting is more complex;
- Composites are inherently corrosion resistant and show substantial cost benefits when used in environments which are extremely aggressive. The resin-matrix is the determinant in the corrosion behaviour since the fibres are fully embedded in the resin. The fibres determine the strength and crashworthiness. In general, an outer layer is used for cosmetic and protective reasons. The most difficult problem is the joining of the composite structure to dissimilar materials. The complexity of the manufacturing process depends on the structure chosen but is generally relatively high;
- Aluminium is being used increasingly for freight vehicle production. It is a lightweight material and has very good corrosion behaviour in a range of situations. Its performance depends entirely on the design and the measures taken to deal with its inherent weaknesses, that is, its relatively low resistance to impact, abrasion and fire. Manufacturing techniques are more complex than for any of the other materials but significant savings can accrue thanks to mass production.

The choice of material thus depends on the application, the expected life and the scale of the production run. In future, it is likely that all the materials listed will be used in a single vehicle, in line with their specific strengths. Steel will continue to be the material of choice for wheels, axles and most parts of bogies. Stainless steel and aluminium are expected to dominate the construction of under-frames although composite materials are attractive for crash-worthy structures because it has been found that they can be designed to absorb more collision energy than metals, when compared on a weight for weight basis [3].

In addition to the qualifying criteria discussed above, there are a number of competitive criteria which facilitate a choice between different materials. The most important of these are: resistance to wear, life-time cost and aesthetic considerations. Wear resistance can be achieved for all the materials listed but this may result in further cost and added mass for the provision of sacrificial abrasion layers and coatings.

The Economic Freight Vehicle
There are several different philosophies relating to the economic operation of freight vehicles. Since the 1960s the first cost of vehicles has increased dramatically and this has led to a situation where operators need to ensure the highest possible levels of utilisation. This has in turn focused attention on regular high volume flows which allow high frequency time tabled trains of uniform composition (block trains). Changing the composition of trains en route is seen as an expensive liability while allowing a customer to load or unload a vehicle at their convenience is seen as detrimental to the economics of freight transport.

Throughout Europe, wagon-load traffic has been decimated as a result of this particular philosophy. The economics of wagon-load traffic change dramatically though if the cost of rolling stock acquisition can be reduced and if the cost of reforming trains can be minimised. The latter can be achieved by the use of auto-couplers, more efficient freight yards and better organisation [4]. The issue of a standard European auto-coupler is not resolved yet, even though the UIC developed its Unicoupler in the 1970s and despite the existence of a widely adopted standard in Russia and the former CIS states, the SA3 Willison derivative coupler. Close co-operation with customers can lead to lower turn-around times and more efficient methods of loading (pallets and trolleys) reduce the number of staff required.

Speed is of the essence in the running of a freight business, however, this statement does not refer to high speed but to the speed appropriate to the needs of the business and the operating environment. Vehicles running at low speeds can be designed to a lower specification, in particular with respect to their running gear, where less demands are placed on unsprung mass and the dynamic behaviour on track. Aerodynamic performance will also not be as important as for vehicles travelling at higher speed although Burlington Northern has reported significant energy benefits from using close coupled coal wagons with smooth sides [5], as shown in Figure 11.7, even at speeds as low as 80km/h. Before designing a vehicle it is thus important to identify all the factors which might affect its top speed as well as its mean travelling speed.

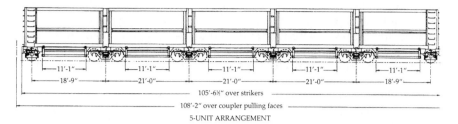

Figure 11.7 Burlington Northern 'Trough Train' Articulated Coal Car
Tare: 117 000 lb, net coal capacity up to 299 tonnes

Shorter vehicles with a higher payload can significantly improve the performance of a railway business since they allow better use of the infrastructure, lower staff cost per tonne km and permit faster loading and unloading [4]. Double stack container movements are typical for this type of operation since the gross mass of containers per m^3 is very often much lower than that of bulk commodities. However, loading gauge restrictions prevent the use of double stack container operation in most of Europe. An alternative to the use of double stack and other high-cube developments is the introduction of more articulated consists where both the load per unit length and the aerodynamics are improved compared with a standard train.

Availability and repairability are major factors determining the economic operation of rail freight services. Both the construction techniques and materials used will have a major effect on whether or not it is possible to achieve the high reliability required from individual vehicles to allow successful operation of trains with 100 or more wagons over long distances. Simplicity tends to be a strong driver for reliability. This should be coupled to a maintenance regime which uses the business' unproductive time [6] for maintenance. Recent development of the LTF25 bogie, shown in Figure 11.6, have been aimed at reducing complexity and component count to achieve higher reliability and lower cost. Careful consideration of the vehicle's design life is also important: the financial return will be poor if it is much longer than the planned period of operation. Low whole life costs are only possible if both first cost and maintenance expenditure are minimised.

The Intelligent Freight Vehicle
There has been a great deal of resistance to the introduction of more intelligent freight vehicles because of the fear that these might require more sophisticated management and maintenance procedures. However, the increased reliability and reduced power consumption of micro-electronic components has changed the railways' perception and American freight operators are starting

to introduce electro-pneumatic braking equipment on most dedicated flow trains [7]. Electro-pneumatic braking is more accurate, reduces the braking distance and minimises buffing and coupling forces since all vehicles, even in a train of 200 wagons, start braking at the same time. This development is expected to lead rapidly to a more general acceptance of the train bus concept.

The authors advocate a system where information is continuously collected on the train, e.g. on the locomotive, and processed immediately to be able to respond to safety critical events. This requires the provision of a coupling including a medium to high capacity data bus, power feed and air brake supplies. While the electro-pneumatic brake system has been in existence for some considerable time for passenger services and some special freight operations, other monitoring and control systems have been developed and proven, including:

1. Vehicle identification;
2. Load identification (for piggy-back and containerised cargo, allowing better information for the shipper);
3. Hot box (axle bearing) detection using bearing mounted sensors;
4. Load weighing using air pressure sensors in the case of air suspension and measurement using strain gauges for spring deflection;
5. Derailment detection using inertial and vibration sensors;
6. Wheel-slide prevention, brake monitoring and prevention of noise and "rubbing";
7. Cargo monitoring (temperature, humidity, presence of noxious fumes, integrity of locking devices).

Currently, (1) and (2) have found widespread adoption, although purely on the basis of track-side interrogators. A large number of freight vehicles with in-board bearings are equipped with temperature sensors (3) using fusible alloy (eutectic) plugs, acting on the main brake pipe via pilot valves. Suitable electronic sensor equipped bearings have arrived relatively recently but are not yet used on freight vehicles. In many cases, hot box detection is still effected by track-side monitors, a notoriously unreliable method which can only ever detect problems in a few critical locations of a network even though it is well known that catastrophic bearing failures can occur within a few kilometres of travel. (4-6) are easily implemented but applications are still on the drawing board. Initial applications for (7) have been trialled.

Major lorry operators are using global positioning systems (GPS) to track their vehicles. The cost of such equipment has dropped dramatically and it may well become feasible to include satellite positioning in future builds of high specification freight cars. However, the authors feel that tracking of individual vehicles may well be less beneficial than that of complete trains using information collected by a master unit. Tracking of individual vehicles and con-

tainers is attractive during the periods where vehicles are waiting to be loaded or unloaded or during marshalling operations but all information gathered in this manner can be made available easily using good databases with frequent updates. Tracking is thus an expensive solution to poor management.

Freight vehicles must thus be equipped, as a matter of priority, with a standard databus which allows communication with the locomotive or a central monitoring and control device elsewhere on the train, not with track-side equipment. Two approaches are gaining favour:

- a European approach strongly supported by German industry and Deutsche Bahn which is based on a high performance freight train databus handling both safety critical and other information. This is illustrated in Figure 11.8, based on a paper by Dorn [10].
- an American approach based on daisy-chained vehicle tags which communicate non-safety critical information to the adjoining vehicle and ultimately to the locomotive. This may include "nearly-critical" information such as hot axle-boxes.

A train borne control system can react more or less instantly to failure reports. Track based systems for detection of hot boxes, derailed axles and failed components will only ever be able to provide intervention opportunities at fixed intervals, often too late for the prevention of loss of life and assets. An additional benefit to be derived from the provision of local intelligence on board vehicles is the "free" provision of train integrity monitoring: subject to regular polling of the vehicle units, the central control unit can easily establish whether the train is complete.

The Caring Freight Vehicle
Road haulage has achieved strong market penetration in some sectors (e.g. fresh fruit and vegetables) because of the high level of care afforded to the transportation of vulnerable cargo. There are two factors which favour road in these markets: (i) the provision of air suspension on individual lorries is straightforward and adds relatively little to the cost, (ii) since the vehicle moves directly from the point of despatch to its destination under the control of a dedicated driver, the transport quality can be guaranteed, even if schedules may not be maintained due to congestion on the roads.

Rail must match this level of care by means of good quality adaptive secondary suspension systems. Innovative approaches are leading to bogies with integral primary suspension, that is, using the bogie frame to absorb high frequency shocks. By gaining space within the loading gauge using this approach, it will be possible to increase the height of the payload or to isolate the underframe and superstructure or inter-modal body from track irregularities using a secondary air suspension.

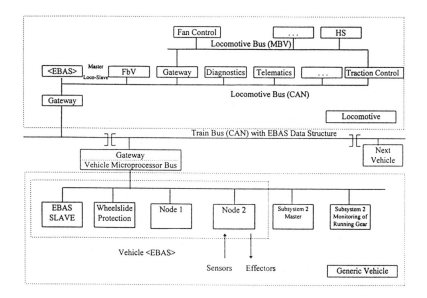

Figure 11.8 Communications Structure of the EBAS System

If wagon-load services are to flourish again it is essential that longitudinal shocks be addressed as seriously as vertical shocks. There are two main causes for longitudinal shock loads on freight vehicles:

- Impacts during shunting movements with the worst situation arising where a wagon is loose shunted. The second in order of severity is a locomotive and several wagons being shunted too fast into a rake of braked wagons. Hump shunting with power assisted closing up of rakes is probably the least damaging method of rearranging trains;
- Impacts as the result of poorly performing brake systems and delays in application of brakes between front and back of train. Such impacts are considerably less significant than those arising from shunting but can lead to cargo damage because of the repetition during long journeys.

Improvements include better operating practice, better training of personnel, auto-couplers with more narrowly defined tolerances on operating force, the introduction of low cost robotic shunting systems incorporating accurate speed sensing, and the development of longitudinal sprung shock absorbers or buffers with good long term repeat performance. These can dissipate energy during both braking and shunting, thus reducing accelerations and jerk during impact. Some freight vehicles already incorporate such devices but recent

131

technological breakthroughs in suspension design could easily be applied to this situation.

Innovative buffers are being adopted in Germany for sensitive cargo, alongside the traction-only automatic coupler [8]. One of the buffer variants is shown in Figure 11.9, taken from Dorn [9]. This buffer can reduce longitudinal accelerations to 1g for impact speeds of up to 6km/h. Other approaches which could help to reduce longitudinal shocks during braking, especially in the case of very long trains, are mentioned in The Intelligent Freight Vehicle (electro-pneumatic brakes) and briefly in The Ecological Freight Vehicle (dynamic brakes).

Thermal insulation of rail freight vehicles may well attract much attention in the future, especially so since new materials have become available offering inherently good heat insulation performance. Burlington Northern has put into service a prototype rail-car made from fibre reinforced plastic with a maximum payload of 95 tonnes, an increase of 23% over an existing metal box car, and a reduction in tare mass of 15% [10]. The multi-layer composite structure provides excellent thermal performance, more or less a "free" bonus from the use of plastics.

Any rail vehicle must be designed to impose an acceptable level of wear on the infrastructure. While it is possible to minimise wear using steerable

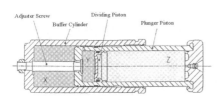

Pictures courtesy of Deutsche Bahn

From left-to-right: Figure 11.9(a) Innovative Buffer Arrangement; Figure 11.9(b) Traction only auto-coupler

bogies and very low unsprung mass this may not be in the best interest of the operator since it increases first cost and maintenance requirements. An operator must thus be compensated for the additional cost of low impact vehicles by the track provider who is able to make savings on the first cost of the infrastructure and of its renewal.

The Ecological Freight Vehicle
Improvements in energy consumption per tkm can be achieved by reducing freight vehicles' tare mass, improved aerodynamic performance, regular bearing checks and steerable bogies or resilient axle mountings, allowing a limited

amount of self steering. Although many railway operators are still wary of steering bogies, major advances have been made, leading to lower first cost and reduced maintenance requirements [11] (see also The Economic Freight Vehicle). Modern train control (signalling) systems can assist in reducing the energy consumption of freight railways and the noise generated.

Minimising the use of brakes through coasting reduces both the energy consumption and the release of potentially harmful brake dust into the environment. The use of more environment friendly brake blocks can also enhance the image of the railway. Better designed brake gear results in less incidents of brakes not being fully released, a major cause of energy wastage, wheel-flats and tread damage. In order to achieve the EU-required noise reduction of 23dB, freight vehicle braking must move to disc brakes using new materials for both discs and jaws. This is an outcome of the Silent-Train programme of a number of European railways on behalf of the Council of European Ministers of Transport. Wheel-slip prevention systems may also be needed in some cases to avoid wheel damage. Cost reduction, in particular with regard to wear parts such as brake pads, is essential to make rail freight more competitive.

In the case of block trains, further improvements could be achieved by including dynamic braking modules at several points along a train. These would be controlled by the drivers for service braking using the train's databus (see the section on The Intelligent Freight Vehicle) and would consist of squirrel cage alternators with static converters and dissipation of braking energy in resistors. Alternatively, it would be possible to use hydraulic motors and to dissipate the energy through unloading the pressurised fluid. In most circumstances, except for very low speeds, it would no longer be necessary to use friction brakes (disc or tread).

When manufacturing freight vehicles, it is essential to use materials whose whole life cost to the environment is minimised. This will include considerations such as amount of energy and raw material used, recyclability (very good in the case of steel and aluminium), toxicity of all emissions during manufacture, maintenance and service, solvent in the paints used and the need for renewed surface treatments after a period in service. The provision of appropriate safety systems and the preparation of incident management plans for hazardous loads is of course of great importance.

11.7 Traction for Rail Freight

Locomotives have traditionally been used to haul freight trains and many electrification schemes were implemented to improve the performance of freight services, e.g. the Gotthard route in Switzerland and the Woodhead line in England. Standard US-type diesel freight locomotives are rated at 2000 –4000kw per unit while electric locomotives can deploy up to 6000kw with only four axles [12]. However, the need for flexibility in routing and direct access to non-electrified terminals is now leading to a gradual reduction of electrically hauled freight, with the exception of countries where most of the infrastructure is already electrified (Germany, Norway and Switzerland) or routes where environmental and regulatory concerns require electric traction (Channel Tunnel). Diesel traction and multiple unit operation of freight services are expected to advance rapidly.

11.8 Conclusions

The authors have outlined the requirements of the rail freight industry in terms of wagon design and have described a range of contributions made by science and technology to the creation of a more effective rail freight industry. Most of the approaches are technically proven, e.g. the low-track-force bogie, or at the pre-production prototype stage, e.g. low cost train databuses. Widescale innovation is not necessarily the solution; in many cases much progress can be achieved by adapting existing technologies and methods.

Solutions must only be introduced on a wider scale if the benefits from their adoption can be provided economically. In most cases it will be the consideration of whole life costs which will determine the outcome. It is certain though that freight operators must improve their approach to the use of information systems on board trains. At moderate investment levels such systems will improve both the performance and safety of rail freight operations.

Rail freight in Europe must at long last be supported by the introduction of a relatively simple automatic coupler which includes a data-bus, power feed and the air brake line. New rolling stock must be equipped with electro-pneumatic brakes and high-speed freight vehicles may well require dynamic braking.

Key parameters for a private operator in the liberalised European and world railway markets include the access charges which may dictate a higher speed than the speed necessary for commercial success. Since the customer is mostly concerned with accurate time of despatch and delivery, a higher speed capability may also need to be built into the vehicle to allow for recovery of lost time. Suspension technology must be improved with regard to both vertical and longitudinal movements, but not at the cost of adding complexity. This is necessary if rail is to compete for flows of high value goods.

Since contracts for freight traffic flows rarely exceed a period of five years it may well be appropriate to develop high performance standard under-frames and running gear with a normal life of between 20 and 30 years. Low mass and good dynamic behaviour could be built in at the design stage. Such under-frames, incorporating a train data-bus and associated interface would be equipped with low cost superstructures and electronic controls suited to a particular freight flow, with a design life appropriate to the particular market. There would be the option of extending the life to cover a second contract where this was commercially viable. Superstructures could thus be tailored to the application and its expected life. Lower cost manufacture should be possible while still retaining the benefits of low mass since the under-frame would support most of the load. Mass production should thus help to reduce the cost of freight vehicles in Europe, currently up to three times as high as standard American costs.

The proposed concept, a form of swap-body wagon, is closely related to that of containerised transport and piggyback transport but avoids the very high tare weights associated with the requirement for stacking containers and the additional weight from the road axles of trailers. Manufacturers of freight vehicles and operators must develop a cohesive technology strategy if they are to succeed in lowering the ownership cost of freight vehicles without losing the benefits of flexibility and high performance.

Mass production techniques have not taken hold amongst manufacturers of rail freight vehicles, perhaps with the exception of the most basic European standard two-axle wagons, the basic bogie wagons familiar on the American scene and, until recently, planned-economy production in the former Eastern Bloc. Flexible mass production is essential though if railways are to be equipped at a substantial level with modern rolling stock.

References

1. Kruglinski, A., 'How scrapping an old rule will affect the used-car market', Railway Age, New York, p12, April 1996.
2. Carruthers, J.J., A.M. Robinson, F. Schmid and D. Tooley, 'Structural Composites for Bodyshells of Passenger Rail Vehicles', Proceedings of the Railtech Conference 1996, IMechE Publications, London, 1996.
3. Hull, D., 'Impact Response of Structural Composites', Metals and Materials, Vol. 1., No. 1, pp. 35–38, 1985.
4. Herbert, W., 'Steigerung der Effektivität beim Wagenladungsverkehr', pp. 34–40, Der Eisenbahningenieur (48) 8/97, August 1997.
5. Kieres, K.C., 'Burlington Northern's articulated coal car', Railway Technology International '95, Sterling Publications Ltd, London, 1995.
6. Matthew, D., 'Freight on Rail, a Customer's Needs', IMechE Seminar 'Freight on Rail, New Horizons', IMechE Publications, London, November 1995.
7. 'Cost Constraints Encourage Innovation, pp. 28,29, International Railway Journal, July 1997.
8. Schelle, E., 'Die automatische Zugkupplung der UIC – Erfahrungen aus der Erprobung der Z-AK', pp. 56–60, Der Eisenbahningenieur (48) 4/97, April 1997.
9. Dorn, K., 'Innovative Güterwagen – Entwicklungsstand und Perspektiven', pp7–13, Der Eisenbahningenieur (48) 8/97, August 1997.
10. Perrella, A., 'Hardcore-DuPont rolls out its first composite railcar', Reinforced Plastics, Elsevier, Kidlington, Oxford, November 1995.
11. Mulder, J.M. and H.M. Tournay, 'Spoornet's experience refines steering bogies', pp. 301–304, Railway Gazette International, May 1996.
12. Gerber, P., 'Class Re465 locomotives of heavy-haul freight service', Journal of Rail and Rapid Transit, Part F of the Proceedings of the IMechE, Vol. 215, No. F1, pp 25-36, 2001.

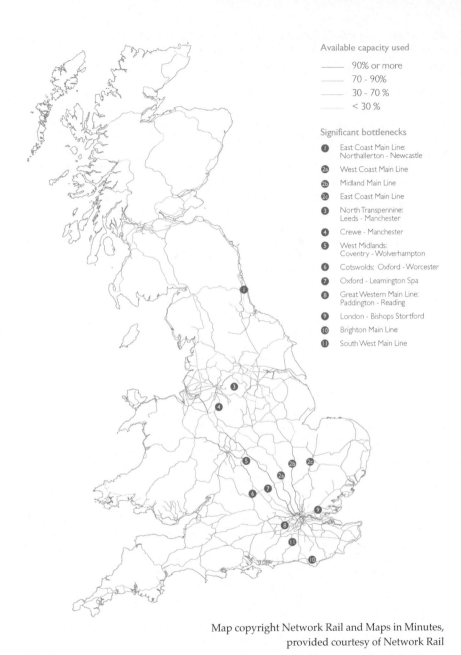

Available capacity used

───── 90% or more

───── 70 - 90%

───── 30 - 70 %

───── < 30 %

Significant bottlenecks

❶ East Coast Main Line: Northallerton - Newcastle

❷ₐ West Coast Main Line

❷ᵦ Midland Main Line

❷c East Coast Main Line

❸ North Transpennine: Leeds - Manchester

❹ Crewe - Manchester

❺ West Midlands: Coventry - Wolverhampton

❻ Cotswolds: Oxford - Worcester

❼ Oxford - Leamington Spa

❽ Great Western Main Line: Paddington - Reading

❾ London - Bishops Stortford

❿ Brighton Main Line

⓫ South West Main Line

Map copyright Network Rail and Maps in Minutes, provided courtesy of Network Rail

Figure 12.1 Capacity Utilisation on the British Railway Network

136

12 Operational Planning

Nigel G Harris, The Railway Consultancy Ltd

12.1 Timetabling Issues

Timing Freight Trains
Freight train timing requirements are ideally defined for a medium-speed unimpeded run between origin and destination. Acceleration and deceleration are both relatively difficult to achieve (especially for diesel-powered services), and should thus be avoided. As it is, gradients may cause problems, and here a free run can be critical in maintaining speed within the target range of 50–70mph. However, at these speeds, it should be relatively easy to carry traffic 500 miles between early evening and factory shift starts at 0700 the following morning.

Time losses often stem from (re-)marshalling and/or border controls en route. Locomotive changes are to be avoided wherever possible; as well as providing a few minutes' delay, they provide a potential source of unreliability if a subsequent engine is not available. Use of multi-voltage or dual-power diesel/electric locomotives can overcome these possible problems, but only at higher capital cost. EU regulations attempting to provide for the technical inter-operability between differing networks are also designed to reduce the severity of this problem in the medium and long term.

Freight and Passenger Slots
On a freight-only line, efforts in finding timetable slots for freight trains are likely to be concentrated on those situations where the line is near capacity. This can include single-track lines, where passing movements are important (and may be critical if some train lengths exceed loop lengths), and double-track lines where signal sections are unduly long.

On an inter-urban mixed-traffic railway, however, the problems are likely to arise from the differing nature of passenger and freight train slots and the fact that passenger traffic is likely to take priority. These issues are again especially important on those parts of the network which are approaching capacity (see Figure 12.1). The basic problem is demonstrated by the examination of train graphs which show distance on the vertical axis, and time on the horizontal axis. Freight trains are often slower than passenger trains, and their paths are therefore represented by less steep lines (see Figure 12.2). Note that slightly fewer freight trains can be run per hour than passenger ones, since freights are usually both longer and slower, so they take more time to clear individual sections of track.

137

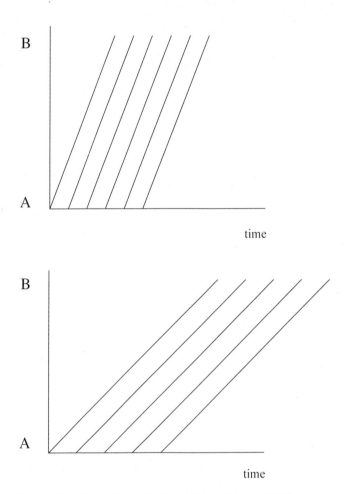

**Figure 12.2 Train Graphs for (a) Fast (typically Passenger) and
(b) Slow (typically Freight) Services**

On a predominantly-passenger railway (such as that in Britain), freight trains may be perceived as taking up several passenger train slots, although the reverse can be argued if the line is predominantly for freight. What is clear (see Figure 12.3) is that mixed use of the line can be very inefficient. Rail network performance enhancement through the unbundling of services and speed harmonisation was a specific objective of Deutsche Bahn's Network 21 strategy [1].

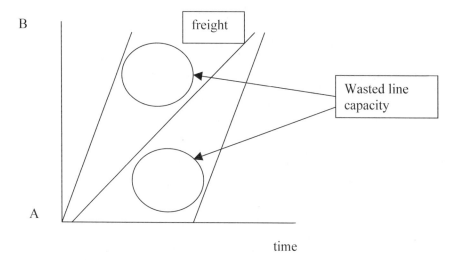

Figure 12.3 Loss of Capacity on a Mixed-Traffic Railway
(Note the difference between the steep gradient of (fast) passenger trains
and the shallower gradient of the freight train)

Typical infrastructure manager responses to this problem include:

- Relegating freight traffic to night-time slots only;
- Bunching freight train slots together ('flighting');
- Allowing freight trains to be overtaken by passenger services; and
- Diverting freights to more circuitous routes.

However, each of these have disadvantages which need to be discussed.

Relegating freight traffic to night-time slots may bring such traffic into conflict with infrastructure maintenance requirements (see chapter 14), and it may not suit the end customer either. Large customers (such as electricity generators) may require either a range of departure/arrival times, whilst small ones (or those with 'Just-In-Time' processes) may require a particular time of arrival to suit their needs. Moreover, grouping freight slots in this manner may also lead to an inefficient use of train operators' resources, since it is creating an artificial peak.

Bunching freight train slots together at various times throughout the day ('flighting') is marginally better. Although suffering from similar problems (albeit to a lesser degree), it has additionally the problem that it is risky (if problems arise, they may affect several freight services).

139

Allowing freight trains to be overtaken is also operationally risky (which may be important in a performance-driven regime) and can result in slow end-to-end journey times for freight, which is becoming increasingly unacceptable. However, 70mph freights may not be incompatible with faster passenger services. If the latter stop fairly frequently, the overall slope of the two types of lines on the train graph becomes similar.

Diverting freights to longer but uncongested routes does lead to an increase in some operating costs (e.g. fuel), but may be the least damaging of the options, if regular unimpeded slots can be provided. Perhaps the best case of this under discussion at present is that of sending North-South freights in the East Coast Main Line (ECML) corridor between Peterborough and Doncaster via Lincoln (along the 'Joint Line'), rather than on the ECML itself.

Freight and passenger slots need to be considered together, if the multi-user railway is not to incur unnecessary capital expenditure. This may involve putting minor constraints on passenger services, in order to benefit freight – which is fine in theory, but may take some negotiation. For instance, the passenger service on the single-track Wrexham-Chester line is timed to turn round so quickly at Chester that it is not possible to run a freight train during the same hour. However, a marginally longer (and hence robust) turnround would enable a freight to run.

Detailed operating knowledge is required, if poor decisions are to be avoided. Infrastructure operators may, for instance, ban all freight trains from peak passenger periods, which seems sensible superficially. However, some of these freight trains may have few if any conflicting moves with passenger services, and banning them from a wide time-band may have dire consequences for locomotive, wagon and traincrew utilisation.

Moreover, it can be argued that it is high-speed passenger services which cause the real capacity problems on railways. Local passenger trains can often work neatly with freight trains, each having similar average speeds, although of course the passenger trains combine a higher inter-station speed with occasional stops. In terms of signalling, higher speeds demand much greater train separation, as braking distances increase with the square of speed. This means that line capacity may be maximised at speeds of around 40mph (see Figure 12.4) – much nearer the typical speed of normal freight trains than inter-city passenger services. This also challenges the suggestion that freight should also be run at high speed in order to maximise rail network capacity (although obviously it has advantages for railfreight customers).

12.2 Assembling the Resources Needed

Loading and Unloading
Traditionally, railway wagons were used as a cheap way of storing goods in transit. Wagon utilisation was appalling, until (through the 1960s-1980s) the railways asserted their need for wagons to be used only for haulage. The time

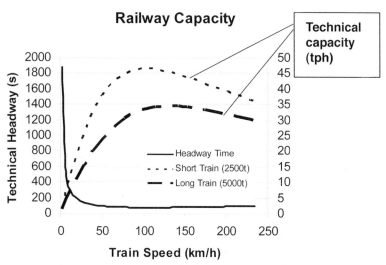

Figure 12.4 Theoretically-Achievable Railway Headway at a Point

taken to load and unload wagons, however, is a key commercial factor in determining the success of a railfreight option. GB Railfreight have recently commented that the success of their Felixstowe – Hams Hall operation is partly determined by the short turnround times (of around 2 hours) achieved at the Hams Hall terminal. Elsewhere, it is not unusual for wagons to spend 6-8 hours being unloaded, during which time the locomotive may stand idle, and the traincrew swapped by taxi from the nearest signing-on point.

As was noted in chapter 2, the advance in coal traffic productivity in Britain took place after the Beeching review in the 1960s. 'Merry-go-round' operation was developed, in which coal wagons are both loaded automatically (from overhead hoppers) and discharged automatically (through the bottom of the wagons, into underground hoppers). This occurs at slow speed (e.g. 5km/h) and is often carried out automatically whilst the train driver takes a meal break, so this is operationally efficient – but at the expense of a cost of several million pounds of capital equipment at the terminal.

At the other end of the spectrum are sidings with hard standing where a JCB-type bucket is used to empty box wagons. Not only does this take longer, but wagons can be damaged and some skill is needed by the operator, in order not to leave substantial quantities of the material behind. Even so, several per-cent of the load may be transported back on an 'empty' train to the loading terminal.

During the 1990s, Redland Aggregates therefore developed a stand-alone self-discharging train, complete with its own underfloor conveyor (see Figure

11.5). This can unload one wagon at a time onto the conveyor, which can be extended outwards from the train to empty into a lineside hopper. These wagons, however, are more expensive to build (and hence hire) than normal box wagons, because of both a slight loss of load and increased complexity.

There is then an important trade-off between the capital expenditure incurred in terminals and the operating cost savings achieved. Regular flows may warrant the investment in terminal equipment, but the capital-intensive nature of the business means that rail can be less competitive for occasional movements.

Resource Utilisation
This is potentially a very difficult area. Relatively few flows are both regular and frequent enough to diagram resources within one traffic flow, although examples may include coal to power stations and the distribution of feeder traffic from marshalling yards. Other flows require the joint use of assets, perhaps on different days of the week. The real problems, however, occur with the multiplicity of 'one-off' traffics which are offered to freight operators. Initially, these may be covered on staff overtime and locomotives spare between other duties. When a larger number of these accrue, however, traffic may have to be planned on an average basis, with locos and drivers booked by the shift, and traffic allocated as it turns up. Nevertheless, this can lead to significant inefficiencies, witnessed through light engine movements passing each other, and drivers travelling back to their home depot on passenger trains. It can also lead to poor financial performance. When short trains run (or none at all), costs are still being incurred.

Although Ed Burkhardt, the figurehead leader of EWS during the mid 1990s, famously offered a service to any branch-line in the British network, the fact is that the administrative costs of doing so may not be very attractive, for reasons including route knowledge and access rights (see below).

Resource utilisation of locomotives, wagons and crews is also tied up with terminal operation, as noted above. Slow terminal turn-rounds may lead to the use of more than one set of wagons, with loaded wagons being left, and previously-emptied ones collected. This at least keeps locomotive and traincrew fully occupied, and may enable them to carry out more return trips per day, if they do not have to wait for loading or unloading to occur.

Ideally, a service will take 3.5 hours driving time, enabling a driver to carry out a return trip within one shift. Multiples of this also work, although subject to a loss of reliability, as driver change-overs have to be arranged. With flexible hours available to most train operators, these arrangements can be stretched slightly on some days. For instance, some Freightliner crews work from Southampton to Crewe and back in a shift, each leg taking nearly 5 hours. The important feature of these issues is the understanding that costs do not rise linearly. Instead, there are steps in the cost function (see Figure 12.5), and effort expended in keeping operations within a lower cost band is worthwhile. Variables which may be amended by a good operational planner, in order to minimise costs include:

- Terminal operation;
- Marshalling points and the possibility of working different parts of a train together;
- Train routeing;
- Line speed; and
- Train length;
- Wagon type (e.g. general purpose or specialist).

All costs are variable in the very long-term, but the cost and time consequences of (say) building a new line for freight (see, for instance, chapter 13) are so high that this is usually prohibitive. Truly variable costs include fuel for locomotives (which varies on a 'per-kilometre' basis), and staffing costs (which vary on a train-hour basis, subject to shift length criteria). Typical short-run variable costs include the annual leasing charges associated with rolling stock, which may not be dependent upon the number of kilometres or even trips operated.

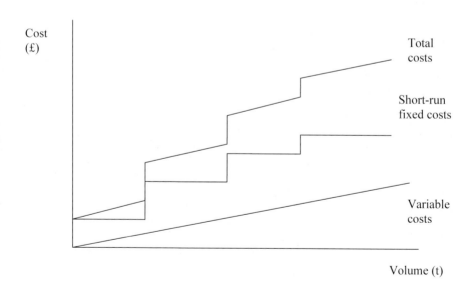

Figure 12.5 Fixed and Variable Costs of Railfreight Operation

Traction and Route Knowledge
Freight train drivers may need traction knowledge on relatively few types of locomotive, especially so as types such as GM's Class 66 become common. Having staff with an ability to fix some smaller faults as well as simply driving is a key step towards increased efficiency and reliability.

However, in Britain drivers also need route knowledge, in order to master the appropriate speeds and track configurations of any particular route. Provided that traffic is not too intermittent, drivers at each driver depot will build up (through training) a knowledge of routes served and this should not be too much of a problem. However, unusual traffics may require the use of a pilotman (conceivably from a passenger train operator) if no staff have traversed the line(s) in question within the period of knowledge (typically 12 months).

With many freight terminals being small and/or remote, significant time can be wasted in getting traincrew to and from them. Having formal, staffed, places for drivers to check in may not be cost-effective, so a number of operators now use methods of drivers signing-on remotely, for instance by telephone, fax or web. This can mean that they can proceed directly on their own to a terminal to pick up a train which may have been left overnight for loading, thereby saving time in place of going to the signing-on point en route.

Access Rights
Open access for freight operators on national rail infrastructure is now an EU directive, so an approach will have to be made by a freight train operator to the relevant infrastructure body. Although there are likely to be designated individuals within the infrastructure company responsible for freight train operators, issues of access and the associated price still have to be agreed.

In Britain, the designers of the structure of the railways as set up during privatisation did not foresee significant traffic growth. Commercial arrangements were therefore predicated on a fixed-price agreement on the basis of existing tonnage. Any additional traffic was to be priced marginally, which was fine whilst there was relatively little of it. However, as Railtrack soon found out, as traffic volumes and distances grew, so did their costs – but not their revenues. Typical prices at that stage were only around £7.50[1] per tonne/train-mile.

Under a new agreement approved by the Rail Regulator in 2002, a higher price was foreseen, but this itself was largely overtaken by events as freight access prices were halved from April 2002, largely for political reasons.

Freight trains in Britain fall into three categories: Long-Term Planned (LTP) trains (for instance, key aggregates trains between the Mendips and London), Short-Term Plan (STP) trains and Very Short-Term Plan (VSTP) trains. The

---

[1] Railtrack received £191.1m for the 25.6m freight train miles recorded by the BRB

last of these never enter the formal timetable as such, but are agreed at the last moment, with relevant details being faxed to signalboxes along the route.

The track access rights associated with these types of trains are contained in access agreements, in which the "quanta" of train slots are set out, sometimes with additional information such as timings at key points, e.g. for attaching and detaching wagons. To ensure that access rights do not merely reflect the timetable, timings are expressed in bands, or with some flexibility e.g. 1900–2100.

LTP services are those expected to last for several years, or at least a whole timetable period. They may be for specific long-term contracts (e.g. in 2002, OOCL signed up with Freightliner for a 10-year contract to move containers from Southampton to Manchester), or for services on key trunk routes where sufficient miscellaneous traffic is expected that reserving a long-term slot is worthwhile. STP services are those which are likely to operate for several months, typically to cover a short-term contract (such as the provision of aggregates for a major infrastructure project). All LTP and most STP services have formal access rights.

Most LTP trains have specific timed slots, but STP and VSTP trains do not. They may be run against a quantum of trains whose characteristics have not been specified, or they may be run against the more general 'spot bid' basis for one-off movements. Over time, if these become regular, there is likely to be pressure for timed rights to be associated with them since, at any stage, Railtrack (as infrastructure operator) can retime such trains, to the potential detriment of one customer, if it helps to fit in other trains. In the short term, VSTP trains effectively run under the general right of freight operators to run trains.

However, freight operators cannot simply reserve huge numbers of train paths without ever using them, because this could be used anti-competitively. Britain's Rail Regulator has therefore imposed caps on the number of paths which may be reserved (for instance) between England and Scotland. Moreover, if paths are not used for a 12-month period, they may be foregone, under a 'use it or lose it' regime.

Train paths are determined through a bid and offer process, with train operators indicating their desires at an annual timetable conference or at other times, and the infrastructure operator responding with an offer. This offer attempts to meet the aspirations of the train operator, but will take into account other bids made at a similar time, as well as other trains (passenger and freight) already running. The fact that this process typically takes several months indicates why so many freight trains (around 50%) run under VSTP arrangements. This is a process simply not replicated on the road network, where delays to other services are not considered, largely because the road network is not constrained in the same way, and overtaking is relatively easy.

Access Rights and Maintenance Requirements

Many freight dispatchers are keen for their traffic to run at night, when factories may be closed. Goods produced one working day can therefore arrive before the next. Unfortunately, it is at night when there is most pressure from infrastructure operators to carry out maintenance on the network.

On 4-track main lines, this does not normally prove to be an insuperable issue but, at other locations, there can be conflicts. Freight trains may need to be diverted, retimed or even cancelled in order for maintenance work to be carried out. Most freight train operators have accepted the need for network maintenance at weekends, and very few freights run between 1300 on Saturday and 1800 on Sunday. Freight operators' access rights are subject to Rules of the Route, which indicate when line closures are permitted. This issue is discussed in more detail in chapter 14.

Infrastructure Design
Although the track gauge (distance between the rails) of much of the world's railways has been standardised at 1435mm, the volume of freight which may be carried on this has not. The structure gauge defines the maximum height and width of vehicles (the loading gauge) which may be carried on this track gauge. Many of Britain's railways were unfortunately built very early in the

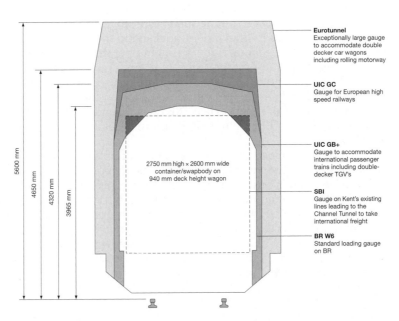

Figure 12.6 Different Loading Gauges

146

19th century, and have allowances which are sub-standard for today's conditions. The Strategic Rail Authority is in the process of funding a major increase in structure gauge to permit the carriage of the latest 9' 6" containers between the ports of Felixstowe and Southampton, and the Midlands, because at present these are simply too large to fit under overbridges (see Table 11.1). An alternative solution in some cases is to build new wagon types of a 'well' design, which permit goods to sit lower, nearer the rails, but these wagons are not only expensive, but permit fewer containers to be carried in the same overall length of train. Tests may need to be carried out to see if wagons fit not only the structure gauge, but also the 'kinematic envelope' – trains overhang the rails on curved track, and the structure gauge itself does not take this into account.

Not all railway lines were constructed to the same standard in terms of weight either. Axle-loads are particularly important, but so is the total amount of weight which may be placed on an under-bridge. As mentioned in section 11.3, in Britain a Route Availability index classifies all routes for freight, with RA10 enabling the heaviest freight trains (of 25.5-tonne axle-load) to run. Even here, though, there may be other operational requirements; for instance, only one freight train is permitted on the Forth Bridge at any one time. Figures 12.7 and 12.8 show loading gauge and route availability maps for parts of the British network – Network Rail's freight section should be contacted for the latest details.

Picture courtesy of Network Rail

Figure 12.7 Loading Gauge

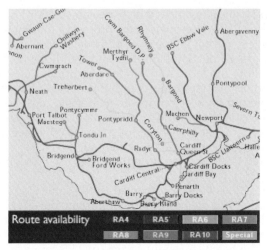

Picture courtesy of Network Rail

Figure 12.8 Axle Load Limits

However, even with a consistent axle-load, operational planners will have to bear in mind the gradients of the route to be traversed. Although freight trains with more powerful modern locomotives may rarely need the assistance of 'banking engines' to reach line summits, their speed when doing so may fall sufficiently to take up train paths unnecessarily.

Line speeds need to be sufficient for today's, not yesterday's, freight requirements. If finances are stretched, infrastructure operators may reduce the maintenance on freight-only lines, compensating in safety terms by reducing line speeds. This, however, increases journey times (rendering the service less competitive to the customer), and increases resource requirements. Regulation of network capability may therefore be necessary.

The issues of speed and weight are interlinked. Because of their relatively-primitive suspension, some freight wagons ride poorly when empty and may thus have speed limitations when empty, unless detailed modifications are undertaken. Other wagons (e.g. the early HAA mgr hoppers), however, may have lower speeds when full.

Traditionally, many freight routes have had relatively low speeds, and infrastructure has not always kept pace with the desires of freight train operators. More subtle problems can arise at junctions, where the slow diverging speed permitted for long freight trains can impinge substantially on the capacity of the main line (for instance at Stechford, on the busy Birmingham-Coventry corridor).

148

Passing loops need to be long enough to accept standard train lengths easily. This may seem obvious, but modern more powerful locomotives can haul trains which may be longer than passing loops installed 100 years earlier. The loops at Trimley on the Felixstowe branch were recently extended to enable two full-length container trains to pass.

Passing loops which only just accommodate the standard length of freight train (775m in Britain) will lead to delays. Freight trains arriving in them will have to slow down considerably, in order not to over-run, and this will lead to their blocking the main line behind them, which may further delay following (passenger) trains which are supposed to overtake them. Moreover, once stationary, freight trains take some time and distance to accelerate, thereby potentially incurring further delay. For such passing movements to take place without any undue delay, loops of around 5kms in length are needed, which would generally be understood as a short section of multiple track, rather than a loop per se. Shorter loops can still be useful in emergencies, but do not have the real benefit of permitting easy train service regulation, planned or otherwise

Relatively-minor expenditure on operating equipment can also substantially improve the efficiency of freight operations. For instance, installing cctv at the rear end of passing loops to check that arriving freight trains are complete can save considerable train time. Where level crossings are not automatic, a second member of traincrew may be required to carry out gate closing activities – a significant additional expense. Provision of cab-signalling equipment to cover short sections of route on key passenger arteries may enable a considerable increase in route flexibility for a relatively minor outlay.

12.3 Case Study: Ikea Rail ÅB

Felix Schmid and *Roberto Palacin,* University of Sheffield

Introduction
The creation and early operational experience of Ikea Rail ÅB provides an excellent example of the difficulties faced (and overcome) by a new entrant to the European rail freight market and thus illustrates the need for European Union directive 2001/16/EC, conventional interoperability. The case focuses on Ikea Rail's use of the Trans European Network (TEN) for its freight services from Sweden to Germany, initially, followed later by services to destinations in most other European countries [2].

Ikea ÅB is the world's largest manufacturer, distributor and retailer of flat-pack furniture, largely made from pine-trees from sustainable sources. It is a vertically integrated business with major manufacturing facilities in Sweden and warehouses and superstores throughout Europe. Ikea Rail ÅB, established in 2001, is an integral part of the furniture company. It was created to switch a substantial part of their international logistics flows

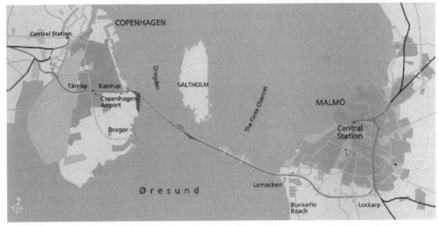

Picture courtesy of Øresund Consortiet

Figure 12.9 Map of the Øresund Rail Link

from road to rail, partly to demonstrate Ikea's commitment to the environment and partly because the company recognised that it would not be able to handle the expected transport requirement without a major development of rail freight.

The Initial Service and Route
Ikea's huge stores require daily deliveries of large quantities of packaged furniture, fabrics and accessories throughout Europe. Due to rapid expansion, particularly in Eastern Europe, Ikea expected a growth in the volume of finished goods shipped of 400% between 2002 and 2010, and thus set a target to increase the rail share of its long distance transport operations from 18% to 40% over this period.

In developing its own rail freight service, Ikea became the first private operator to benefit from the deregulation of European rail freight ordained by the European Commission [3]. The first Ikea Rail ÅB service was launched on 27 June 2002, with two trains a day, 5 days a week, moving goods for its stores from Älmhult in Sweden to Duisburg in the German Ruhr area. The journey initially took just over 16 hours, achieving an average speed of 65km/h over the 1044km journey.

The initial Ikea Rail service uses three essential components of the TEN, namely, the Øresund Link, the Great Belt Link and the North-South Rail Freight Freeway (NS-TERFF). The completion of the two combined rail and road links between Funen and Zealand and between Denmark and Sweden,

Systems Issue	Sweden	Denmark	Germany	Poland
Loading Gauge	UIC'A' except Kiruna to Norway	UIC 'C'	UIC 'C'	UIC 'B'
Axle Loads	25t	22.5t	22.5t and 18t	18t
Electrification	15kVac, 16.7Hz	25kVac, 50Hz	15kVac, 16.7Hz	3000Vdc
Signalling Type[2]	Speed Signalling	Speed Signalling	Speed Signalling	Speed Signalling
Automatic Train Protection (ATP)	EBICAB	ZUB123	INDUSI, LZB and ZUB222	INDUSI
Signalling Examples	2 green light = slow, stop next signal[3]	2 green = line speed, next signal clear	1 green = proceed at line speed[4]	1 green = proceed at line speed
Regulations and Language	Swedish	Danish	German	Polish

Table 12.1 Differences in Technical and Operational Characteristics (partly from [5])

shortly before Ikea Rail's formation, allowed for the first time the establishment of through rail services between Sweden and Germany without the need for train ferries.

The Great Belt Link and The Øresund Link
The Størebaelt separates the Danish provinces of Funen and Zealand. Although the ferry operation across these straits had been very efficient, it offered only limited capacity for rail freight services. The construction and opening of the combined rail tunnel/road bridge solution in 1999 increased

---

2 In Europe, only the railways of Britain, Norway and Spain use route signaling. However, many trains operate through between Norway and Sweden and this issue can thus cause problems.
3 In Norway, 2 green lights signify that operation is permitted at line speed AND will continue at line speed
4 In Germany, there are several signalling systems in concurrent use, e.g. H/V and Ks

151

capacity and reduced the rail journey time via Nyborg, Korsør and Padborg to a level where it became competitive with the ferry link via Rødby and Puttgarden.

The Øresund Link between Malmö in Sweden and Copenhagen in Denmark was towards the top of the list of priority projects adopted at the European Railways' Essen summit of 1994. It was opened in July 2000, almost ten years after the governments of Denmark and Sweden had signed the agreement for its design and construction [4]. As shown in Figure 12.9, the link across the 16km wide Øresund involved the construction of an artificial peninsula next to Copenhagen's Kastrup airport, an immersed tunnel, an artificial island and western and eastern approach bridges. These lead up to a high level bridge, about 4km from the Swedish coast, to allow the passing of ships heading for the Baltic Sea.

The North-South Freight Freeway
The infrastructure managers of Finland, Norway, Sweden, Denmark, Germany, the Netherlands, Austria, Switzerland and Italy set up the North-South Freight Freeways organisation to provide and manage access to some of the major European transit routes for freight traffic. The organisation set up a One Stop Shop (OSS) as the mechanism to market the services of the NS-TERFF. The OSS was part of the original concept of the Community of European Railways (CER) for the TERFFs. Potential customers, such as Ikea Rail, can contact the OSS to book either a pre-established path or a tailor-made path for the movement of their train(s). It also provides operators with complementary services such as consultancy, intermediary negotiation and information management, as well as helping with administrative procedures and advice on technical conditions. It thus forms the only contact required by the customer for the complete international journey.

The NS-TERFF was set up in anticipation of the European legislation allowing open access to some European corridors from 16 March 2003 and the extension of this to open access to the Trans European Rail Freight Network (TERFN) from 2008 (see chapter 2). In effect, it is a pilot project for the implementation of TERFN.

Obstacles
In setting up the new operation, Ikea Rail ÅB was faced with many obstacles, of both a technical and operational nature. Some of these were related to the need for interoperable traction (locomotives), some to the different safety standards and regimes and some to the variety of rulebooks dealing with standard operational situations. A summary of the differences faced for the first services, in a number of areas, is shown in Table 12.1.

The main problems were encountered in obtaining suitable traction (locomotives) whereas there was no difficulty in sourcing appropriate freight rolling stock, largely thanks to the long-standing standards of the UIC for internationally used wagons, covering issues such as buffer and coupler heights and the braking system. For the initial service from Sweden to Germany, the locomotives needed on-board equipment to deal with four automatic train protection (ATP) systems and two electrification systems. The latter problem was resolved by leasing diesel locomotives of the type of the GM built Class 66 locomotives in Britain. However, this still left environmental issues to be resolved, most notably noise issues.

Design and installation of the ATP equipment was very involved since the Swedish system is relatively simple while the Danish system is complex, expensive and requires a substantial space for installation. Also necessary was an interface system to switch automatically from one to the other in the middle of the Øresund Link [6]. It took 18 months to resolve the technical issues and then several more months to complete the certification procedures for the modified locomotives. Staff also had to be trained to be able to work across national borders. STIs (Standards for Technical Interoperability) and harmonised rule sets are reducing these problems but conversion of all of Europe's railways will take a long time still.

The Future

In late 2002, Ikea Rail ÅB extended its operations into Poland and Italy and, in 2003, it started with services connecting Duisburg with the Benelux area and with Hungary using traction and drivers provided by national railway undertakings. This was necessary to overcome the technical obstacles of supply voltages, signalling systems and operational rules. Building interoperable locomotives for more than three or four combinations of signalling and three types of power supply was not feasible. However, the experience of Ikea Rail ÅB shows that a major shipper can improve control over its logistics operations by running its own railway operation.

12.4 Conclusions

Finding train paths is not as easy as it might appear, given the non-standardisation of the rail network across key parameters such as axle-loads, loading gauges and line capacity. Indeed, it may appear that the operational planning of rail freight flows is impossibly difficult, and it is clearly more difficult than making simple arrangements with one lorry driver. However, this is an issue of which rail freight operators are only too well aware, and a number of initiatives are taking place to reduce this gap. For instance, the 'One Stop Shop' offered by a number of European railway administrations attempts to reduce the number of industry players a potential consignor needs to deal with.

There remain some problems, however, especially where any link of the chain is a monopoly – most obviously in the supply of infrastructure, but also potentially in the availability of specific rolling stock. The key advice is to identify from Figure 12.5 the particular combinations of throughput and train capacity which maximise profit opportunities for the flow under consideration, and to persevere in achieving them. Finding creative solutions (for instance, in different loading points or equipment, or transit routes) can unlock very substantial gains for the consignor which road hauliers can never achieve.

References

1. Fricke, E & Pohl, M (2001) 'Network 21: Impact on Rail Freight Traffic', Proc. Instn. Mech. Engrs Vol 215 F, pp. 37–44.
2. King, M. and G. van Marle, 'Ikea on track to do it itself', International Freighting Weekly, p 20, 19. November 2001.
3. Kadeřávek, P. (2002) 'Ikea Rail. The Freeways Concept Live at last', Railvolution, vol. 2, no. pp. 36-38.
4. Øresund konsortiet, 'Interim Report', p 6, 1 January to 30 June 2002.
5. Bailey, C (ed) 'European Railway Signalling', Institution of Railway Signal Engineers, A & C Black, London, 1995.
6. Hove, K. and N.B. Buch, 'Integrated signalling, ATP and train radio on the Øresund Link', Railway Gazette International, vol. 156 no.7, pp 428–430, 2000.

13 New Freight Lines

Charles Watson, University of Sheffield

The issues surrounding route selection for passenger railways are well documented, and many of these are similar when choosing a freight route. There are, however, some important differences, and this chapter examines these in some detail. The chapter then discusses the reasons for constructing freight railways, and provides some examples.

13.1 Issues of Route Selection for Freight Lines

There are a number of reasons that might prompt a promoter to construct a new freight line but, whatever the reason, the same rigorous route selection method outlined in [1] needs to be followed. There are, however, some specific issues which apply to freight and they will have a great effect on the selection of a route, the components and the structures that will be used in its construction.

Especially in the European context, it may be possible to re-use parts of other railway alignments, either those which have become completely disused, or where spare land remains alongside lines still in use. Where completely new construction is required, however, the fundamental characteristics of rail freight need to be understood, although the planning process itself also needs to be considered, as there may be trade-offs with political and environmental issues (see section 16).

Freight trains tend to be considerably heavier and have much higher axle loads than passenger trains. They also lack an effective wheel slide protection system on the brakes of freight vehicles (which have no power to operate such a system), but use mostly tread brakes. These factors mean that freight vehicles are more prone to both wheel flats and higher wheel roughness, which lead to high impact forces and increased dynamic forces in general. This means that any bridges must be constructed to withstand this greater vertical loading and the formation must also be robust enough to withstand the loads. Additionally, rail sections and sleeper spacing must be chosen to avoid any undue stresses in the rail, and to distribute the load evenly into the formation. Another important factor is the higher tractive effort and braking forces transferred to the rail by the train which, if not properly accounted for, can cause longitudinal motion of either the track or any structures supporting it.

The maximum gradient over which a freight train can operate successfully is also much less than for a passenger train, with 1% (1 in 100) considered a steep grade. This could result in long diversionary routes being required or

Train	Mass (tonnes)	Speed (km/h)	Speed (m/s)	Radius (m)	Force (kN)
Passenger ICE-3	544	330	91.7	3000	1524
Freight 1 X 150 tonne loco 52 X 100 tonne wagons	5350	80	22.2	3000	881

Table 13.1 Mass, Speed and Curving Forces for Typical European Trains

considerable sections of railway located in tunnels, especially in hilly or mountainous terrain. Curving forces for freight trains are generally less than for passenger trains, due to the lateral force being proportional to the square of the speed and Table 13.1 shows that, for typical European freight trains, the curving force is only half that of high speed passenger trains.

Usually the maximum length of train that can be operated on a given route is governed by the siding length, so any passing loops must be constructed to accommodate the longest train expected. 775m is becoming the standard length for passing loops in Britain, but far longer trains are operated in the heavy haul environment (see chapter 6).

As the drive for greater efficiency continues, it is likely that freight trains will get heavier, longer and faster. Thought must therefore be given to the future of the line and consideration given to what properties trains may have in the future, for it is very expensive to upgrade a route that has become obsolete because the designers did not recognise that trains may evolve over time.

13.2 Reasons for Building New Freight Lines

Reasons for constructing a new freight line include:

• To exploit newly-discovered mineral deposits;
• To create, or improve access to a convenient port for import/export of goods;
• To reduce journey times;
• To free up capacity on mixed traffic railways;
• To reduce gradients on mountainous sections;
• To improve/create larger loading gauge to allow piggyback or container traffic;
• To remove a physical barrier for freight traffic.

There are, however, very few freight-only lines currently being constructed, and most of the examples found have, at the very least, a few passenger services operating on them. This is due, in part, to the great expense involved in constructing a railway and the desire of the promoter to gain maximum revenue from the investment. Additionally, where lines are constructed through towns that had not previously been in the vicinity of a railway, there will be the demand for a passenger service to link these towns to other centres, in order to increase the mobility of the population. It could also be argued that the economic case for building a new railway may be enhanced if additional traffics can be found and the case studies given below also demonstrate benefits in other areas.

Exploitation of Newly Discovered Mineral Deposits
A new freight line may be constructed to exploit newly discovered mineral deposits where the increase in road traffic would be unacceptable to residents living along the road, or to provide a cheaper method of transporting the large amounts of material excavated from the earth. In Nigeria, a 51km rail line was constructed between the iron ore mine at Itakipe and the Ajaokuta steel mill, being commissioned in 1990. Prior to the construction of this railway the ore was transported by barge and road. The rail line is being extended a further 300km to Warri to supply the Delta Steel plant at Aladja; however, due the poor economic conditions in Nigeria this line has yet to be completed.

Create Access to a Convenient Port
A new freight line may be needed to create or improve access to a convenient port for the import/export of goods. This may be in conjunction with the building of a new port or container terminal. There is currently a $AU 1.3 billion railway line being constructed in Australia, heading North from the current railhead at Alice Springs to the Port of Darwin; the 1420km single track line is due for completion in December 2003. This link to Darwin's new East Arm Port, which includes railway connected wharfage and an intermodal container terminal, will greatly reduce shipping times to Asia and the rest of the world. For example, the current time from Sydney to Singapore is 11 to 15 days and, upon completion of the new rail line, it will be 8 to 11 days; similar time savings are expected from shipments originating in Melbourne. Freight currently travelling between Adelaide and Darwin goes as far as Alice Springs by rail and then must be transferred to road for the completion of the trip, a time and expense which will be eliminated.

Reduce Journey Times
The Botniabanan is being constructed to reduce journey times from Umea to Nyland along the East coast of Sweden, halving the distance by rail between these two cities. This 10.9 billion SEK project will result in a single track line that is expected to reduce journey times for freight trains by over 3 hours. Currently, freight traffic travels by an inland route originally chosen to reduce the need

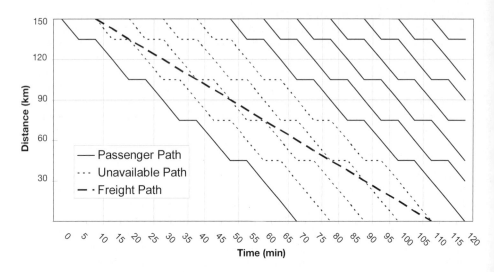

Figure 13.1 Freight Paths and Available Capacity

for long tunnels and, once the new 190km Botnia line is opened in 2008, it will allow 750 metre long trains to travel at 110km/h. This route will also be used by 250km/h high speed trains and 200km/h regional trains, meaning that it is effectively a mixed traffic railway.

Free up Capacity
Freight railways may be constructed in order to free up capacity on mixed traffic routes for passenger trains. Freight trains generally travel at a lower speed than passenger trains and, as shown in Figure 13.1, can reduce significantly the capacity of a predominantly-passenger railway line.

The Betuweroute is a 160km double track railway in the Netherlands which is being built to carry freight from the port of Rotterdam to the German border. This freight-only line is due to open in 2006 and will form a key freight artery, where traffic otherwise has to share tracks on the congested Dutch rail network. The line will operate at a speed of 120km/h and accommodate a 25t axle load. The line will operate with a six-minute headway, allowing 10 trains per hour per direction. Initially the line will only be able to handle single stack container trains but the 20km of tunnels have sufficient height to allow for double stacking, should the need arise.

Not only is the lack of spare capacity a problem on rail, roads are also becoming increasingly congested, resulting in longer journey times and decreasing delivery reliability. This of course provides a stimulus for freight railway development.

158

Reduce Gradients on Mountain Railways
Many of the world's railways were constructed in the 19th Century. At that time trains were slow and not very long, so gradients could be steeper. When the Canadian Pacific Railway was constructed through the Rocky Mountains in the early 1880s the ruling gradient for Westbound trains was 4.5%. However, as trains became longer and heavier, the line was regraded so that the ruling gradient was reduced to 2.4%. The discovery of significant coal deposits in South-Eastern British Columbia provided the railway with a major traffic flow; however, to transport this coal, the railway was forced to operate trains of 14,000t made up of 100 or more wagons with several locomotives at the front, more in the middle of the train (controlled by radio) and pusher loco-motives at the rear of the trains, to help them over the steepest sections. The use of these pusher locomotives means that the trains must stop at the bottom of the steep sections so that they can be coupled up and they must also stop at the top of the hills to uncouple the pushers. There is an added drain on railway capacity as the pusher locomotives must run light down to the bottom so they can assist another train. In 1988, the Canadian Pacific therefore opened the 34km Mount MacDonald Line, which reduces the ruling gradient to 1% and eliminates the requirement for pusher locomotives. Railway capacity is also sig-nificantly enhanced because, although westbound trains use the new line, eastbound traffic continues to use the old line due to its ruling gradient being downhill and since the traffic mainly consists of empties returning to the mines.

Create Larger Loading Gauge
When railways were first constructed, the loading gauge in many countries was quite small in order to keep construction costs down, especially where sig-nificant tunnelling was required. As shippers' requirements changed, con-tainerisation and piggyback operations became more popular due to the greater flexibility in reaching destinations not directly connected to the railway. Piggyback operations in particular require a generous loading gauge because the road trailer sits directly on a rail vehicle, which will require overhead clearances greater than 5.5m, as shown in Figure 13.2.

An example of this is through the Swiss Alps, where freight traffic from Germany to Italy passes through using one of two main routes. One route runs from Basel on the German border, through Luzern and the St. Gotthard route to Bellinzona in Italy. The other trunk route travels through Bern and the Lötschberg and Simplon route to Domodossola. In 1991 some work was done on the existing Lötschberg tunnel to make it suitable for piggyback opera-tions, but high vehicles still had to have their tyres deflated to allow them to fit within the loading gauge and pass unrestricted through the tunnel. It was therefore decided to construct a new, longer tunnel further down the mountain. The Lötschberg base tunnel will be an important element in the Alp Transit concept. Measuring 34.6km in length, and expecting to cost

Figure 13.2 Piggyback Train

CHF 3.25 billion, the 9-metre diameter tunnel runs from Frutigen in the Kander valley to Raron in the Rhone valley. The project commenced in 2000, and the tunnel is expected to be in operation by 2007 but, due to cost constraints, initially only one of the twin tubes will be used for rail traffic, the other tunnel being completed at a later date. A new base tunnel is also being constructed on the St Gotthard route and these two routes are expected to take in excess of 40MGT of freight off the roads every year by providing a rolling highway service through Switzerland.

Remove a Physical Barrier
The opening of the Channel Tunnel between England and France in 1994 marked the removal of one of the key barriers to international trade in Europe. Although a comprehensive system of ferries (including train ferries) oper-

ated to carry traffic across the Channel, time was wasted in loading and unloading the ferries, which also ran to a fixed timetable, which may not always have been convenient for shippers. Eurotunnel's business case minimised risk by spreading its capital costs across four market segments (Eurostar passenger trains, their own passenger and freight shuttles, and conventional freight trains), but the key benefit for all of these was the reduction in transshipments. Although there was an associated reduction in journey times, this was perhaps less significant for shippers, because the time spent on the ferries was traditionally used to give lorry drivers their breaks from driving. The shuttle is sufficiently fast (30-minute transit) not to provide a long enough break in all cases.

Similar physical barriers have been removed elsewhere in Europe in recent years, most notably the joining of the Danish mainland with Sweden (through the Størebelt and Øresund links). Although the time savings and reductions in shunting or reloading are significant, rail has not yet fully taken advantage of the new opportunities, because of differences in network characteristics (e.g. traction voltages and signalling systems) of different countries (see section 12 for the problems encountered by Ikea in using the new Danish links).

Mixed Benefits
Some rail freight schemes are clearly designed to overcome more than one deficiency in the existing network. A fine example of this is the proposal by the Central Railway Group to develop a rail freight route between the Channel Tunnel and Liverpool, via the Midlands. This fits the aim of improving import and export opportunities for British industry.

However, at present, the British loading gauge is too small to accept continental gauge wagons (see section 12), and even the Channel Tunnel Rail Link only provides one route for such wagons to the outskirts of London. The Central Railway Group's line aims to provide a larger loading gauge to new terminals in the Heathrow, Leicester, Sheffield and Liverpool areas, enabling British companies to take advantage of efficiencies associated with larger wagons.

Nevertheless, even if traffics can fit within the British loading gauge, there is a shortage of line capacity. London acts somewhat as a barrier at present, with only two rail routes available for freight crossing the River Thames, plus potentially the route at Reading. Moreover, all of these routes have heavy passenger traffic, and there is simply not the line capacity to accept significant increases in freight.

13.3 New Branch Lines

The need for new branch lines is much more common than for completely-new main lines and, fortunately, construction requirements for these are less onerous. With design speeds likely to be lower and train weights possibly less, if wagonload traffic is envisaged, sharper curves and steeper gradients may be permitted. However these can still generate unnecessary operational costs (from increased maintenance) and noise (which is unpopular with the local community). Even for branch lines though, costs are not insignificant (easily running into tens of £m), and it is not uncommon for freight flows to start up with a connecting road journey to the nearest rail terminal. Only when the general feasibility of using rail has been established will some shippers invest in their own branch line.

13.4 Conclusion

The route selection process for a freight line is much the same as for a passenger line, but must take into account the length, weight and speed of freight trains, as well as considering the properties of the trains that might use the line in the future. There are a number of reasons for constructing a new freight railway, but many lines are going to be justified on their solving more than one problem. Unfortunately, very few freight only lines are currently being built because of the large capital investment required and the difficulty for promoters in ensuring an adequate return on the investment.

Reference

1. Catling, D (1992) 'Civil Engineering: Finding an Alignment', chapter 14 pp. 152–164, in Harris, N G & Godward, E W (eds) 'Planning Passenger Railways', TPC, Glossop.

14 Infrastructure Maintenance

Luke Ripley, The Railway Consultancy Ltd

The need to undertake maintenance and renewal of the railway infrastructure is an oft-overlooked aspect of railway freight planning, perhaps because most work is, of necessity, carried out largely unseen, in the dead of night. However, such work is crucial to the continued safe operation and good performance of any railway, whether it carries predominantly passenger or freight traffic, or a mixture of both. The inclusion of this chapter in a volume on planning freight railways is because of the dual impact of maintenance on rail freight operations – whilst maintenance work hinders the development of conventional rail freight, it also provides opportunities for railfreight operators to run trains for the infrastructure companies carrying out those works.

On a unitary railway, all infrastructure trains are regarded as non-revenue traffic. However, under a railway privatised as in Britain, with separate Freight Train Operating Companies (FOCs) and an infrastructure company (Network Rail), the FOC is therefore simultaneously a customer (since it must still bid for paths to run the trains) and contractor of Network Rail. Engineering traffic currently consists of around 6% of freight on the British railway network.

14.1 Infrastructure Trains

Maintenance and renewal works themselves generate considerable volumes of railway freight. Because of the large amounts of heavy material (e.g. ballast, rails) required, and the relative inaccessibility of many worksites, delivery of material to site can often only be achieved by rail. Various types of infrastructure freight are needed, to support the different elements of the infrastructure itself (permanent way, structures, signalling, OHLE, etc). Although wiring trains carrying miles of cable are an integral part of maintaining the electrified railway, the majority of infrastructure freight relates to the carriage of new ballast to works sites and the removal of spent ballast away from them.

Traditionally, ballast trains ran directly from source (e.g. quarry) to a location near to the site of works, finishing their trip when required (which would often be the following weekend). Sometimes these trains covered considerable distances. Whilst this was inefficient in terms of wagon utilisation, most of the wagons used were 'hand-me-downs' from revenue-earning freight, and were completely life-expired. However, they were often limited to very slow speeds, and could cause pathing difficulties when mixed with modern higher-speed trains over a busy network.

Figure 14.1 Trunk Haul of Bottom-Discharge Ballast Hoppers

Railtrack instituted a quantum change in operations, through a complete overhaul of the distribution system. They decided to invest in modern high volume wagons (see Figure 14.1) which could run at higher speeds. To make maximum use of these, however, they also set up, through their National Logistics Unit, a number of ballast dumps located strategically around the network. These are served regularly by trunk hauls of ballast from sources including both quarries and ports (see Figure 14.2). From these points, the relevant wagons and equipment can be dispatched locally to the relevant possessions.

14.2 Possessions and Blockades

Some types of minor maintenance work can be undertaken while trains are running. In general, however, it is necessary to close a section of line to normal traffic in order that the civil engineer or his contractors can have unrestricted access to the line; this is known as "taking a possession". Increasingly onerous safety requirements have, in recent years, tended to reduce the proportion of work which can be undertaken without taking possessions, or in single-line

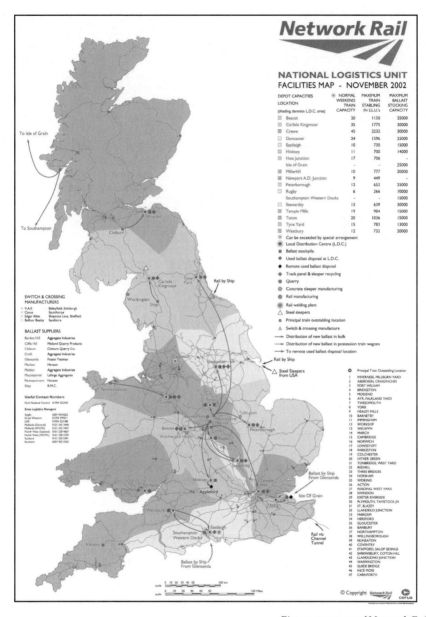

Picture courtesy of Network Rail

Figure 14.2 National Logistics Unit Facilities Map

possessions. While this has led to a welcome improvement in the safety of on-track workers, it has also tended to make maintenance and renewal works more difficult to plan, more costly, and potentially more disruptive to traffic.

In order to minimise the disruption to normal traffic, most possessions are taken at times when the railway is less busy – for instance, at night or at weekends. Shorter possessions are commonly taken overnight, when the passenger traffic which dominates many railways in Europe is relatively scarce. However, this can cause significant problems for rail freight, especially in such sectors as the overnight express parcels business. Longer possessions may be taken at weekends (when freight may be less affected) or even over periods of several weeks, when a "blockade" may be used to undertake very significant works using the latest large hi-tech equipment. Blockades will inevitably require alternative arrangements to be made for freight traffic; in extreme cases, these might even jeopardise the business, without freight benefiting from the improvements which may be targeted at higher-speed passenger trains.

A possession may extend to only one, several, or all of the running lines in a particular area. On a double-track line, for example, where work on one line can safely be carried out without interference to the adjacent line, single-line working can be instituted over the unaffected line for the duration of the possession. However, arrangements may need to be made for a special driver to 'pilot' trains past the affected section. By this means, the route can remain open to traffic, albeit with much-reduced capacity. Similarly, on a quadruple-track main line, a double-line possession can sometimes be taken, with the remaining pair of lines open for traffic. However, this depends partly on the track configuration, as shown in Figure 14.3.

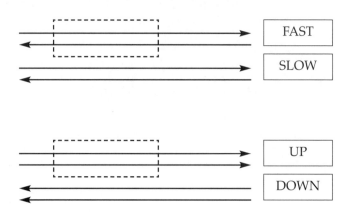

Figure 14.3 Impact of Line Configuration on Ability to Maintain Traffic During Engineering Works

Picture courtesy of Rail Link Engineering

Figure 14.4 Beechrook Farm Railhead for CTRL

Where lines are paired by speed, a possession of any two adjacent running lines leaves one line in each direction open for traffic. Where lines are paired by direction, wrong-line running must be instituted over one of the unaffected lines.

In some cases, where the work permits, it can be arranged for the possession to be "given up" for the passage of a particular train or trains, and retaken immediately afterwards. However, this obviously reduces the amount of work which can be carried out and may be completely infeasible when tracks are being replaced. Any trains which are required to pass through the possession (e.g. ballast trains required at worksites within the possession) do so under the authority of the person in charge of the possession (PICOP) and not the lineside signals.

The resources required for possessions and (particularly) blockades can be very significant. Even in the modern era, large numbers of staff are required – usually to work at anti-social hours. For the rail freight operator, however, there is considerable scope for business for the infrastructure provider. Specialist track-laying equipment may need to be hauled to the site. Large numbers of trains may be needed to take ballast to, and remove spoil from, the worksite. For the largest projects, special temporary railfreight terminals may be set up, to manage the resources. For section 1 of the Channel Tunnel Rail Link from Dollands Moor to Fawkham Junction, a rail head was set up at Beechbrook Farm (see Figure 14.4) which was later returned to agricultural use. Other materials (such as rails) may need to be left at the worksite beforehand, and picked up afterwards.

14.3 Operational Capacity versus Possession Availability

For any particular stretch of line, maintenance and renewal requirements, in general, increase with increasing density of traffic, but, conversely, the availability of possessions decreases. There exists a fundamental trade-off between the availability of network capacity for normal train operations and the availability of possession time for maintenance, renewals and capacity enhancement projects.

From an "operating" perspective, engineering works are ideally undertaken solely during periods when traffic levels are low or non-existent (typically midweek nights and weekends). Permitting possessions only at such times (i.e. within "Rules of the Route" – see below) results in minimal disruption to the train service. However, this approach tends to result in very short duration possessions and this can be inefficient and costly from a construction perspective. The nature of railway work is such that it generally involves fairly lengthy set-up and clear-out times, plus the time required to take and give up the possession. These often reduce the productive time to as little as an hour or two. An extreme example is on underground "metro" type systems where long operating hours coupled with the relative inaccessibility of worksites can routinely result in only an hour of productive time being available.

If, because of unforeseen circumstances (e.g. a late-running last train), the possession cannot be taken on time, it is only the productive time which can be reduced. If the remaining time is insufficient to complete the job, this may result in the possession being lost altogether. Figure 14.5 illustrates a typical possession time-line for both "as planned" and "delayed start" scenarios.

The situation can be eased, to some extent, by curtailment of the late-evening or early morning train service. Passenger trains at these times are often relatively lightly-loaded, and substitution of a few trains by buses can extend the available length of the possession significantly. The time gained is all productive time.

The "construction" perspective favours the use of lengthy possessions or "blockades" which substantially reduces the total duration and cost of works. Being able to work continuously obviates the need for staging works that are usually required in order to open the line to traffic during the day; it minimises time wasted in setting up, travel times to/from site and facilitates the assurance of safety for those working on site. Its drawback, of course, is the increased disruption to the train service during busy periods. The volume of logistical support required (ballast trains, etc) can further reduce the already restricted capacity available for normal operations. Freight railroads in the US are increasingly adopting the "blockade" strategy for track relaying. Complete closure of a route for a short period permits high output relaying equipment to be used continuously until the job is complete. If planned properly in advance, alternative facilities or routes can usually be found for traffics, in an attempt to minimise the disbenefit to existing users.

14.4 Structure of the Railway Industry

The organisational structure of the railway industry has a considerable bearing on the way in which this conflict between operational and maintenance requirements is handled. For a vertically integrated railway which controls both infrastructure maintenance and operations, the conflict is internal, and can be resolved by simple consideration of the trade-off between costs and benefits of various alternative strategies. For example, a more disruptive possession strategy may reduce the costs and duration of a particular project, but at the cost of an anticipated loss of revenue.

In a fragmented industry, such as that which currently exists in Britain, the position is much more complex. The structure of the privatised railway industry in Britain is extremely complicated. Essentially, Network Rail is responsible for managing the maintenance, renewal and enhancement of the railway infrastructure by its contractors and for providing timetable paths to passenger train operating companies (TOCs) and freight train operating companies (FOCs) in order that these companies can operate a train service in accordance with their franchise obligations and commercial objectives. The conflict between maintenance and operations requirements is therefore governed by contractual relationships between the companies. The times during which Network Rail's contractors may freely book posses-

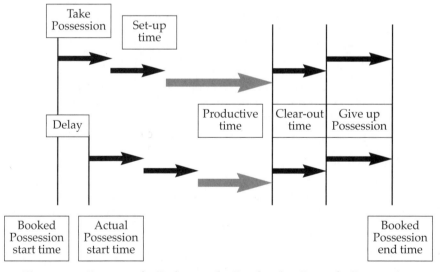

Figure 14.5 Impact of a Delay on the Productive Part of a Possession

sions are laid down in "Rules of the Route" (see below), and compensation is payable by Network Rail to train operators for any disruption outside these times. Compensation is determined according to Schedule 4 of the train operators' track access agreements. This is a somewhat complex set of calculations which is intended to reflect some measure of the revenue lost by the train operator.

Rules of the Route

Rules of the Route (RoR) define, for each section of route, the time periods when the route is considered to be either open for traffic, or available for possessions. This can vary from a simple open/closed arrangement to a more complex regime allowing various permutations of running lines and route sections to be taken. The permissible permutations may also vary by timetable period – the aim being to ensure that when one through route is blocked during normal traffic hours, its natural diversionary route(s) is/are not blocked simultaneously. For example, on the British West Coast Main Line (WCML), during those timetable periods when long weekend RoR possessions are available on the Trent Valley line (Rugby – Nuneaton – Stafford), no possessions can be taken in the Coventry Corridor (Rugby – Coventry – Stechford), since the latter provides the diversionary route for through trains between London and the North West and Scotland.

Rules of the Route are formulated by Network Rail (NR), based on a consideration of the previous year's train service, and the volume of maintenance/ renewal/ enhancement work it intends to carry out on the route. Train operators may, however, appeal against the proposal, and negotiate changes before the Rules are finalised.

Possessions are normally planned by NR's contractors; in most instances they are taken within Rules of the Route and can be booked directly by the contractor into NR's Possessions Database (PRIDE). Where the volume of work is very heavy, it may be necessary (or advantageous) to seek extended possessions, or even "blockades", outside the scope of Rules of the Route. In such instances, NR will normally issue a Major Project Notice to the TOCs/FOCs in advance, and consult with them in an effort to gain their approval.

14.5 Major Schemes

As outlined above, where volumes of work are relatively low, as is normally the case where only routine maintenance and renewals are concerned, it can usually be carried out within Rules of the Route. This is essentially the situation which Railtrack has been expected to manage when it was set up. At the time of privatisation, it had been envisaged that demand for rail transport in the UK would, at best, remain static, or, more likely, continue to decline slowly; the dramatic growth which has in fact occurred was not anticipated. This has resulted in Network Rail being largely constrained to attempting to deliver major capacity enhancement schemes using a mechanism designed to manage routine maintenance.

Processes which may be adequate and manageable at low levels of activity become unworkable at high levels. For example, planning by various engineering disciplines/contractors is normally carried out in isolation. When the volume of work required is relatively low (as will usually be the case with routine maintenance), the probability of a conflict between different contractors planning incompatible work at the same location at the same time is small. However, heavy work volumes are likely to result in frequent conflicts which may only be identified at a late stage, resulting in high levels of replanning, late changes, cancellations, and increased risk of possession failures. In addition, maintaining protected paths for possession trains becomes increasingly difficult and, with the frequent changes, planning of possession train requirements is more difficult.

To mitigate these problems, there is a need for good integration/sharing of planning information across disciplines/contractors at an early stage. In the West Coast Route Modernisation programme, which has demonstrated the problems resulting from a very high level of construction, maintenance and renewal activity on a very busy mixed-traffic route, this was recognised and developed into the Routeway Integration Plan.

14.6 Alternative Strategies

In the late 1990s, Railtrack sought to develop alternative approaches to delivering major projects, and pursued the "blockade" strategy in various forms, with mixed success. Different traffic types tend to have different peak/off-peak demand characteristics and, hence, operators may have different views on when long possessions or even blockades may be considered.

Long-distance passenger traffic tends to fall into two categories: business travel, which is heavy in early mornings and late afternoons on weekdays, and leisure travel, which peaks on Friday evenings and Sunday afternoons. Friday afternoons/evenings are particularly busy, since both peaks coincide. The periods of lightest demand, and hence the least disruptive time for lengthy possessions or blockades, occur at weekends, that is, late Friday evening to mid Sunday afternoon. Long Bank Holiday weekends (especially Easter and Christmas/New Year) are particularly favourable[1].

Suburban passenger traffic is very heavily peaked towards weekday mornings and evenings. Given the difficulty of handling heavy volumes of passengers on alternative routes or services, these times are generally best avoided.

---

[1] Evidence from other European railways would indicate that the British public has been conditioned to accept poor railway services at weekends and bank holidays rather than there being inherently low demand. On the Spanish high speed railways (AVE), all trains have to be in service at weekends to cope with available traffic.

Possessions of longer duration than a standard midweek night are normally accommodated by curtailment of the late evening service, or at weekends, when traffic is lighter. However, since the TOCs' peak-time costs, revenues and subsidy are effectively fixed, its off-peak revenue is a crucial factor in its profitability (off-peak costs being marginal). Such a TOC may actually favour a blockade strategy, rather than face many months of disruption to off-peak weekend traffic, as well as the inherent risks of Monday morning overruns. A high level of planned disruption to regular commuters for a relatively short period can sometimes be tolerated, especially during holiday periods (August is particularly favoured) when peak ridership is lower than normal.

Freight traffic tends to be heaviest on weekday nights, but very light at weekends. A freight operating company (FOC) may therefore be agreeable to long weekend possessions, including Sunday night, but not Friday night. There is also a tendency for freight volumes to reduce somewhat during traditional holiday periods (e.g. August).

On a busy mixed-traffic railway, these conflicting objectives make it very difficult to reach a solution agreeable to all operators. In a unitary railway, as noted above, a single authority can trade-off the costs and benefits to each traffic category and determine the optimum solution. In a multi-operator situation with contractual obligations, any single operator can effectively veto any proposal. The infrastructure authority is then left with no choice but to plan the work as far as possible within Rules of the Route.

The situation is somewhat easier on a railway carrying entirely, or predominantly, one type of traffic, since it is then generally possible to identify periods of low or zero demand. France's high speed TGV lines, for example, are closed to traffic overnight (when very high speed running has less commercial benefit), and often have long daytime "white periods" at off-peak times as well.

The way in which infrastructure work is spread over time affects the efficiency of the methods used by the railfreight operators to assist infrastructure owners in that work. The possessions approach, whilst maximising the use of specialist track equipment, can lead to locomotives not being required at other times. When possessions are limited to weekends, railfreight operators may find it easy to find other productive work for locomotives on revenue-earning trains during the week. However, a 'big bang' approach lasting several weeks can lead to conflicting requirements for the railfreight operator.

14.7   Diversionary Capacity

It has been a long-standing objective to increase railway efficiency by eliminating excess capacity, reducing infrastructure capacity to not much more than the minimum required to sustain existing traffic levels. From an economic perspective, this is a worthy objective. However, difficulties arise when major upgrade of a route is required, since there is little excess capacity elsewhere on the network to absorb traffic diverted away from the route in question. In general terms, there is a trade-off between the maintenance of excess capacity and the level of disruption to be expected during major infrastructure upgrade works (e.g. WCML). For the freight operator, there is effectively no equivalent to the high level of substitute buses used by passenger operators during a blockade.

15 Terminal Design and Technology

Matthias Beth, Kombiverkehr

15.1 Introduction

Intermodal transport was introduced in chapter 10 and is based on moving goods from origin to destination using two or more modes of transport, for example, Road – Ship – Rail – Road. Each mode has a place in the sequence because it excels at a particular skill. Modes are generally linked at "terminals". The design of railfreight terminals is critical to the ongoing success of the business using them. Chapter 16 deals with the land-use planning elements of the process needed to establish a new railfreight terminal. This chapter concentrates on the internal design of the terminal and the technologies which can enable the swift transfer of goods between modes. It stresses the equipment needed for the transfer of freight to/from road, although many large terminals are designed for other purposes and have other equipment, e.g. specially-designed rapid loading bunkers for transfer to/from ships or power station coal stores, or unloading facilities for liquid products directly to/from pipelines. The design and operation of terminals must take into account the very different properties of the transport modes involved, e.g. road with single load-units carrying stochastic traffic flows, as compared to transport by trains, planes or ships that is based on the timetabled transport of consolidated loads. The following description of the approach to create a well functioning intermodal terminal is based on standardised, widely accepted rail-road technology, available throughout Europe.

15.2 Locating an Intermodal Terminal

General Terminal Requirements
Intermodal terminals, even in a standardised format, are expensive facilities and therefore need to be intensively used to justify the investment. Generally, the promoter first needs to know the transport requirement and then uses the predicted traffic flows and any related activities to design an appropriate terminal. Satisfactory traffic sources could primarily be expected in proximity to a harbour or port (deep sea or inland), within an industrial zone or a distribution centre, near to a main highway interchange or railway hub, or possibly within a single major industrial complex.

Where the political will exists to move traffic onto the railways, additional traffic flows can be created by carrying bulk products in containers. This includes many loads in quantities not sufficiently large to go via pipeline, ship or specialised wagons operated in unit trains, for example, domestic coal

Figure 15.1
(a) Dörpen terminal, Germany; **(b)** Köln-Eifeltor terminal, Germany

in Britain. Obviously, the terminal needs connections to rail and road links, described in more detail later.

Flat terrain is a very important requirement, as all operational activities get more difficult or dangerous where gradients occur, other than those required for rain water drainage. The start and stop of rail and road vehicles (energy usage, noise and air pollution), running away of wagons, and safe and easy operation of unit handling all improve considerably in a horizontal site.

Public Terminals
An independent terminal operator can try to find a single major potential customer who is willing to use rail services or who is being forced to do so by law, e.g. for dangerous goods. An accumulation of some similar industries could provide an equally sensible traffic source. A major population centre might also promise a reasonably aggregated traffic volume, be this parcels traffic or supermarket logistics.

That last option will be difficult to assess in the early design process. Even though many parties may be interested in using such a terminal, it may be difficult to secure sufficient unit numbers for day-to-day operation once the terminal has been built. On the other hand, the former two options could prove fatal to the terminal's financial viability, should a major customer experience a swing of opinion on the most suitable transport modes or a downturn in the segment of the economy concerned. Few businesses are prepared to guarantee a fixed amount of traffic to be carried by intermodal rail services, without the right to change shipping methods if the cost base changes significantly.

Minimising distances between terminals and the origins and destinations of the major freight flows is important to achieve the core idea of intermodal business, namely, to cover short distances by road and long distances by rail. Even with an optimised location, access journeys may well involve some 80 km of road transport for national services and some 150 km for international operations, e.g. areas as large as Belgium can be connected to a single terminal for certain long distance transport tasks.

Company Terminals
The future traffic volumes and commodities to be carried should be quite clear for a manufacturing company that is eager to send considerable traffic flows by rail and is therefore willing to build an intermodal terminal. Depending on the range of products, dividing volumes between wagon load and intermodal rail traffic units may well be a significant issue. In companies with an output large enough to operate complete railway trains, an internal industrial rail system is often available, allowing a controlling influence on terminal railway operations. Difficulties in designing a terminal within the company site may be created by the need to find the necessary terrain, devising the layout of the terminal area and placing the feeder roads.

15.3 Size and Throughput

Intermodal terminals are rarely designed from only a theoretical point of view. The high level of complexity of the issues involved makes learning from existing examples a wise move. With an approximate idea of the traffic flows and the traffic segments primarily to be handled, one can roughly pick hours of operation and calculate necessary track lengths and storage area requirements. Typical factors influencing these dimensioning tasks are:

Deep Sea Containers may be stacked several high and, when loaded, generally leave the terminal area shortly after arrival. Empty containers are sometimes left for longer term storage. Containers include specialised equipment, such as tanks, flat rack, open top and fold away containers. Sea going containers tend not to be time critical, due to the length of sea journeys, so they generally arrive at terminals evenly spread over the hours of operation.

Swapbodies, generally containing a mixed cargo, may not be stacked and have to be transferred by bottom lift. These units need a large storage area, but are generally collected soon after train arrival and are delivered back to the terminal shortly before train departure.

Tanks with twist lock fittings, mainly used for bulk chemicals, can be handled by top lift and may be stacked, but they can be expected to be left by the customer for some time in the terminal, mainly when empty, to avoid expensive cleaning procedures (note their typical use for a single product). Chemical products tend to arrive at terminals evenly spread over the hours of operation.

Semi-trailers can be hauled into the terminal area without the need for a terminal crane operator. After a crane lift they need to be manhandled to set them down on their front supports, but do not need the crane for a second lift onto the road tractor, if parked staggered.

Determining the terminal size should then start with an estimation of the track lengths and the storage capacity required. The traffic forecasts for different cominations of destination and origin terminals have to be translated into train lengths. Depending on land availability, one might try to have one track per destination served, which reduces short term re-organisation of track occupation when trains arrive delayed. Selecting the number of storage lanes to be equal to the number of railway tracks is a reasonable approach to determining the necessary storage area immediately linked to the tracks. It might seem inappropriately high to calculate storage capacity as lane length multiplied by number of stack layers but there are several reasons for such extensive land take, most of them influenced by technical and usage-related load unit properties:

(1) To allow some form of book-keeping of stored units, the operator will allocate numbered storage areas, generally some 40 or 45 feet in length. The real-world unit mix would always leave parts of these lots not occupied, e.g. due to placing a 30' tank container on a 45' lot.
(2) In order to avoid lifts[1] of containers in addition to the one needed for hand-over to the road haulier, stacking is generally restricted to long term storage. Daily throughput would thus be stored at ground level only.
(3) Not all units accepted for despatch by rail may be loaded immediately onto a departing train. Some extra area is needed for these units, preferably easily distinguishable from units having arrived by rail and waiting for road pick-up.
(4) As described in more detail elsewhere, semi-trailers are parked staggered and neither semi-trailers nor swapbodies may generally be stacked.
(5) The late arrival of trains raises the maximum number of units which must be stored within crane reach, because customers will not readily accept additional delays due to the delayed train waiting outside the terminal yard.

All these general practical aspects reduce the theoretically available stacking capacity, simply calculated as area times stacking height.

Apart from different load unit types with their widely diverging handling needs, throughput tends to vary greatly depending on the day of the week and the time of the day and, indeed, the season. Where a terminal is closed at weekends (i.e. Saturday afternoons and Sundays) or, for that matter, where the industries served work on a five-day basis, one can expect some congestion within the terminal on Monday mornings, when arrivals which departed Friday and early

---

[1] A "lift" is the action of handling a container once and includes the three tasks of raising from current position, moving and depositing in a new position.

Saturday are waiting to be picked up. Customers are bound to need most urgently those units still loaded on wagons outside the crane area!

Later additions to the terminal surfaces are generally difficult, if not impossible, and create additional complexity for terminal operation so that thoughtful choice of the terminal size is a good starting point for successful running of the facility for many years to come.

15.4 Design of the Terminal Layout

Once a rough calculation has been carried out for the number and types of load units to be expected as a maximum at any given point in time, and once the outline of the piece of ground to be used is known, the terminal layout can be planned. The design process generally starts with the establishment of the number and length of railway tracks, adding storage and vehicle lanes within crane reach, followed by check-in and check-out areas and, if desired, long term storage areas outside the immediate track vicinity.

Rail operations facilities (i.e. servicing, parking and storage sidings), as well as repair and maintenance facilities must be planned properly early on. Outside the crane area, additional storage sidings are normally provided because intermodal traffic generally has significant daily and weekly demand fluctuations, in terms of train loading, train arrivals and departures, pick-up and delivery by road vehicles as well as parking of rail vehicles. These matters generally are aggravated by the late arrival of international trains.

Flat terrain has been mentioned earlier. Sharp curves should be avoided as they reduce speeds allowed and produce additional noise and wear to vehicles and rails alike.

A new terminal should allow for standard continental gauge (see chapter 12), even if connecting lines are not yet equipped to accept such a generous gauge. The same holds true for axle loads: 20t per axle must generally be allowed, 22.5t or 25t would be the provision for future demand, even if not needed from the outset.

The choice of track length against split trains is to be considered thoroughly. Intermodal trains with their low weight per unit length can generally run with 600m or even up to 700m of length. Having train-length tracks raises travel distances of cranes as compared to half-train-length tracks. Dividing trains inevitably means delays in arrival times and additional shunting before departure. Where the available land does not prevent long tracks, it is currently considered to be more advantageous to have longer tracks rather than additional shorter tracks. The need for fewer turnouts is another favourable factor.

Level crossings should be avoided. Not only do they present an imminent danger of accidents but, with trains having to cross lanes, road vehicles could be delayed waiting for the crossing to clear. Generally road and rail access should be from different sides of the terminal, so that tracks and tarmac areas comb into each other. Where crossings are necessary, heavy duty crossing elements (rubber or concrete segments) have to be provided to secure trouble free passage of vehicles and easy maintenance and replacement.

Buffer stops provided should be of the sliding type or be equipped with high capacity, long travel buffer elements to minimise damage to loads and equipment. Points generally do not need to be electrically operated. If point machines are provided, local actuators should be fitted that can be operated by the shunter riding at the front of the train while the train is moving.

Air brake hoses with a supply from a fixed reservoir and compressor (see Figure 15.9(a)) help to speed up operations, since they can be used to fill up and check brake equipment before the locomotive arrives and thus reduce the locomotive hours spent idling just to fill up brake reservoir tanks. Storage capacity for minor replacement parts, mainly brake blocks or pads, allows technicians to keep wagons in traffic without the need to shunt wagons out of their train consist and into a repair shop and back.

The *road vehicles'* movements inside the terminal area must also be considered carefully in the layout design:

- Tight curves not only cause serious wear on the tyres and surfaces; they also result in additional exhaust fumes.
- Delivery lorry waiting areas must cover rush hour business needs.
- Possible causes for accidents should be avoided. These include:
  - Crossing lanes at oblique angles where drivers cannot easily see conflicting movements;
  - Walkways or lanes hiding behind building corners;
  - Narrow lanes leaving no leeway for walking personnel or for avoiding movements of trucks;

Pictures courtesy of M. Beth / Kombiverkehr

Figure 15.2
(a) Medium-sized terminal
(Note one track left, road surface with central gutter, reachstacker, second covered track, third track, lighting masts left and right)
(b) Trailers parked staggered ready for pick-up by tractors

179

Pictures courtesy of M. Beth/Kombiverkehr

Figure 15.3 Köln-Eifeltor terminal
(a) Road vehicle return lane with staggered storage beneath cantilever arm, in centre radio antenna mast with control cubicle
(b) gate area, in the centre vehicles parked for check-in and paperwork done; in the foreground gates for entry checks and driver information

- Two-way traffic;
- In contrast to public roads, pedestrians must be expected during all operating hours, night and day, in rainfall and fog or snowfall. As these persons would be conducting their work, they might be less aware of the dangers of approaching road vehicles.

The *terminal operation buildings* and associated areas (e.g. for load unit repair and maintenance services), parking lots for employees' cars and emergency response areas need to be placed appropriately.

Providing check-in and check-out facilities, e.g. personal shelters or camera supports, and fencing off the terminal area are important factors to prevent theft, damage and claims regarding load units being inside the terminal.

It is by no means cheap or easy to get satisfactory automated pictorial records of units and trucks entering and leaving the terminal area. Key problems are:

- Units loaded end to end onto lorries or wagons prevent optical scans of end sides;
- Unit identification numbers other than ISO container numbers are not necessarily attached horizontally (e.g. onto oblique frame struts), sometimes they are not even to be seen laterally (e.g. when fixed to circular tanks where the lift pocket struts provide the only flat surface);
- Vehicle license plates have different sizes and fonts of letters, often enough they are covered in grime;
- Damage must be of a certain size to be seen on scans; higher resolution obviously takes up more storage capacity and slows the scanning process.

180

Appropriate assessment of units entering or leaving the terminal helps to minimise liability claims which not only always cost manpower but influence customer satisfaction as well. The available choices (e.g. personnel vs. automated cameras (including numbers of both), high speed cameras vs. slowing down of trucks, storage of pictorial records without comments or with text messages after processing of pictures) depend on the traffic actually handled. Visiting existing terminals with a similar traffic range might again help to make reasonable choices.

Helping terminal personnel, lorry drivers and visitors to the terminal to find their way around will speed up operations and reduce accident risk. Key elements to ensure this include:

- Signage for vehicles, e.g. along traffic lanes;
- Signage for people, e.g. building entrances and inside buildings;
- Lighting of roads, storage areas and tracks.

Special equipment for these tasks is readily available, e.g. hinged lamp masts which can be swivelled from the erect position to the horizontal position to avoid the need to climb lamp posts to replace bulbs. The hydraulic equipment can be quickly attached to appropriate hooks on the post.

15.5 Lifting Equipment

Amongst the most important questions to be answered is in respect of the type and quantity of lifting equipment. The main choice is between reachstackers and gantry cranes.

Reachstackers are quite flexible in their movements within the individual terminal as well as between terminals. They need an operational area of roughly 15m width to move around between trains, lorries and storage positions. Wherever they need to move, it must be considered that the front axle

Pictures courtesy of M. Beth/Kombiverkehr

Fig. 15.4
(a) Reachstacker   (b) Empty container stacker

181

carries up to 100 tonnes of static load on compressed wheel surfaces of about one square metre.

The time needed to handle a single unit is quite short (1 to 1.5 minutes) but, in the track area, the reachstacker practically cannot serve more than one track and not more than two storage lanes, even though in dedicated storage areas third or fourth row stacking is achievable. However, reachstackers can easily cope with curved tracks. The noise generated by combustion engine-powered container and swapbody stackers is considerably greater than that of electric gantry cranes and must be expected to rise with the age of the machines. In the reachstacker's favour is that the terminal driver can be tasked to exchange paperwork with the customer driver, e.g. during off-peak service times, thus helping small-scale operations to become less marginal.

Where three or more machines work with a high percentage of ISO containers, it is worth considering employing one empty-container stacker (8 tons), which often is not operated with twist locks but with rigid bolts fitting into lateral openings of ISO top corner fittings. These machines are cheaper to buy and maintain and they also operate substantially faster.

Rail running gantry cranes need less surface, basically two one metre wide lanes for the running gear, but the civil engineering requirements for the crane rail foundations are quite impressive, with static wheel loads of up to 30t (see

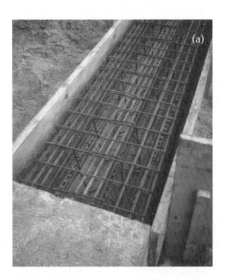

Pictures courtesy of M. Beth / Kombiverkehr

Figure 15.5 Gantry crane rail foundation erection phases
(a) framework with steel reinforcing bars
(b) rail baseplates grouted in and rails fixed

182

Figure 15.6 Gantry cranes:
(a) Crab out on the cantilever arm
(b) Steel wheel running gear, with end of track equipment, emergency stop
button, warning flash light

Figure 15.5). The operation of electric cranes minimises noise and pollution.

The loading and unloading cycle is somewhat longer than with the reach-stacker (1.5 to 2.5 minutes), but the number of lanes served is considerably greater, e.g. up to a total of nine tracks, road lanes and storage lanes between the running rails and two more lanes outside the crane rails, either on one or both sides.

Generally, cranes have a rotating crab running on top of lateral main crane girders and are equipped with a spreader and bottom lift equipment supported from wire ropes, some of which are hung at an oblique angle to suppress horizontal movement of spreader and unit. The lateral sections of the main crane, outboard of the running gear, are described as cantilever arms.

The spreader allows the lifting of containers of different lengths using the twist locks on top while bottom lift prongs can be used for swap-bodies and semi-trailers used for piggy back operations. The operator cannot see the load grip elements and thus cannot assess their proper functioning, so that electric sensors check safe status and visualise the status via coloured lights.

Crane tracks, and thus the associated railway tracks, have to be straight. Transfer of used cranes to a different location is rarely possible because crane rails generally differ in gauge.

Some typical values for crane capabilities are:

- Crane track length (net) 100-750m, with some 30m extra for running gear length and emergency braking equipment.
- Lift height 10.5m, allowing it to lift one container over three others. Heights of up to 14m may be provided to allow stacking.

Figure 15.7
(a) Truss girder gantry crane; and **(b)** Lozenge shaped box frame crane

- The width of area covered can be between:
  14m, i.e. 4m (1 track) + 6m (2 storage lanes) + 4m (1 truck lane) and
  48m, i.e. 18m (4 tracks) + 8m (2 truck lanes) + 12m (4 storage lanes)
  + twice 10m cantilever arms (two storage lanes each side).
  (even wider movement coverage areas are in use for ship loading, with
  partly automated operation).

Crane construction comes in two main types: truss girder and box
frames. Box frames are easy to produce and their welding lines can easily be
checked. Truss girder frames necessitate a high standard of proficiency in

Figure 15.8
(a) Rubber tyred gantry crane; and **(b)** running gear

manufacture and examination, because of the many circular elements connected at three-dimensionally oblique angles. Their main advantages are less girder weight and lower air resistance forces which in turn allow designs with less overall weight, leading again to savings through lower steel usage, lighter foundation construction and lower operational costs, mainly relating to energy consumption.

Box frames can come in different shapes as well. A lozenge shaped main frame, for example, with an underslung single running beam might reduce crane weight, when compared to the standard, right angle construction.

The running gear of gantry cranes would usually be placed somewhere between storage lanes and tracks to avoid damage to crane running gear caused by street vehicles. If this is not advisable, because a second crane area is placed directly adjacent to another, a concrete slide wall would stop road vehicles from getting into the crane path.

Rubber-tyred gantry cranes reduce the space requirements and improve parked unit numbers, compared with reachstackers, and offer greater flexibility than gantry cranes. These cranes exist in an electrically driven form or with a diesel engine, the latter version allowing to serve segregated areas because wheels may be steered. The running gear always limits the lateral movement of lifting gear and load units as the available tyre pressure allows no cantilever arms.

This is a crane type that can be used to serve a low-throughput terminal with just a pair of short tracks; with added demand, tracks can be lengthened or another track element can be added. This variety is generally operated from a hand-held control panel, i.e. without an operator's cab.

Lifting gear: Lift capacity of the different cranes is a factor to be determined early as this influences the dimensioning of the crane's mainframe and, subsequently, the civil engineering requirements.

The heaviest lifting gear would include full endless turning capacity, a top lift spreader and bottom lift prongs, currently generally able to lift some 41t of nominal service weight, requiring the twist and main lift elements to carry some 50t.

Depending on the required unit mix, some of these positioning facilities can be omitted. Where only deep sea containers are to be handled, the main cranes do not require a turning mechanism, reducing the weight to be moved with every unit handled. Where semi-trailers are to be lifted, the ability to turn units is mandatory to avoid counter-sense road movements.

Within a privately owned terminal with a single type of load unit, a crane might be procured with a limited lift capability (e.g. 15t for loaded swapbodies), with defined unit turning capacity (e.g. 90° horizontally) and without a spreader, with only prongs provided. Where the limited expected amount of traffic allows provision of only one crane, hire of a mobile reserve machine at short notice should be planned and prepared to reduce the down time of terminal operations.

Emergency provisions need to be considered at the early design stages as well because lifting heavy loads, handling dangerous goods of different kinds and movement of heavy rail and road vehicles, often during times of low vision, can cause the need for urgent, external help. Easy access for fire brigade and ambulance vehicles is important. Even at rush hour times quick access must be possible.

Building legislation often requires a separate storage area for leaking load units where an independent sump allows the retention of evasive materials. In reality moving a leaking unit around the terminals would lead to the whole length of the terminal needing clean-up treatment. Thus, enough mobile fencing and drainage materials provided quickly often do a better job towards quick recovery of normal terminal operation. Less drastic, but still urgent activities follow failure of lifting equipment, permanent way components and rail motive power.

Railway-related defects will usually be handled by the adjoining railway company. However, failure of loading machinery might be anticipated by a short notice contract with a local crane rental company. Providing a crane as part of the terminal equipment could be a useful alternative. The most important failure situations to be considered here are breakdown of an only machine and blocking of a part of the terminal by an impaired machine, so that a second crane cannot get to the units inside the blocked area.

Additional services to be offered depend on the requirements that cannot be fulfilled by nearby external facilities. Services might include:

- Repair shop;
- Customs office (incl. phytosanitary and veterinary check facilities);
- Restaurant;

Pictures courtesy of M. Beth/Kombiverkehr

Figure 15.9
(a) Rolling Highways: Munich terminal, with ramp, brake air hose (in the background couchette car on separate track)
(b) Manching terminal with ramp (centre) and waiting lorries

- Fuel station;
- Toilets & shower.

15.6 Crane-Free Terminals

There are a number of specific operations, however, where lifting is not required.

The *Rolling Highway* (Rollende Autobahn/Rollende Landstrasse) business is a completely different concept from the craned terminals described above. This rail transport solution is currently only employed over a very restricted number of routes, most of them crossing environmentally sensitive areas. Lorries are directly carried on trains, often with a separate railway coach for the drivers to rest in.

The relatively limited number of rolling highway operations is mainly due to the rather low percentage of allowable payload and the very specialised nature of the rail equipment with very delicate small diameter wheels.

The only terminal infrastructure needed is a straight piece of track (train length: 400m) with a short section of levelled-in straight track (~ 50m) and a separate track to have the couchette car for the drivers treated. This involves dealing with waste disposal, replenishing fresh water reservoir and bed clothes etc., compartment heating, and battery charging. Providing a short-wheelbase tow vehicle helps minimise the disruption caused by disabled trucks. Finally, waiting lorries must be parked in an organised manner that secures first in/first out treatment of lorries, without having to move parked vehicles, as the drivers often sleep in their trucks while waiting for train loading to commence. Theoretically, operation is possible with unloading happening at one end and simultaneously reloading at the other end but this has not been done in practice.

Pictures courtesy of M. Beth/Kombiverkehr

Figure 15.10
(a) Train of Trailerzug type semi-trailers with bogies;
(b) Trailerzug terminal tractor, Cologne

Trailerzug and *RoadRailer* are two systems where the road vehicle's main frame is strengthened to bear the longitudinal forces of a train consisting of similar semi-trailers. Thus trailers can be pushed onto specialised bogies. End bogies of a wagon group have buffers and standard brake hose connection pipes in contrast to internal bogies.

These systems have improved aerodynamic performance (due, for instance, to the reduced distance between units), but at increased price and with tare loads of the semi-trailer increased by 1 – 1.5 tons, thereby reducing road transport capacity.

The civil engineering requirements are a straight piece of levelled-in track (train length: 400m), a separate track on which to park bogies, and parking areas for arriving and departing trailers. A terminal tractor will push trailers onto bogies prior to departure and tow them off their bogies after arrival. This tractor variety has additional air cylinders to feed and operate the train brake system and the trailer suspension system and is equipped with a strengthened frontal shock absorber to push bogies along the track. A fork lift truck is used to pick up bogies to permit changes in the length of the train consist, according to the number of trailers actually arriving at the terminal.

The *Modalohr* system carries trailers, tractors and complete artics on wagons equipped with a load bridge to be swung out for loading and unloading. Requirements in the terminals are base plates for load bearing cylinders, lowered from the swivelled load bridge, and ramps leading on and off the swivelled load bridge.

The *Eurotunnel* service for public road vehicles is another similar service allowing any standard sized road vehicle to be carried by rail, to avoid combustion engine pollution in the "environmentally sensitive area" of the Channel Tunnel.

15.7 Small Scale Terminals

Rail operation is at its best when running long trains without any shunting. Unfortunately, this is not always possible. The physical change over the years in the types of commodities carried (in the past heavy machinery and bulk goods, today light-weight consignments) adds to the necessity to consolidate transport volumes at several stages. A number of solutions have been proposed to address the problem of small scale intermodal operation (see chapter 8 for a description of three ongoing projects in Britain).

Several makes of sidelifter are available which can pick-up a container from the rail wagon, carry the unit on public roads at standard speed, then set down the unit at the customer's premises (see Figure 15.11(a)). This technology works without any preparation necessary on the rail side of the business: a short track section alongside a road-vehicle-carrying surface suffices. Different lengths of container can be carried with the same vehicle. Chains are hooked to bottom corner fittings. The drawback of this chain-lift solution is the heavy weight of crane machinery carried around with the road trailer.

There are systems available (e.g. Mobiler, see Figure 15.11(b)), which can move the container horizontally, but can not set down the unit at road level. This bottom-lift system requires non-standard mobile units with a tunnel accommodating the transfer beam. Horizontal loading and unloading limits the expense for big lifting machinery and allows handling beneath any catenary.

Other intermodal systems allow:

- Rail vehicles to be carried on public streets;
- Containers to be picked up from street level using a hydraulic "back hook" system, e.g. ACTS (Abroll Container Transfer System) approach;
- Standard semi-trailers to be taken onto wagons without the need to lift the road vehicle;
- Specialised containers swapped on and off wagons on passenger platforms, e.g. Minimodal system.

15.8 Operational Demands

When unit mix, equipment choice and terminal layout have been established, daily operational demands need to be considered and solutions must be devised.

Track occupation: Generally, intermodal trains between particular terminals run at a frequency of one departure per day, requiring similar departure times for many trains: each working day, Monday to Friday, trains should leave the facility some time after the end of shifts of manufacturing companies (e.g. 1900 to 2100). There may be constraints on terminal operations planning as a consequence of timetabling restrictions on the rail network. Availability of paths (slots) on the railway servicing the site may not allow all trains to leave

Pictures courtesy of M. Beth/Kombiverkehr

Figure 15.11
(a) Sidelifter Trailer **(b)** Mobiler system transfer beam being retracted

189

together. Spreading train departures over twenty-four hours a day might not be allowed due to local planning restrictions, because of noise, fumes and lighting emitted during terminal operating hours.

More than one departure per day can be expected:

- At rolling road terminals;
- For high density connections (e.g. Germany to Northern Italy);
- At seaport terminals.

In a start-up period, some international services can run successfully and viably less than five times a week (e.g. on Tuesdays and Fridays every week), saving wagons on the railway's side but requiring increased track length to store the trains between services. Once the number and daily schedules of planned departures have been established, a track and sidings occupation plan can be devised, hopefully not showing overloading. This might only be accepted in cases of late arrivals.

Client data flows and customer information are important factors in detailed operations planning:

a) Handling of bookings:
   (1) Take in booking from customer;
   (2) Compare with available capacity;
   (3) Return acceptance to customer;
   (4) Handle changes to accepted bookings.
b) Freight document transport railway-related: how can the paperwork best be transferred between operations building and train locomotive driver?
c) Freight document transport not railway-related: this is best handled within the load unit to avoid loss and subsequent annoyance, or in a document box as an integral part of intermodal units.
d) Status of unit and transport between booking and pick-up: internet data presentation is state of the art, no longer requiring the customer to operate a special data processing system.
e) The handling of units which have to change trains between rail services must be treated differently, as no client lorry driver is available to claim the unit and to do the necessary paperwork, e.g. where check-in reveals damage or theft to unit.

Internal data and information transmission via cable transmission is less flexible, but much more reliable and with better quality of information received. Connection would generally be between fixed buildings, e.g. operations management, and to rail cranes.

Radio transmission covers a complete area but is susceptible to information deterioration or loss, mainly due to catenary arcing and the rail crane main frames acting as radio wave shields. Radio links would be provided between train crews, reachstackers and single persons working in the terminals. To achieve acceptable transmission quality, the antenna mast should have nearly crane height. A control cubicle needs to be positioned close to the mast (see Fig. 15.3 (a)). Depending on the size of the terminal there could be one or two voice transmission circuits, i.e. one each for loading activities and for railway related activities. Note also that a rail crane operator cannot generally communicate with the outside world except via radio or cables.

Other operational issues: In any case, some provision should be prepared to avoid conflicting movements between cranes and trains. Some safety authorities request shutting down cranes completely as long as rail vehicles are being moved. Operational practice shows verbal communication to be much faster and less intrusive, while the risk of accidents is not at an unacceptable level.

Differing production cultures between nations make co-operation at times very difficult: Lax handling, which may be acceptable within one country, is not acceptable in an international context. Experience shows that these differences occur even between different units of international companies. The intermodal operator as the link between both sides sometimes has to bear the task of negotiation between both. Damage from daily handling of containers may be seen as standard somewhere, but will be seen as liable damage elsewhere.

Terminal operational details having an influence on operation thus include:

- Employees, i.e. numbers, skill levels and flexibility between tasks;
- Locomotives, wagons, rail infrastructure, overhead line equipment;
- Train arrivals, departures and expected delay patterns;
- One train per track or several trains per track and shift;
- Cranes, reachstackers, terminal tractors;
- Unit transfer between separated terminal areas, e.g. in "gateway operation";
- Need for double handling;
- Bottom lift versus top lift;
- Provisions for handling dangerous goods;
- Irregularities, emergency situations;
- Load unit repair facilities.

Operation of an intermodal terminal should try to achieve an average terminal stay of road vehicles of twenty minutes, during peak times a lorry should not need to spend more than thirty minutes inside the terminal.

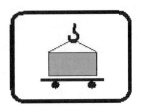

Figure 15.12 Terminal road signage

15.9 Terminal Connections

Intermodal terminals must be connected to the outside world, i.e. to the local road and rail networks.

Road connections must consist of streets wide and strong enough to carry heavy lorries, including extra weight for rail-link services where allowed by relevant legislation, e.g. 44 tonnes as compared to 40 or 41 tonnes regular maximum laden weight. As intermodal business is intended to reduce road congestion, one should avoid delivery vehicles running long distances between highway exits and terminal entry roads. This can influence the choice of terminal location, but could be handled with construction of new exits to existing highways. Motive power for road operation is not a matter for the terminal operator.

Outside the terminal, easy recognisable signage on the road network is an important element to achieve the goal of combined transport i.e. to reduce road traffic (see Figure 15.12). Where HGVs can easily find their way to the terminal, trips are not wasted and customer satisfaction rises.

Regarding *rail connections,* the quickest means of obtaining terminal connection facilities is obviously the use of existing railheads, if there are enough paths available at suitable times and if available tracks can cope with extra wagons or trains. Rail operation properties may vary greatly, partly depending on available track properties (vehicle gauge, axle load, weight per unit length), partly depending on the proposed business volume.

Very small volumes can be handled easily by a low-horse power diesel locomotive or a road-rail vehicle (see Figure 15.13(a)) that can haul a small consist to another yard to make up a complete train. With small scale handling equipment, even existing non-container related rail heads can be used.

Tracks in terminal areas must never be part of main running lines. First, it is not wise to use a main line track to park wagons; secondly, it is not safe practice to carry out loading activities close to running lines.

Where complete shuttle train services need to be moved and where the

Pictures courtesy of M. Beth/Kombiverkehr

Figure 15.13
(a) Road-rail vehicle; **(b)** Terminated overhead lines for four tracks

192

route gradients are not very favourable, more power may be needed than diesel engines can deliver at a satisfactory acceleration and line speed. Swapping diesel and electric locomotives requires another brake check and is therefore time consuming so that container terminals may need overhead line equipment to allow powerful electric locomotives to pick up or deliver their trains directly. Overhead equipment is not provided within the crane sweep area (see Figure 15.13(b)), so that for successful arrival of electric-powered trains, the topology must not prematurely bring the consist to a standstill. Even outside the terminal, flat connecting tracks are then important.

Net train journey times are generally favourable when compared to road traffic. Departures once a day may seem to reduce available service speed, but night-time running usually allows evening departure times and morning arrival times, which is the basic requirement of most intermodal customers.

Long distance main line travel data has to be derived by an iterative method, taking the first approximation of travel time from existing services. Today, intermodal rail services are expected to run at a line speed of 100km/h, resulting in international end-to-end transit speeds of 30-50km/h, national average speeds varying between 40 and 90km/h.

Once the required departure and arrival times have been defined, a first schedule must be sought from the participating infrastructure controller, usually via the former state railway infrastructure department (not necessarily the railway providing local shunting). The resulting path sequence will in most cases differ from the requested timings. A second schedule run might be necessary, depending on the priority of departure or arrival times (e.g. customs handling of units at the destination terminal excludes late afternoon arrival times). The more countries that are involved, the more difficulties in obtaining a satisfactory schedule will be encountered. Often a compromise schedule will have to be accepted as a start and, before the next timetable period, improvements may have to be requested.

The main restrictive aspect of the railway business is the structure gauge (see chapter 12). Weight and length of freight items will generally not prevent transport by rail. The kinematic gauge issue in itself is difficult enough: where most European railways accept standard sea containers up to 8½ ft high for national and international movement without special preparation, the British rail system has to check transport against tighter gauge restrictions and special Channel Tunnel safety requirements.

Most Central European Railways' lines can cope with 4 metre high road vehicles without any problems, but some routes need lower vehicles to allow their rail transport. Checking gauge availability with infrastructure operators prevents misconception.

Terminal connections of a different kind include the neighbourhood. Emissions of noise, fumes and light have been mentioned in several chapters. Depending on surrounding areas being industrial zones or housing areas, local circumstances will obviously influence necessary protection schemes, sometimes certain operation elements must be ruled out, e.g. night time operation or restricted operation modes, e.g. through forbidding the use of combustion driven equipment.

15.10 The Impact of Rolling Stock Requirements on Terminal Design

Rolling stock is obviously not part of the terminal planning business, but is a necessary requirement from a systems point of view. The load mix greatly influences rolling stock choices, e.g. chemicals carried in tanks need more rigid wagon frames than swapbodies. Semi-trailers need their own special wagon equipment as well.

All wagons should be able to run at 100km/h, empty and loaded, as lower train speeds could incur higher track access charges. Continental European railways' procurement currently specifies all wagons with empty and loaded speeds of 120km/h.

Wagon load traffic requires different railway and terminal operation as compared to merry-go-round shuttle trains. Available route clearance or load unit height would either allow standard UIC wagons to be used, or might result in the use of special low level wagons. Some 30cm can be gained with low level frames and small wheels and some 60cm can be gained with loading wells between bogies. Further discussion of these issues can be found in chapter 11.

Depending on the scale of operation, it may be necessary to find out whether a sufficient number of appropriate wagons is available for the planned services, as delivery of wagons from manufacturers takes at least a year and the market for rental intermodal wagons is only just emerging. Also, some former state railways of continental Europe will not readily provide wagons to see them hauled by competitors' locomotives, so wagon leasing arrangements may need to be investigated at an early stage

(a)  (b)

Pictures courtesy of M. Beth/Kombiverkehr
Figure 15.14
(a) Pocket wagon; **(b)** Low level wagon

194

Load Carrying Units
There is a great variety of unit types available. Some of these are described below in (a) to (e):

(a) Standard lorry
Standard lorries may be carried on "Rolling Highway" type low level wagons or Modalohr load bridge wagons. The permissible undercarriage loading gauge is defined by ramp angles and wagon floor details, excluding only very special road vehicles (see Figure 15.15(a)).

Standard vehicles may also be carried by Channel Tunnel lorry shuttle wagons without any size restriction. Planning of parking, storage and waiting areas for these types of service follows standard road lay-by practice.

(b) Container
Containers are carried on flat wagons. ISO deep sea containers are carried unrestricted, other container types if coded to combined traffic rules. Road transport generally takes place on articulated lorries. However, container types may have different properties, e.g. chemical bulk containers weigh 34 tons in 20 feet of length and may have differing internal and external width, height and length.

Containers may be stacked several high, deep sea containers up to nine, other types three, with the handling usually done via corner fittings.

(c) Swapbody
Swapbodies are widely used in continental Europe where they travel on truck-trailer combinations and are carried on railways generally on flat wagons and can be parked standing on folding legs; they are basically similar to general road swapbodies with grab pockets added to allow bottom lift (see Figure 15.15(b)).

Pictures courtesy of M. Beth/Kombiverkehr

Figure 15.15
(a) Rolling Highway train with loaded lorries
(b) Pair of 7.82m swapbodies on wagon

Pictures courtesy of M. Beth/Kombiverkehr

Figure 15.16
(a) Pair of 7.15m swapbodies on truck and trailer
(b) Swapbodies parked, truck and trailer moving away

There are two standardised length classes,

• Class A of 13.6m length without legs;
• Class C of 7.15m, 7.45m and 7.82m length with legs.

Legged swapbodies can be parked standing on their feet, avoiding a second lift but needing time for lowering and raising the legs and making theft easier.
(d) Semi-trailer-piggyback
Standard height semi-trailers may be carried in pocket wagons or EuroSpine wagon units. They are derived from road semi-trailers with added grab pockets and with a stronger frame and need additional ground personnel helping with the support props and guiding the king pin into recess.
(e) Semi-trailer-bimodal
These specialist vehicles can be turned into rail vehicles with the use of specialised rail bogies, therefore there is no need for lifting equipment or major surface works (see Figure 15.17).

General Aspects of Load Unit Operation
The large number of intermodal units currently in service does not allow fast changes to present technical details such as twist lock dimensions (top lift), grab pocket dimensions (bottom lift), bottom lock dimensions (road vehicle and rail vehicle connection via pins). There are also differences in load unit properties between countries, e.g. swapbodies are widely used in Germany but in the UK flat semi-trailers are dominant in the road business.

Automated unit data transfer, counting units in and out of terminals could happen via electronic tokens. These would not only bear constant unit data, but transport related data as well. The difficulty in this is that the large number of units which might at some time be carried by rail could not successfully be fitted with one single transmitter system, because it is always possible to have

196

Figure 15.17
(a) Semi-trailer sitting on front supports and with rear bumper folded away; (b) Semi-trailer-bimodal

units introduced into an equipped terminal from distant countries. This is an as yet undecided interoperability issue.

From a terminal operator's point of view, the optimal choice of units would be very close to the deep sea container mix: 20′ and 40′ units, with their similar cross-sectional sizes, as these can be stacked several high, and are clearly and uniformly marked. They can carry loosely loaded goods staying within original unit gauge and minor damage is acceptable without endangering rail transport. This is not the case with scratched tarpaulins which could be ripped completely open and blown into the overhead-line equipment.

Use of stacking areas could be dealt with by flexible pricing: as the terminal gets going and increasingly needs allocated storage areas for the current day to day business, prices could be raised.

15.11 Finance and Other Sources of Assistance

Terminal owners are typically large private businesses, railways, port authorities or government agencies. In the current economic situation, local or state governments tend not to involve themselves in new undertakings. Thus, almost inevitably, a private company will be responsible for designing, planning, building and operating the terminal.

Intermodal terminals require a major landtake, include expensive customer-built equipment and take quite a long time to get them from the planning stage to the fully operational status, including technical and other risk factors. Even a minor terminal would require at least €3 million (~ £2 million) to turn an existing rail connection into a functioning transhipment facility. Usually the money cannot be provided by private companies so that finance has to be achieved using different providers.

European and national monies may be available to provide funding, as intermodal transport is seen as a useful tool to reduce road congestion and air

197

pollution, as described in directive 92/106/EEC which provides a number of supporting activities.

In the *European* legislation and funding framework, over the past ten years, PACT (Pilot Actions for Combined Transport) monies have been available. In the years 1997–2001, around €35m (~ £50m) was spent on the evaluation and construction of many international railway related activities, particularly in favour of small enterprises. 160 projects have been funded by PACT since 1992.[2]

The funding has not ceased but has been relaunched under the new name of Marco Polo and now efforts are directed less towards evaluation, but more on activities to introduce new international services. Available are €75 million (~ £120 million) in the years 2003–2006, for rail freight in general, not restricted to combined transport. Up to 30 % of the actual projects may be subsidised, and up to 50 % of project feasibility evaluation tasks.[3] Like PÁCT, the Marco Polo programme is intended to improve the environmental performance of the transport system by promoting the shift of freight from road transport to short-sea shipping and to rail and inland waterway transport.

The EU has other funds that promote local development which might include railway infrastructure projects, the most prominent of which is the European Regional Development Fund ERDF. The Research and Development in Transport (RTD) programme finances new ideas when they are in line with the general policy to reduce road usage. Additionally, directive 92/106/EEC made indirect funding by member states available through tax exemption on vehicles used for combined transport and these transports being exempted from compulsory tariff regulations.[4]

It is also always worth applying to local governing bodies for assistance. If no monies are available to fund terminal construction costs themselves, there might be a chance of support for improvements to rail or road connections to the terminal site.

Financial support is also available at country or state level. For instance, the *German* organisation of public railway line planning is based on federal laws[5] which include certain intermodal terminals where the central government has established a need for a new terminal. These would be seen as an integral part of the national railway network.

Additionally, the transport ministry introduced a federal funding guide line in spring 1998, allowing private companies to draw money towards the construction and enlargement of intermodal terminals, if these could be used

2 Commission Staff Working Paper: Results of the PACT programme (Pilot Actions for Combined Transport) 1997–2001 Situation on 30 September 2001.
3 This programme was announced in the Commission White Paper "European transport policy for 2010: time to decide".
4 Directive 92/106/EEC on the establishment of common rules for certain types of combined transport of goods between Member States.
5 Bundesschienenwegeausbaugesetz.

by everybody, i.e. in a nondiscriminatory manner. This guideline was re-introduced in November 2002[6], changed mainly to allow funding:

- A higher percentage of pro bono public monies (85 %);
- The modernisation of existing terminals, especially safety measures;
- The replacement of reachstackers because of their shorter life span as compared to gantry cranes.

If projects can prove their usefulness to the ministry, virtually no company-owned money is needed beforehand, as the amount not covered by pro bono public money is provided by an interest-free loan to the promoter of a future terminal. In addition to promotional tax and tariff regulations based on directive 92/106/EEC, German legislative ruling allows a higher vehicle weight of 44 tons[7] and permits running road vehicles as part of combined transport during weekends[8] and on certain holidays[9].

British government assistance for investment in combined transport is available through the Strategic Rail Authority on behalf of the Department for Transport (DfT) (see chapter 3).

The *Austrian* government gives special financial incentives to the Rolling Road business. Not only are direct subsidies given to the companies operating Rolling Road trains. Using these trains helps trucking companies with "Ökopunkte", allowing additional transfers to be done on the road. Tax reimbursement for Rolling Road shipments is available as well.

Technical assistance for international traffic within Europe can be obtained from organisations including:

- UIC (Union Internationale des Chemins de fer), 14, rue Jean Rey, F-75015 Paris
- UIRR (Union internationale des sociétés de transport combiné Rail-Route) avenue du port 100, bte 3; B-1000 Brussels; and
- ICF (Intercontainer-Interfrigo), Margarethenstraße 38; CH-4008 Basle

15.12 Risks of Terminal Construction

Once the design process has been carried through to a final version and money has been secured, then the erection process can get underway. Still, many risks can play havoc before the terminal can actually serve its purpose.

---

6 Richtlinie zur Förderung von Umschlaganlagen des Kombinierten Verkehrs, Bundesministerium für Verkehr, Bau- und Wohnungswesen, 1. November 2002.

7 Dreiundfünfzigste Verordnung über Ausnahmen von den Vorschriften der Straßenverkehrs-Zulassungs-Ordnung vom 2. Juli 1997.

8 Straßenverkehrsordnung § 30 (Fassung vom 1. September 2002), Absatz 3, Verbotsausnahme Nummer 1.

9 Verordnung zur Erleichterung des Ferienreiseverkehrs auf der Straße (Fassung vom 30. März 1992), § 3 in Verbindung mit § 1.

Irrespective of the technology chosen, the ground must be able to withstand heavy loads during construction and during operation of the terminal. With soil being a natural material, economically viable preliminary checks can never fully exclude unwanted changes in sub-surface properties which could delay erection and make works more expensive. Similarly, the natural habitat or fauna might provide surprises, e.g. rare or even endangered species, that would not be allowed easily to be moved.

The customer-built nature of major terminal equipment always includes the risk of delivery failure, caused by financial troubles of the manufacturer or by technical properties not achieving set limits.

Usually these risks (which are a genuine part of any major construction work) can be overcome eventually and the terminal successfully opened to traffic. Nevertheless, costs will inevitably rise. Financial reserves must therefore be available to keep the construction process rolling to avoid financial failure of the project.

However, risks associated with the planning process and policies, and politics can also be significant, and are discussed in chapter 16 at greater length.

15.13 Outlook

Planning for intermodal terminals requires specific knowledge which is not very often used. It is therefore not uncommon for planners to ask for assistance from terminal operators or intermodal companies. The two-ended nature of the intermodal rail services allows the assumption that helping to set up a smoothly functioning new terminal, if not too closely situated, might add some traffic to an existing rail terminal.

Public intermodal traffic currently only has a low percentage of automation employed, due to the large number of participating companies and businesses. Steady financial pressure and the need to carry more freight on consolidated rail shipments to reduce road traffic should result in a growing number of automated processes in the next few years.

Further Reading

Commission Staff Working Paper: Results of the PACT programme (Pilot Actions for Combined Transport) 1997-2001 – Situation on 30 September 2001
Commission White Paper "European transport policy for 2010: time to decide"
Directive 92/106/EEC on the establishment of common rules for certain types of combined transport of goods between Member States
Dreiundfünfzigste Verordnung über Ausnahmen von den Vorschriften der Straßenverkehrs-Zulassungs-Ordnung vom 2. Juli 1997
European Agreement on Important International Combined Transport Lines and Related Installations, 1 February 1991
European transport policy for 2010: time to decide, Commission White Paper, 2002
Förderrichtlinie Kombinierter Verkehr, Bundesministerium für Verkehr, vom 15. März 1998

Gesetz über den Ausbau der Schienenwege des Bundes (Bundesschienenwege-ausbaugesetz) Fassung vom 15. November 1993

Richtlinie zur Förderung von Umschlaganlagen des Kombinierten Verkehrs, Bundesministerium für Verkehr, Bau- und Wohnungswesen, 1. November 2002

Straßenverkehrsordnung, Fassung vom 1. September 2002

Verordnung zur Erleichterung des Ferienreiseverkehrs auf der Straße, Fassung vom 30. März 1992

16 The Planning Process for New Terminals

Roland Niblett, Colin Buchanan & Partners

16.1 Introduction

The Strategic Rail Authority's freight strategy contains a thoughtful section on the provision of new freight terminals and the many factors which tend to conspire together to prevent their construction. This chapter draws on the SRA's work, and on two specific case studies – of the proposed Colnbrook and Solihull terminals.

Although there remain some 1500 rail-connected terminals on the Network Rail network, the vast majority handle very little traffic. Conversely, on the Pareto principle, a small number of terminals handle the majority of current freight traffic. These are concentrated on the ports (Felixstowe, Tilbury, Southampton, Liverpool), industry-specific locations such as power stations, steel works and car factories, and at a few inland intermodal terminals, as noted below (see also Figure 16.1):

London:	Willesden
Midlands:	Lawley Street (Birmingham)
	Hams Hall
	Daventry
North-West	Trafford Park, (Manchester)
	Garston (Liverpool)
North-East	Middlesbrough
	Tyne Dock
Yorkshire:	Wakefield
	Doncaster
Scotland:	Coatbridge
	Mossend
South Wales:	Wentloog (Cardiff).

The distribution of intermodal terminals matches the main population centres of the UK, with some major exceptions. These exceptions tend to be where facilities do not match demand. The most obvious of these is the London area, where a population of ⅙ of that of the country relies on one inadequate site – Willesden. The Strategic Rail Authority believes that 3 – 4 major new facilities are required in the London area, one of which could have been the London International Freight Exchange at Colnbrook. This is described in more detail later in this chapter. These major interchanges, likely to be located close to

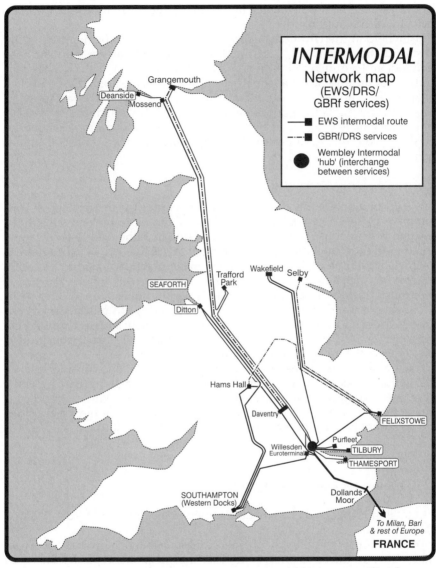

INTERMODAL
Network map
(EWS/DRS/
GBRf services)

■— EWS intermodal route
■-·-■ GBRf/DRS services
● Wembley Intermodal 'hub' (interchange between services)

Grangemouth
Deanside
Mossend
Trafford Park
Wakefield
Selby
SEAFORTH
Ditton
Hams Hall
Daventry
FELIXSTOWE
Purfleet
Willesden Euroterminal
TILBURY
THAMESPORT
SOUTHAMPTON (Western Docks)
Dollands Moor

To Milan, Bari & rest of Europe
FRANCE

Map courtesy of Freightmaster

Figure 16.1 Map of Intermodal Terminals in Britain

the M25, should be supplemented by several smaller facilities within the M25, each of which would handle 2–3 trains per day.

Elsewhere in the UK, new facilities are most likely to be required in the West Midlands, the North East, the South West, and Eastern and Northern Scotland, and a number of proposals exist (Gallop, 2002). The SRA has concluded that the absence of adequate rail terminals in the South East and elsewhere does represent a constraint on rail's market share of the fast-growing general freight market, e.g. consumer goods. The result is an inability of rail to compete adequately with road. Subsequent sections of this chapter examine the constraints on the development of new terminals and ways of overcoming them.

16.2 The Function of New Terminals

The main function of any new terminal is to permit the interchange of containers or pallets between trains and lorries, but an important subsidiary function is warehousing so that goods arriving by either rail or road can be stored until they are required. The timing of this is likely to be when there is a sufficient volume of different goods to make up a lorry load to a specific destination, such as a supermarket.

Terminal tracks must be long enough to cater for trains of up to 775m without having to divide them into separate portions. Speed of transfer of containers is essential, using mechanical handling equipment such as reachstackers and gantry cranes (see chapter 15), which can lift containers either from ground level or from the top of a stack of containers.

The amount of land needed for a successful terminal is considerable; as well as the rail sidings and adjacent roadways for the reachstackers to operate, there must be space to store full and empty containers. Whereas rigid containers can be stacked up to six high, swap-bodies do not have rigid sides and so cannot be stacked. Other space-consuming activities are:

- Warehousing;
- Security;
- Customs (for international traffic).

In total, this means that a site needs to be of the order of at least 1000m x 200m in size.

The economics of rail freight operation are such that no terminal can expect to be viable on the basis of cargo transfer income alone, typically £15 – £20 per container. Financial success depends on income from ancillary activities, such as warehousing, stockholding, materials processing and the repair of containers. It is these activities which are more likely to provoke opposition from local groups, but yet without them the rail terminal itself cannot function. On the other hand, the value added by warehousing at a purely road-served interchange is such that rail facilities could be provided as planning gain, whilst maintaining viability. Consequently, in searching for suitable sites for rail interchanges, it is essential to take into account the activities and requirements of road-based transport.

These issues are illustrated by the search for a suitable location for a terminal to serve Cornwall. Being peripherally located within Britain, so that average trip lengths are high, rail transport can be competitive with road. Consequently, Cornwall is capable of generating a significant volume of containerised rail freight, although it is unlikely to be able to support more than one terminal within the County. The criteria which should be fulfilled by the site, and indeed any other location for a new terminal, are as follows:

- Large level area of land available;
- Land has relatively low value;
- Adjacent to a railway;
- Close to major road;
- Centrally located within the Country;
- Close to sources of suitable labour.

With so many constraints, it is not surprising that the number of sites which satisfy them all is very small. Indeed there is no perfect site; the one which has the highest combined score has been assessed as Roche, on the Newquay branch railway line, and close to the dual carriageway A30 Trunk Road. It is hoped that a terminal can be built with the help of EU funding, through Objective 1 (urban regeneration).

16.3 Land Availability

Potential sources of land for rail freight interchanges are:

- Land already in the ownership of Network Rail, i.e. part of the operational railway;
- Land formerly in use by the railway, under the control of Rail Property Ltd. and now in the ownership of the Strategic Rail Authority;
- Brownfield land owned by local Authorities or other statutory bodies;
- Privately owned brownfield land, such as former power stations, which were at one time rail-served;
- Privately owed greenfield land.

One of the difficulties associated with the construction of rail terminals is that their revenue-earning capacity is less than several other potential uses of the same land, such as housing, retail or leisure. For example, former rail freight sites in Brighton, Cambridge, Cardiff and Maidstone have all been used for housing. Consequently, owners of sites which could be used for rail freight are likely to seek higher prices for it from developers interested in one of these other uses.

The SRA has recently taken over the administration of the long-standing Freight Grants system from the Department of Transport. As noted in chapter 3, Freight Grants can be either for capital expenditure on rolling stock or terminals, or for revenue expenditure, e.g. on track access charges. In either case, grants are only given if the promoter can prove that the project will divert an existing freight flow from road to rail. The amount of grant is then related to the number of lorry kilometres saved. However, in the case of an open access terminal it is not possible to identify in advance the actual flows which will use the terminal, consequently the Freight Grant regime is powerless to help.

Instead, the SRA is proposing to assist the provision of new terminals through loans and equity, paid for over time by traffic receipts, in such a way that the risks inherent in rail freight are shared between SRA and provider. To ensure that new terminals do not compete with each other in a damaging way, it is intended that there shall be regional competition. The SRA intends to call for proposals in a particular area by a certain date, but only to offer financial assistance to the most promising scheme within that area.

In its Planning Policy Guidance on Transport (PPG 13), the Government advises Local Authorities to identify and protect sites for freight interchanges through the statutory Development Plans. They should also seek to influence the location of freight-generating development so that it is close to the rail network. These measures will go some way to overcoming the financial barriers to the creation of rail freight terminals already outlined.

In some parts of the UK, notably the South East and the West Midlands, land suitable for freight interchanges is very scarce, since it has nearly all been developed already. Since these are the two areas most in need of new facilities, the whole future growth of the UK rail freight industry appears to be at risk because of this land shortage. To try and counteract this problem, the Strategic Rail Authority is working with Network Rail Property and the Rail Regulator to ensure that any Network Rail-owned land which could conceivably have potential for freight use is not released for alternative uses. The SRA is also advising local authorities in these and other areas about the identification of suitable sites in the future for designation in emerging Local Plans.

16.4 The Planning Process

Before a freight interchange can be built, it must receive Planning Permission from the Local Planning Authority (the District Council or Unitary Authority in which the site lies). The Planning Application for a major project such as a freight terminal requires a large amount of preparation and detailed work – if it is to have any chance of succeeding.

Planning Application
The main pieces of information which should accompany the application will
be:

* The purpose of the interchange;
* The types of goods expected to use it, based on a survey of the market;
* The way in which the terminal is expected to operate, i.e. when and how
  goods will arrive and depart and how they will be moved around the
  site;
* The reasoning behind the choice of this particular site;
* The layout of buildings on the site;
* The benefits which the interchange will bring, including the creation of
  new jobs;
* An environmental appraisal;
* A transport appraisal;
* Proposed mitigation measures to overcome identified problems.

Probably the most important of these are the environmental and
transport appraisals. A great deal of detailed guidance on the content of these
appraisals was published as DoE Circular 2/99. The main environmental factors are visual intrusion, noise and air quality, whilst the main transport factors are congestion on the roads around the site and on the railways serving
the site.

In the case of both noise and air quality, there will be significant benefits of
transferring freight from road to rail transport, since a large number of long-
distance lorry movements will be replaced by a much smaller number of long-
distance rail movements – the capacity of a freight train being some 30 times
that of a lorry. However, the main function of the freight terminal is to bring
lorries and trains together so that there will actually be more lorry movements around the terminal itself than would be the case if there was no terminal. In order to benefit a dispersed majority, a minority of people who live
near the site will suffer from additional lorry movements. Furthermore, it
will be these people who will be the most vociferous in lobbying their local
councillors to reject the Planning Application, however much painstaking
public consultation is carried out beforehand. Consequently most Planning
Applications for major freight interchanges are initially rejected by the Planning
Authority.

Appeals
Of course this is not the end of the matter, because a developer can appeal
against a refusal of Planning Permission, in which case Central Government
may decide to hold a Public Inquiry before deciding whether to uphold the
appeal. The Public Inquiry, held before an Inspector appointed by the Secretary

of State, is an opportunity to bring out all the arguments for and against a particular project. It therefore requires much careful planning and hard work by the developer and his team. They must put together a series of witnesses who are prepared to stand up in the Inquiry and be cross-examined by the opposition. This may be the local authority, local residents or landowners affected by the scheme.

It is at this stage that the developer needs not only to develop his case, but must also enter detailed discussions with opponents, so as to try and find ways of meeting their concerns. The inquiry inspector always takes a lot of note of the efforts made by the developer in this way, as well as statements in support of the proposals. The Strategic Rail Authority's support is likely to be particularly influential. Nevertheless, some of the recent acts of Central Government (of which the SRA is in effect a part) appear to be making it harder for rail freight to compete with road freight. Examples are the increase in permitted weight of lorries and abolition of the fuel duty escalator by which the duty increased faster than the retail price index.

16.5 The London International Freight Exchange

The London International Freight Exchange, or LIFE for short, was to be a large-scale road/rail freight terminal near Slough in Buckinghamshire. This proposal was the subject of a lengthy planning inquiry in the Spring of 2000, following an initial rejection of the planning application by Slough Borough Council. The issue was then handed to the Secretary of State for the Environment for a final decision. He rejected the application after the first draft of this section had been written.

The proposed site for the exchange was in a near ideal location from the point of view of road and rail access – it lies close to the M4/M25 intersection just to the west of London, close to Heathrow Airport, Slough and Staines (see Figure 16.2). It lies on a freight-only branch railway which links onto the Great Western Main Line at West Drayton. Unfortunately, it also lies within designated Green Belt. In addition, because of its location in such a thriving area, both the road and rail networks in the area are very close to capacity.

Nevertheless, despite the outcome of the Inquiry, it is worth describing the design of LIFE here, because it represents current best practice in the field. Figure 16.2 shows the proposed layout. Perhaps the most striking feature is the large amount of land taken up by the warehouses, which are included in the proposal in order to make it viable. LIFE would not have been simply a road/rail interchange, but a place where goods were stored for periods varying from a few hours to several months.

The freight interchange effectively had three elements:

(a) An intermodal interchange, i.e. where containers are transferred directly between lorries and trains, with no requirement for a warehouse.

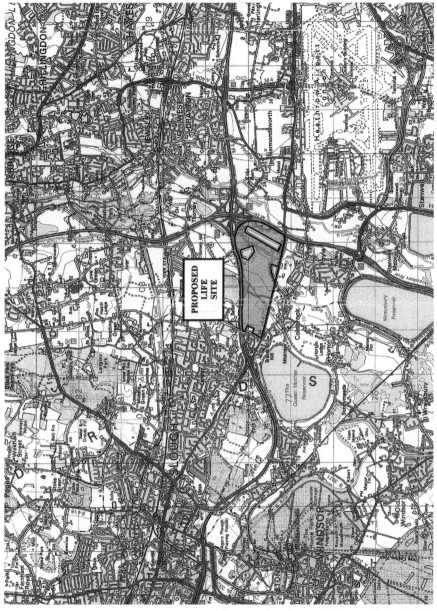

Map reproduced uner OS Licence No 100038073

Figure 16.2 Proposed Site of London International Freight Exchange

209

Slough

RAILFREIGHT PROPOSALS
A1 RAILWAY SIDINGS
A2 TRANSIT WAREHOUSE BUILDING
A3 CONTROL BUILDING
A4 RAIL SERVED DISTRIBUTION UNITS
A5 RAIL NETWORK
A6 ROAD ACCESS
A7 LORRY PARK
A8 ESTATE OFFICE
A9 FORMAL RECREATION FACILITIES

RESIDENTIAL NEIGHBOURHOODS
B1 BRANDS HILL
B2 COLNBROOK
B3 POYLE

HIGHWAYS
C1 M4
C2 M25
C3 A4(T), (COLNBROOK BYPASS)
C4 A4 OLD BATH ROAD (COLNBROOK HIGH STREET)

NATURAL FEATUR
D1 OLD SLADE LAKE
D2 ORLITTS LAKE (N)
D3 ORLITTS LAKE (S)
D4 COLNBROOK WE
D5 OLD WOOD
D6 COLNE BROOK
D7 EXISTING PUBLIC
D8 PROPOSED FOOT
D9 PROPOSED VISITC

Figure 16.3 Detailed Plan of the Proposed London International Freight Exchange

210

FREIGHT EXCHANGE

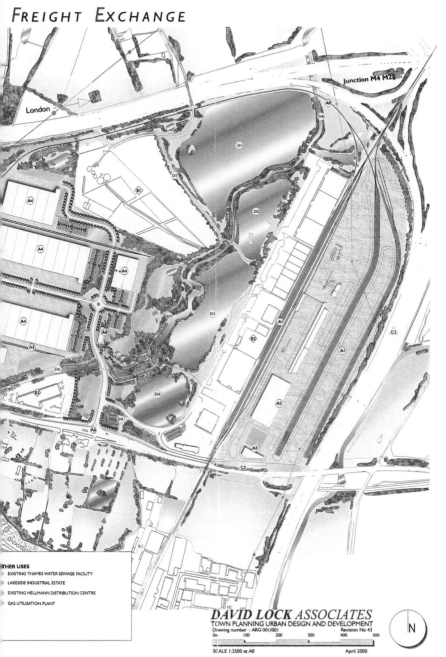

London

Junction M4 M25

A5
D6
D1
D7
E1
A4
D2
A4
AA
A4
D7
D3
A1
AB
E2
A5
A1
C2
D6
A1
E3
D4
A2
D9
A6
A3
C1
B3

THER USES
- EXISTING THAMES WATER SEWAGE FACILITY
- LAKESIDE INDUSTRIAL ESTATE
- EXISTING HELLMANN DISTRIBUTION CENTRE
- GAS UTILISATION PLANT

DAVID LOCK ASSOCIATES
TOWN PLANNING URBAN DESIGN AND DEVELOPMENT
Drawing number : ARG 001/001   Revision No 43
0m   100   200   300   400   500

SCALE 1:2500 at A0   April 2000

N

Map courtesy of Slough Borough Council

211

(b) Warehouses for UK-manufactured goods, 25% of which were to be brought in by rail. All these goods were to be distributed by road to local consumers. The kind of goods anticipated were groceries, beer, chilled foods and plastics.
(c) Warehouses for continental and overseas manufactured goods. Again, 25% of incoming goods were to arrive by rail. In addition, 25% of goods (not necessarily the same ones as arrived by rail) were to depart by rail to northern Britain. The remaining goods (e.g. consumer durables and food) were to arrive and depart by lorry.

10 intermodal trains (i.e. carrying containers) per day in each direction were proposed, plus 4 so-called conventional trains each way. These were trains to carry bulk goods, possibly loaded on pallets, which were for some reason unsuitable for carrying in containers. This fairly small number of trains were to be matched by about 1300 daily lorry movements in each direction, which is an indication both of the much greater capacity of a train, but also of the fact that the majority of movements are both in and out by lorry. This is inevitable, bearing in mind the function of the warehouses.

Figure 16.3 also shows how the design was affected by the requirement to be able to cater for very long trains, of up to 775m. The sidings are arranged so that each one is within 10m of a roadway, this being the maximum reach of the proposed mechanical handling devices. The entire site was to be surrounded by security fencing, because of the incidence of freight going to and from continental countries and there was to be extensive landscaping, with lakes and woodland.

The importance of the scheme is that, had it been authorised, it was expected to attract some 500 million ton-kilometres per year from road to rail. Put another way, this one scheme could have increased the entire UK rail freight market by about 2.5%.

16.6 Land-Rover

The Land-Rover plant in Solihull, Warwickshire lies some 4km west of the London – Birmingham railway, but is separated from it by Birmingham International Airport. Figure 16.4 shows the site. The Land-Rover Company is proposing to build a new double track rail link to its factory, to enable completed cars to be exported, and to bring components into the factory. A capital grant has been applied for, from the Strategic Rail Authority, justified on the basis of the number of lorry-miles removed from the road network as a result of transferring goods from road to rail.

A quite separate proposal to extend the length of the runway of Birmingham International Airport, means that the Land-Rover branch will have to deviate south of the most direct route. More importantly, the presence of the M42 motorway, which is difficult and expensive to bridge, means that the Land-

Map courtesy of Land-Rover

Figure 16.4 Proposed Link to Land-Rover Plant at Solihull

Rover branch will curve towards the north and have a north facing junction with the London – Birmingham line.

The majority of the origins and destinations of the rail traffic to and from Land-Rover lie to the south, for example, the ports of Purfleet and Southampton and the Rover factory at Swindon. Thus it will be necessary for most trains to reverse at Birmingham International station, which lies just to the north of the proposed junction. The railway widens out to five tracks through the station. Providing most of the freight trains operate at night when there are few passenger trains, there should be sufficient capacity to accommodate the freight train reversals. Up to 12 trains per 24 hours in each direction can be catered for.

Inside the Land-Rover works, the rail terminal will consist of five parallel sidings, with a shunt neck at the far end. One of these sidings will be located under cover within the plant. Of the remaining four tracks one will be for intermodal containers bringing components to the factory, one will be a locomotive run-round loop and the other two for completed cars for export. These cars will be driven directly onto the trains. Figure 16.5 shows the proposed layout of the terminal, with the car despatch storage area adjacent to the more southerly rail sidings. A different road is adjacent to the tracks carrying intermodal containers, and will be used by reachstackers.

Altogether this proposed investment in a freight link to Land-Rover represents a well thought-through attempt to transfer traffic from road to rail (over 400 lorry movements per day), and deserves to succeed.

213

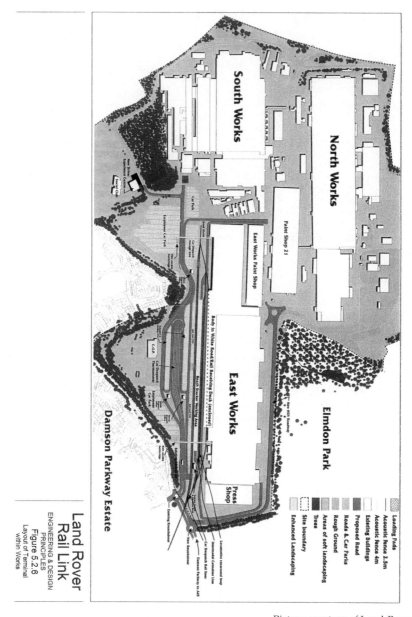

Picture courtesy of Land-Rover

Figure 16.5 Proposed Land Rover Rail Terminal at Solihull

16.7 Conclusion

Railway freight economics requires long trains which in turn imply large sites. Associated warehousing activities also increase the size of site required for multi-user and multi-modal terminals. This makes planning and implementation that much more difficult. On the other hand, without such terminals, the rail freight industry will not be able to penetrate those key new market segments of food and consumer durables which it must reach in order to increase its currently very low market share.

Editors' Notes:
As mentioned in the text, in early 2003, the Deputy Prime Minister ruled against the LIFE proposal, largely on the grounds that it was indeed a large development within London's Green Belt. This decision caused considerable anguish amongst property developers and the railway industry, especially since the Strategic Rail Authority had supported the scheme. Clearly, the problem of insufficient railfreight terminal capacity within the London area is even more of an issue without LIFE

In a further blow to railfreight development, Land Rover pulled out of the proposed rail terminal connection at their Solihull plant, during the period of rail industry problems in 2002.

On a potentially more positive note, however, the British Government recently introduced new legislation into Parliament, with the intention of speeding up the planning system whilst improving the involvement of local communities. At present the 'Planning and Compulsory Purchase Bill' is still undergoing discussion at Westminster (see also R Owen's article in Modern Railways July 2003, pp.52–53.)

Reference

Gallop, N. (2002) 'Can Railfreight Break the Non-Bulk Market?', Rail 439 pp. 42-45, July.

17 The Economics of Rail Freight

Nigel G Harris & David McIntosh, The Railway Consultancy Ltd

If rail freight is to continue in business, if not to grow, it must have an economic rationale for doing so. This may be couched either in terms of innate financial profitability or on the basis of economic value including external benefits (such as road congestion relief) for which governments may be willing to pay. But some traffics are more amenable to carriage by rail freight than others and it is important to understand where best economics within the industry may be found. The authors of this chapter consider the relative profitability of various sectors of the rail freight industry, using worked examples which are representative of conditions as at the time of writing.

17.1 The Economics of Different Products

Bulk

Rail freight has a number of overheads which its road competitors do not have. For instance, in Britain the Vehicle Excise Duty for a 44t lorry (including trailer) is currently in the range £950-£1150 (depending upon the level of emissions). After paying that, it may be possible for a road haulier to operate for an entire year without any further payments for the use of road infrastructure, other than fuel duty, the revenues from which are not hypothecated. Typical British rail freight track access charges even after the Regulator's 2002 intervention halved their cost, are 0.15 p per tonne-km. However, the cheapest North American railroads quote all-inclusive charges as low as 1p per tonne-km. On the Continent, rates of €0.5-0.9 per km for a container or lorry (on piggyback services) are typical; for 40t vehicles, this too reflects a price around 2p per tonne-km, although terminal handling charges of €20 may be added at each end. Whether or not these low costs actually permit the long-term economic replacement of assets, however, is another issue.

Bulk flows minimise any disadvantage of track costs by replacing a large number of road vehicles with only one train. Even if train crew costs are relatively higher than those of lorry drivers, because of route learning considerations and higher safety requirements, a 1000t (net) freight train requires only one driver, whereas the equivalent flow by road will need 40 lorries each carrying 25t of the product.

A key problem to avoid is that of terminal costs. Automatic loading and discharge equipment for major rail flows can easily cost several million pounds to build, and hundreds of thousands of pounds to operate p.a. In addition, this can be doubled by the construction costs of rail sidings, especially if the site concerned is not immediately adjacent to a main rail line. Even where the link is short, the costs of signalling a connection to that main line can be significant. Although the cost per tonne may (over time) be relatively low, the up-front nature of the costs, and the relative difficulty of scheme implementation, mean that many otherwise-profitable rail freight flows never get off the ground. If facilities can be minimised, e.g. through the provision only of hard standing next to a siding and a mechanical grab, capital costs can be kept down to around the £1 million mark if starting from scratch – and, of course, many locations have such facilities available already.

Table 17.1 gives a typical example for a 1000t (net) flow over 300 km, where loading can occur directly onto rail wagons, but final distribution to the customer needs to be by road. Also shown are typical road haulage costs, which may alternatively be expressed as around £1 per lorry mile.

The key driver in profitability here is the length of haul, with road competition's variable costs rising directly with distance. However, these costs are not entirely linear – for instance, there is a discontinuity at that maximum point where a return trip can be undertaken by one driver in one shift. The same effectively applies to rail freight – but here the primary cost driver is probably the utilisation of wagons, which is itself driven by the time taken to load and unload (itself a function of the investment in terminal equipment), as much as by the length of haul. Unfortunately, longer trains typically take longer to load and unload, since only one wagon is usually loaded at once, in order to minimise terminal capital costs. As an order of magnitude, freight wagon leasing costs in Britain are around £5000 p.a.

Many people ask the question 'What is the break-even distance over which rail freight can compete?' They cite rail's higher fixed costs, including terminal costs and the possibility of needing a lorry feeder to the terminal,

	Rail costs	Road equivalent
(all figures in £ per tonne)		
Loading equipment – capital	0.05	
Loading equipment – operating	0.05	
Rail terminals – capital	0.25	
Rail terminals – operating	1.25	
Rail track/signalling capital	0.30	
Rail trunk haul	8.00	
Rail wagon leasing	0.15	
Road distribution – fixed	1.00	1.00
Road distribution – variable	1.00	20.00
TOTAL	12.05	21.00

Table 17.1 Typical Costs of 1000-tonne flow over 300km

but lower variable costs. In some ways, they are correct – as Figure 17.1 shows, rail is indeed more likely to be profitable over longer distances, whilst its costs may be above the prevailing haulage price for short-distance traffics. It is though in the medium-distance range where modal competition is likely to be most severe and in the shorter and medium-distance markets where environmental grants in favour of rail (see chapter 3) are most likely to achieve modal shift.

However, whilst the generality of this relationship holds good for the majority of freight flows, there is no simple answer as to the break-even distance, because it varies dependent on such factors as:

- The quantity of traffic involved;
- The requirement for investment in terminal facilities;
- The length of time over which any capital expenditure may be recouped;
- The availability of back-haul flows on either road or rail;
- The quality of the competing transport networks;
- Any planning restrictions or conditions, or environmental regulations ruling out road use (e.g. Boulby potash in the North York Moors in England, or Valser water between Ilanz and Ems in Switzerland)

Where rail facilities have been reduced, the rail distance may be considerably longer than the road distance. A well-known case is that of the move-

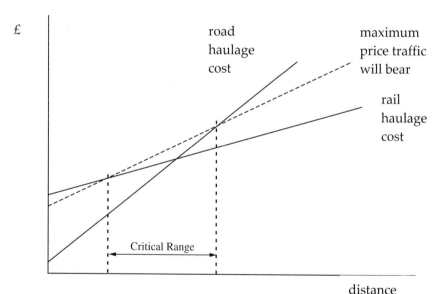

Figure 17.1 Relationship between Modal Costs and Price by Distance

ment of cement between Ketton (near Stamford) and London. There is no crossover at Ketton between the two running lines, so empty trains returning to Ketton have to travel a further 50 miles to Leicester and back in order to reach the loading point again. Increasingly, road and rail congestion is also preventing the optimum use of vehicle capacity, and the less-congested mode will have an advantage. This may be coastal shipping, which may have longer distances to cover, but at lower cost and suffering little congestion.

However, all this being said, rail is likely to find it difficult to compete over distances shorter than 100 miles, in current conditions. Particular combinations of origin and destination may also find their traffics susceptible to competition from coastal shipping.

Merry-go-round coal
In some ways, this is merely a special case of bulk traffic. The difference is perhaps that the volumes of traffic are such that expenditure on capital equipment can be repaid. Automatic loading and discharge equipment may cost £5m and £10m respectively but, at the largest power stations, 1500t trains run hourly.

Investment here has also produced loops, rather than sidings, and trains are automatically set to run at 3–4 mph during unloading. Without the need for shunting, and with drivers potentially taking their meal break during unloading, efficiency rises substantially. With similar facilities at the loading terminal, return trips can be made within six hours, and each train of locomotive and wagons may complete as many as four return trips per day.

At this level of efficiency, the break-even distance for rail is perhaps as low as 10 miles, below which conveyor belts may be used instead.

Containers
Intuitively, the transport of containers by rail ought to be economically successful, but it does not always work out in practice. Many containerised flows are relatively small in volume (perhaps one or two containers per day), which is not economic for rail. Rail operators have therefore concentrated their attentions on ports, where ships may offload hundreds (if not thousands) of containers. Finding 100 of these to take together to a key inland urban area is the basis of the Freightliner operation in Britain.

However, this has become a very competitive market, with margins as low as 1%. The reasons for this include:

(1) Some shipping lines require rail operators to transport all their containers, whether or not they are over a distance where rail is likely to be profitable. For instance, it is unlikely that Freightliner's operation from Southampton to London is profitable, but it may be seen as the price that has to be paid to gain Southampton – Manchester traffic.

(2) Some shipping lines do not pay (either road or rail) for the transport of empty containers. This has naturally depressed transport rates.

(3) Some of the traffics brought to Britain for onward shipment by rail are partly seasonal, with a peak in the Autumn, prior to Christmas. However, rail operators may be required to provide an equal level of service through the year, despite low loadings (for instance) in the Summer.

Wagonload traffic

It has been suggested that, in a typical wagonload operation, 50% of the rail costs are attributable to the trip working at each end of the journey, 30% to the shunting and only 20% to the line haul [3]. It is important to understand the three main reasons for this.

First, some rail costs accrue per mile – for instance, track access charges and fuel. Others, however, effectively accrue per hour – for instance, some vehicle leasing charges, and traincrew costs. Freight trains worked locally are likely to be on secondary lines or even freight branches, with lower speeds than on the main line. For a given hour of movement, then, distances travelled will be smaller – yet the hourly costs will be the same.

Secondly, train lengths on trip workings are usually shorter than on the main line (indeed, if they were the same, the train would operate throughout as a block working from terminal to terminal). This means that the costs accrued are spread across fewer wagons.

Lastly, the need to split and shunt trains generates additional resource requirements, such as the provision of a shunting yard and locomotive. These are often relatively poorly utilised, compared to resources used on line-haul movements. Shunting locos may sit around for hours between the departure of one train load and the arrival of the next. Worse, since several trip workings may depend upon one block train, there may be the demand for several trips to take place simultaneously (e.g. immediately after the arrival of the block

Type of Railway	Average haul *km*	Average revenue *$/load*	Average load *tonnes*	Average revenue *cents/t-km*
Class 1	1356	1191	56.8	1.55
Regional	256	467	79.8	2.30
Local	56	268	79.8	5.98
Switching & Terminal	23	188	77.1	10.86

Table 17.2 Impact of Distance on N American Rail Prices
N.B. Loads are much lower on Class 1 railroads because of the higher proportion of intermodal traffic. (Source: 4)

train), requiring several locomotives then not used for the rest of the day until collecting wagons simultaneously for the block train's departure.

If the trip working is instead made by road, then again the hourly costs may provide the stumbling block. Instead of perhaps £1 per lorry mile, a daily charge of £150 may be made for the lorry, during which time it may only undertake one collection and delivery (C&D) trip, even if this is only to a place 15 miles away. Freightliner have attempted to improve their financial position by owning their own road tractor units.

These three issues raise the interesting possibility that it may be more worthwhile to run a short freight train as a separate block train throughout, rather than shunting it to and from an existing mixed freight train.

There are genuine costs associated with terminal working which inevitably drive up prices, compared to longer-haul flows, as shown for the US situation in Table 17.2.

We reject the analysis carried out as part of the decision to close the 'Speedlink' wagonload network in 1991. That suggested that wagonload rail services were uneconomic unless one could pick-up or drop off 10 wagons per day on a flow of total distance of 600 miles. We believe that changes in the competitive situation since then (for instance, the lower maintenance costs of Class 66 locomotives, and increased road congestion) render those figures unnecessarily pessimistic. However, all this being said, wagonload rail freight is likely to find it difficult to compete over distances shorter than 200 miles, in current European conditions.

International Rail freight

Potentially, the opening of the Channel Tunnel offered huge opportunities for the expansion of rail freight to/from Britain. Distances of key traffic flows (e.g. to/from Germany) are typically 500 miles, and the volumes of traffic quite sufficient. In practice, these markets have performed poorly. Key reasons include:

(1) Rates charged by Eurotunnel for rail transit through the tunnel are not cheap, when compared to their own lorry shuttles;
(2) Quotes for charging and timetabling have often been very slow, as several railway administrations have had to be consulted, whilst customers want a "one-stop shop";
(3) The apparent advantage of avoiding interchange at both Dover and Calais has largely been negated by competing lorry companies using the cross-Channel ferry time for drivers' rest;
(4) Different technical standards (e.g. traction voltages) prevent the smooth through running that is desirable;
(5) Border crossing procedures have often been slow, reducing overall transit speeds. EU Commissioner Kinnock has paid special emphasis on tackling this problem;

(6) Delays at borders have sometimes caused onwards slots to be missed, generating further delays;

(7) Industrial action (particularly in France) has reduced levels of reliability;

(8) Deutsche Bahn pursued a pricing policy of charging as much for this traffic from the Ruhr to their border at Aachen as to their competing ports (e.g. Hamburg)

(9) From 2001 onwards, difficulties in securing traffic from the unwanted attentions of immigrants attempting to gain access to Britain meant that around half the services due to run were cancelled for around a year;

Despite these difficulties, rail has gained a key share in particular markets, of which the most significant is to Northern Italy. Rail has a second advantage here: not only does it avoid the sea crossing of the Channel, but it avoids problems crossing the Alps, where Switzerland requires much transit traffic to travel by rail anyway. Based on carrying the same amount of goods, typical costs compare as follows:

Lorry costs Milan – Birmingham £1000 (ca 1200km)
Rail costs Bari – Birmingham £2000 (ca 2100km)

Even with relatively poor performance, rail can often quote transit times for long distances significantly better than by road. For instance, for one flow between NW England and northern Italy, the initial rail quote was for a four-day transit, compared to six by road.

Shuttle Operation
Where there are significant natural barriers, e.g. short sea crossings or mountain ridges, rail may have a competitive advantage. Short sea crossings can lead to goods having to be transshipped anyway and certainly leads to lorries queueing to board and leave ships, whilst mountain ranges can lead to significant environmental disbenefits, as well as providing difficult terrain for lorries. In either case, a shuttle operation of piggyback wagons may provide the solution.

Two of Eurotunnel's market segments are, respectively, shuttles for private cars and lorries, whilst a number of Alpine routes carry shuttles between Germany and Italy (e.g. Freiburg – Novara, Munich – Verona). The latter attract Government support per lorry unit carried.

The secret of success for such operations is in the efficient use of resources. With dedicated wagons and terminals and non-stop transits through a barrier where rail investment in a tunnel gives it an advantage, costs can be brought down. However, the high charges levied by Eurotunnel for through freight services tip the market in favour of their own freight shuttles, compared to through-running by conventional freight trains. Moreover, not all of the Alpine operations would be profitable without both planning regulations and Government subsidies.

In fact, hauliers have been able to exploit rail shuttle services to their own advantage. By using these relatively-short times as break- or meal-times for lorry drivers, the net driving time wasted may be minimised. This has made lorry + shuttle + lorry stiff competition for the 'rail throughout' option, for instance between Britain and the Continent.

17.3 The Economics of the Industry as a Whole

There are undoubtedly economies of scale in the railway industry. Doing more of the same activity leads to a reduction in per-unit costs, as some costs, such as the high fixed costs of infrastructure, can be spread across more output. Perhaps more importantly, there are economies of density, i.e. carrying more traffic within the same cost parameters (numbers of terminals, wagon-sets, traincrew, line) certainly improves performance.

However, there is also clear evidence [1] that there are diseconomies of scope, i.e. railways carrying a variety of traffics incur greater costs than railways of similar size concentrating on only one type of traffic. Unfortunately, increasing scale tends to result in higher complexity. Complexity is a highly relevant factor in determining the cost of an operation. Factors affecting the complexity of operating a railway include:

- The number of markets served (e.g. freight/urban/suburban/ intercity/airport express or, within freight, bulk vs. containers vs. wagonload);
- Route length and the extent of geographical dispersion;
- The numbers of lines, terminals and depots;
- The number of technologies (e.g. types of trains or signalling systems);
- Different corporate objectives (e.g. from government and the operator itself).

Accepting that these factors are valid, one might reasonably assume that the efficiency of a railway operation changes with both scale and complexity, as shown in Figure 17.2. The volume dependent development of fixed and variable costs is shown in Figure 17.2(a). This also indicates that complexity and its associated costs related to short-run fixed costs may have to increase to attract increasing volumes. Figure 17.2(b) is based on the assumption that revenues grow more slowly as more and more marginal business is attracted. Profit (a measure for efficiency) therefore has a clear peak, as reflected by Preston's research into the optimum company size for railways [2]. Initially, efficiency increases as the available resources are utilised more and better but, with volume and diversity rising, efficiency starts to decline through traffic congestion and the dilution of management effort. Where the balance is right, railways can compete successfully. Railways devoted to freight can generate

(a) Costs of Operations

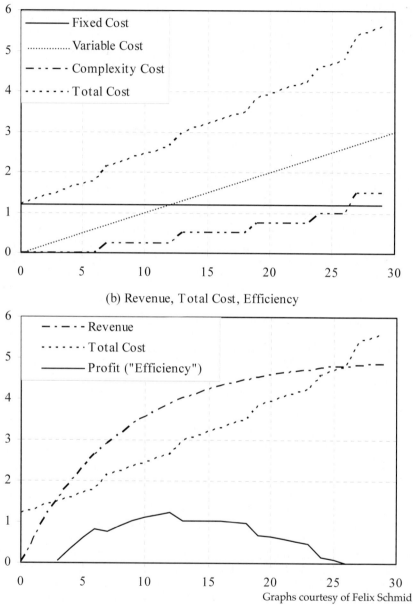

(b) Revenue, Total Cost, Efficiency

Graphs courtesy of Felix Schmid

Figure 17.2 Company Efficiency v Size and Complexity

profits for their owners and investment levels are rising slowly in countries such as Brazil and in Central America where rail privatisation has created smaller and more focused organisations (e.g. the Companhia Vale do Rio Doce in Brazil).

17.4 The Wider Picture

In addition to the business perspective of examining the value of particular rail-freight solutions, there is a wider picture which also needs to be considered. Indeed, it is this wider picture which provides the rationale for Government support, such as through the Rail Freight Grant scheme outlined in chapter 3.

Rail freight is good for industry, in providing cost-effective transport – for instance, in Britain, coal is carried to 16 power stations in 800 trains a week [5], whilst a wide range of companies supplying goods ranging from bananas to steel scrap find the railways a useful and punctual element of their distribution strategy. The recent upward trend in rail freight in Britain (tonne-miles up 50% between 1997 and 2002) suggests that these benefits are increasingly being recognised by companies.

Rail freight also supports government (for instance, in the process of disposing of local authority domestic waste), and the wider world (through its supply of transport at lower environmental cost, with lower accident levels, and whilst incurring less road congestion). In Britain alone, these latter impacts have been valued at around £400m p.a. Companies looking for a wider stakeholder base beyond the traditional 'profit for shareholders' target may also find these additional benefits worth pursuing.

17.5 Options for Improving Economics

At present, some rail freight operations are only making a profit if loaded to 90% capacity. Given the variability in traffic flows in different months of the year, the Summer period typically being slack, this makes true profit extremely difficult to achieve. It also makes the start-up of new services difficult, as it may take a year or two to become profitable. So what can be done about this?

The 'easy' approach is to wait for road congestion to swing the balance between modes in favour of rail. However, this is risky, since new roads or improved (e.g. 44t) lorries may work against the railway. Evidence shows that the road lobby is powerful and has managed to gain concessions from governments otherwise minded to improve their environmental credentials.

There are, however, a number of more pro-active approaches. In general, these must address one or more of the three key issues of (i) captial expenditure, (ii) operating expenditure and (iii) revenue (either through pricing or service quality). In many cases, however, different solutions impact on all three but, as in the USA after the Staggers Act of 1980, investment is often the key to improvements in productivity and service levels [6].

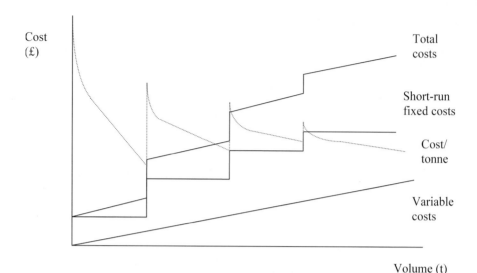

Figure 17.3 The Economic Solution to Railfreight Competitiveness

Figure 12.4 identified the non-linear costs associated with rail freight. These provide us with a clue as to finding profit-maximising solutions, if we develop the argument to consider the implied costs per tonne.

The important consequence of the relationships shown in Figure 17.3 is that, when considered against competitors from the road haulage sector, only specific operational solutions may be worthwhile. For instance, rail may be competitive at 1.9Mtpa if this can be achieved with two sets of wagons each completing two round trips per day, but not at 2Mpta, if this requires additional capital input, whether this be operationally-based (e.g. further wagon sets) or infrastructure-based (e.g. a new passing loop or enhanced signalling). This is because many road haulage solutions are effectively based solely on variable costs, such that the cost/tonne is almost constant across a wide range of volumes. Rail freight planners should therefore aim to offer services which use a relatively high proportion of their capacity. They should also remember what their relative strengths and weaknesses are – strengths include the ability to reduce operational costs through running longer trains, whilst weaknesses include high capital requirements for terminals.

Expressed in practical terms, possible approaches to enhancing the economics of rail freight include:

(1) Reduce rail's generalised cost (see chapter 7) e.g. by using vehicles with a higher top speed (although this may increase train maintenance costs), and/or travel more directly between origin and destination (although this may prevent other traffics being carried).

(2) Reduce operating costs by:

- The more efficient use of resources ("sweating the assets") (although this can have performance implications);
- Implementing new technologies, for instance, in wagon design (see chapter 11);
- Ensuring efficient company performance (at first, there are increasing returns to scale, but these eventually become inefficiencies).

(3) Reduce handling costs by increased capital expenditure in:

- Providing direct access to the rail network through new sidings;
- Using containers/swapbodies/pallets

(4) Combine less-than-trainload traffic into a block train by:

- Not running a train every day, although this may lead to inefficiencies in terminal investment (i.e. large terminals used infrequently);
- Putting several freight forwarders together in a freight village, with all of them having immediate access to the rail sidings (see chapter 15);
- Reducing the costs of a block train by developing Freight Multiple Unit options (see chapter 8).

(5) Reduce capital costs by using self-discharge trains not requiring major investment in terminal facilities.

Prices offered to customers may, of course, be manipulated in other ways, not only through attractive pricing, but by transferring costs (e.g. of wagons, terminals) to the customer.

17.6 Summary

The economics of rail freight operations are relatively poor in many situations due to the current state of competition and legislation governing the different modes. Many commentators have written off rail outside specific markets. They feel that rail is only suited to bulk haulage of low value high-density commodities, such as grain, aggregates and iron ore, or the long distance transport of reasonably time critical brown and white goods, particularly in the USA. Rail's high fixed infrastructure costs and limited responsiveness to some opportunities have allowed its competitors to make inroads even in its own traditional markets. This includes short-term flows of traditional rail served cargo such as coal and steel. For too long, rail had relied on its perceived environmental and efficiency advantages.

Yet, even where planning or environmental regulations do not demand the use of rail, the mode can compete across a wide range of traffics. Increasingly, road congestion and lorry drivers' hours regulations are putting pressure on hauliers, thereby reducing the minimum trip length over which rail can compete effectively.

Not only can rail be competitive but, in an increasing number of markets profits can be made in the rail freight industry, provided that set-up and terminal costs can be minimised. Specific geographic and topographic situations may provide opportunities – for example through the new alpine tunnels and in international traffic across barriers such as the English Channel. However, there are still many interoperability issues to be tackled in order to minimise costs and maximise service performance. Also, very large and complicated freight operations must be assessed and managed carefully because of the potential risk to the bottom line. Operational complexity must be minimised and resources must be used close to their capacity level to ensure acceptable cost.

In summary, profits can be made in the rail freight industry if operators can exploit rail's key strengths of:

• Tightly timetabled operations;
• Comparatively high line-haul speeds; and
• Ability to carry large volumes.

For these critical skills to result in new customers, competitive prices have to be offered and other areas, such as reliability and customer service have to be managed to a consistently high standard.

References

1. Bouf, D, Crozet, Y, Guihery, L & Peguy, P-Y (1999) 'Compared Performance of Railway Companies in Europe', PTRC ETF Stream A pp. 45–59.
2. Preston, J, 'Does Size Matter? A Case Study of Western European Railways', *Jnl. Transport Economics & Politics*, 1993.
3. Hansford, T (1991) "Speedlink's Final Trip', Rail.
4. Burns, D (2002) 'The Cost of Being Profitable', Railway Gazette International pp. 417–420, August. (data from the Association of American Railroads)
5. Smith, G (2003) 'Rail Freight – Perception and Reality', Modern Railways 60, no. 656 pp. 58–62, May.
6. American Association of Railroads, website.

18 Summary and Conclusions

Nigel G Harris (The Railway Consultancy Ltd)
and Bob Goundry (Freightliner Ltd)

Introduction
Freight transport begins with the customer, an individual or a corporate entity that needs to move goods from one place to another. The need for this function has existed since the earliest days of trade, thousands of years ago. However, its importance grew in the late 17th century when the regular and efficient transport of large volumes of heavy freight was a pre-requisite for the success of the industrial revolution. In some ways, the railways can be seen as the enabler of the industrialisation of society.

Rail freight's role in servicing heavy industry has reduced in importance in recent years, largely because of changing methods of production. However, increasing congestion on the competing road network means that rail continues to be an option worth considering in a significant range of situations. In specific circumstances, rail can even reduce the need for short-distance air-freight operations.

Conditions for Success
Rail can thus offer competitive services in the right environment and in situations where its strengths can be deployed, that is, timetabled operation at relatively high speed, weather- and congestion-independent performance and a comparatively low wage cost per unit carried. The following freight flow criteria though should be satisfied if rail's strengths are to be used to best effect:

(1) Regular major flows between origin and destination pairs, e.g. process plants and major customers, or between pairs of railheads which are acceptably[1] near to major traffic generators, i.e. where they serve a substantial catchment area;

(2) Flows that can be easily transferred between modes thanks to unitisation or automated handling;

(3) Haulage charge levels that allow a commercial return on the investment required or availability of grants to supplement the revenue stream where defined non-user benefits can be identified;

---

[1] "Acceptably" means that the cost of transfer, including transhipment, between railhead and origin/destination does not reach such a high level that insufficient money is available to operate the rail element profitably.

229

(4) The required quality and an acceptable cost for the rail movement as perceived by the customer, when compared with the other available options.

In Britain, the road haulage industry is efficient and effective, transport distances are relatively short and the road network is both comprehensive and in fair condition. Many major traffic destinations are within easy reach of transport by sea and primary manufacturing has declined and is likely to continue to decline. Rail freight thus tends to satisfy niche demands, namely, where goods and materials have to be moved either in significant bulk and/or over longer distances, such as between ports in the South and the North West of England.

Rail has a substantial future market where it can move highly time-sensitive freight reliably and fast over distances that can be covered in either up to 10 or up to 30 hours when operating at average speeds of 80km/h. Road cannot compete on this basis and air transport may not be price competitive. Currently, rail is not performing well in this sector but there is great scope in retailing and logistics if rail improves.

Limiting Factors
Today, the major passenger routes essentially determine the shape and size of the British and European rail networks. "Freight only" lines usually exist only where there is a demand for a link between the passenger network and centres that despatch and/or receive substantial quantities of freight by rail. In the British and several other European contexts, freight traffic does not of itself justify long segregated through routes, nor indeed separate freight tracks in existing corridors. Almost all freight flows run for the greatest part of their journeys on the passenger network. In countries with different geographies and population concentrations, however, rail freight on its own can be able to support considerable infrastructure, particularly where it is operating at its most efficient, carrying bulk goods or large flows of unitised cargo.

With rail's competitors being treated differently in many countries, it is important to use the strengths of the rail mode, as noted above. Some countries offer favourable taxation and may provide the infrastructure at a cost which is comparable to road, e.g. in Sweden. Particular combinations of traffic may offer much greater opportunities for profitable operation, in terms of technology, terminal size and location, and wagon utilisation. Even in apparently less favourable environments, however, good operational management can allow the exploitation of profitable opportunities.

The Need for Flexibility
Although situation-specific solutions may offer new opportunities for rail freight, it is very difficult to forecast in detail future traffic flows. It is therefore not easy to plan investment (be this rolling stock or specialist infrastructure for the long term). Because train service patterns can be changed relatively easily,

the design of freight terminals should allow for changing circumstances. For instance, the Seaham terminal in County Durham was opened with the expectation that it would serve the forestry and coal markets, but it has succeeded with cement and steel. Conversely, the layout at Didcot power station faces North, the direction from which coal originally arrived. It is less suited to accept traffic from the West, where imported coal now reaches the UK market via the port at Avonmouth. The good freight planner therefore needs to keep options open for future traffic flows, as well as ensuring good value for money for proposals currently being investigated.

The Future
With the changes in manufacturing and distribution patterns forced on the markets by globalisation, the importance of transport is increasing dramatically. Rail freight has a potentially bright future where it can satisfy the new demands, in particular, where it can assist in minimising inventory. However, whilst opportunities are there to be taken, they require initiative, thinking outside the box, a determination to drive the project through and continuing customer focus. There are potential gains for customers (in terms of faster and more reliable transits), freight train operators (in terms of larger and more profitable businesses), and society (in terms of reduced transport externalities).

Sources of Further Help

THE UNIVERSITY OF SHEFFIELD

Msc Programme in Railway Systems Engineering

A modular taught postgraduate programme leading to Diploma and MSc (Eng.) in Railway Systems Engineering (PT & FT):

The programme allows new rail industry staff to acquire the broad knowledge to supplement a specialist engineering degree while specialists from the industry learn to understand and appreciate the thinking of specialists of other disciplines.

The MSc (Eng.) programme in Railway Systems Engineering was developed in 1994 as a joint initiative of the University of Sheffield and of the British Railways Board, at the suggestion of the Railway Division of the Institution of Mechanical Engineers (I.Mech.E.). It is unique in the world in that the course team views the railway as a system in a holistic and integrative manner.

Railway systems engineers are concerned with establishing the processes and systems to manage and control the resources required to conceive, design, build, operate and maintain railways of all types within the constraints imposed by the natural technical, operational and organisational characteristics of the rail mode of transport, in an effective and efficient manner. They also ensure that the complex and safety critical interfaces of the system railway are controlled in a dependable manner.

The interdisciplinary activity of Railway Systems Engineering was created in response to the substantial new challenges faced by the railway industry in the 1990s. Some of these relate to the demands imposed by the directives of the European Commission, others to financial requirements of national governments and some are the result of increasing demand for railway services. The University of Sheffield was instrumental in creating some of the concepts involved in RSE, transferring know-how from the well-established fields of manufacturing and aerospace systems engineering.

RSE requires a multi-faceted approach, involving technologies and methods from civil, mechanical and electrical engineering, as well as from the social sciences. The programme consists of eight taught modules, ranging from railway operations management to track design and train control. MSc level study involves an industry relevant dissertation project. Some modules are suited to Continuous Professional Development.

'Planning Freight Railways' contributors M. Beth, R. Palacin and C. Watson are graduates of the MSc Programme in Railway Systems Engineering and read for their degrees under Dr. F. Schmid.

For Application Details Please Contact:

Postgraduate Admissions Secretary
TEL: +44 (0) 114 222 7802

For Further Information Please Contact

The Programme Director
TEL: +44 (0) 114 222 0160

Department of Mechanical Engineering, University of Sheffield
Mappin Street, Sheffield S1 3JD, England
FAX: +44 (0) 114 222 7890

Which is better for the economy and the environment?

This....

....or this?

The Rail Freight Group exists to promote the use of rail for freight transport. If you are a user or supplier, why not join us?

Further information: Rail Freight Group,
17 Queen Anne's Gate, London SW1H 9BU, tel 020 7233
3177, fax 020 7223 3178, Email phillippa @rfg.org.uk, website
www.rfg.org.uk

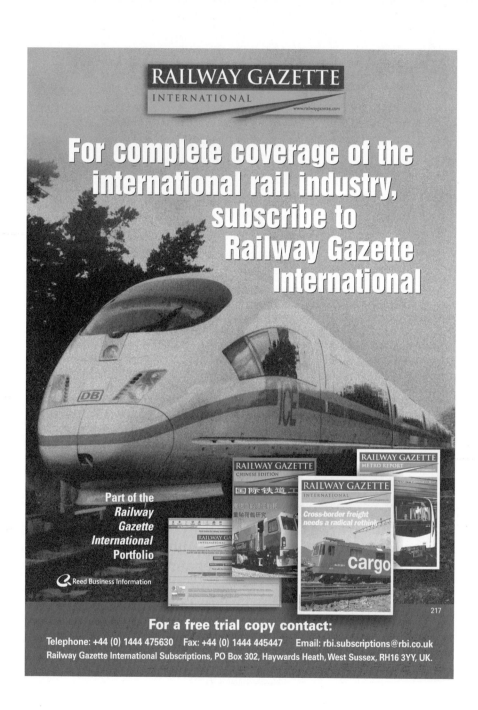

Glossary

CIM	standard international rail freight conditions (Regles uniformes concernant le contrat de transport international ferroviaire de marcandises)
combined transport	has most of the route travelled by rail or by ship to reduce road usage, minimum distance covered by rail/ship 100km, maximum distance covered on road 150 km at either end. This segment is in the focus of European transport legislation, i.e. activities of the member countries are co-ordinated and special funding is available for research and operation expenses. Includes both piggyback and container operations.
Glw:	Gross Loaded Weight (Mass)
Gross Mass:	Tare mass of the vehicle plus payload
intermodal	transport with load units swapped between transport modes
kg	kilogramme = 2.205lb
kN	1000N (100kgF)
kW	1000W
lb	pound (avoirdupois) =16oz=0.4536kg
MT	1 million short tons
Mt	mega tonne or 1 million t
multimodal	any transport that uses more than one transport mode
Net mass	Payload
OHLE	OverHead Lineside Equipment (the 25kV power supply)
Payload:	Net quantity of goods or cargo carried by a vehicle or train for which a haulage charge can be levied
pkm	passenger kilometres (=number of passengers times distance travelled)
RID	conditions pertaining to the rail transport of dangerous goods (Réglements uniformes concernant le transport international ferroviaire de merchandises dangereuses)
RIV	Regolamento Intercambio Vehicoli, rules for the international exchange of railway rolling stock between national railway administrations.
Service Weight:	Empty mass of the vehicle but including any essential equipment and fluids etc. Generally greater than tare
sh ton (or T)	short ton or American ton (2000lb=907kg).

STI	EU directives on standards for Technical operability, passed into national law in 2001 for high-speed operators, and 2003 for conventional operators
t or tonne	(metric) tonne (1000kg)
Tare Mass:	Empty mass of the vehicle
tkm	tonne kilometres (=load in tonnes times distance travelled)
ton	(long) ton UK (2240lb=1016kg)
tr lb	troy pound=12 oz tr=0.3732kg
TEN	Trans-European Network
TERFN	Trans-European Rail Freight Network

About the Contributors

Nigel G Harris is amongst Britain's leading railway planners, with a reputation based initially on technical advances in fares policy research (at Newcastle University) and network modelling (during eight years at London Underground). In addition, he has expertise in service planning, operational simulation, demand forecasting, scheme appraisal and railway business planning, which gives him one of the best understandings in the country of railway economics. He has managed The Railway Consultancy, specialists in demand forecasting and operational planning, since 1995. He co-authored the key texts "Planning Passenger Railways" and "The Privatisation of British Rail", and has published over 50 other papers. He is a visiting lecturer at the Universities of Newcastle, Sheffield and Oxford Brookes, and has spoken to a wide variety of groups including railway staff and international conferences in Europe and North America.

Felix Schmid is a Senior Lecturer in Railway Systems Engineering at the University of Sheffield. He has lived and worked in Britain since 1978, with three and a half years spent in industry designing locomotive control systems for GEC Traction before moving in to the academic sector. His main teaching interests are in the areas of train operations, human factors, electric traction systems and the economics of rail transport. His research interests are in the areas of train control, systems engineering and associated human factors issues. He is the director of the postgraduate programme in railway systems engineering at the University of Sheffield but has also practical experience of railway operations through a year spent working for the Swiss Federal Office of Transport as a railway inspector.

Allen Marsden joined British Rail's freight sector in 1980, helping to run Crewe marshalling yard. Since then he has spent 17 years of his career in freight. A "founder-member" of English Welsh & Scottish Railway, Allen joined its Planning Directorate in 1998. Besides strategic business planning, his responsibilities include managing EWS's relationships with regional and local government and industry associations. Allen represents EWS at the "Freight on Rail" group which encourages support for rail freight from regional and local tiers of government, and he has written the EWS response to several consultations on UK and EU transport and spatial planning policy.

Robert Goundry has been Director of Strategy for Freightliner since October 1997, and is responsible for commercial and industrial policy development for the company. Before joining Freightliner he was Managing Director of

North West Regional Railways Ltd. Between 1982 and 1985 he was Railfreight Manager, Chemicals and Industrial Minerals, for the British Railways Board, being responsible for the rail freight business in those commodities for the West of the country, from Cornwall to Ayrshire.

Arthur Durham has over twenty years of experience in permanent way construction, design and maintenance in the Heavy Haul industry. He has specialised in the management of the wheel and rail interface, the development of maintenance and replacement decision models and the design and testing of network compatible subsystems. He has delivered a number of technical papers at the International Heavy Haul Association and for the South African railway fraternity. He has managed various multi-disciplinary infrastructure refurbishment projects on the South African Heavy Haul Coal Line. He was also involved with the design, re-engineering and testing of various permanent way heavy haul subsystems. Since joining WS Atkins, two years ago, he has been involved with various track asset management projects in the U.K, Denmark and Greece.

Charles Watson began his railway career in 1975 when he worked for the Canadian Pacific Railway as a train order operator in his home town of Galt, Ontario, Following redundancy, he spent some years working for a road haulier as a fork lift truck driver and warehouseman. Thus Charles has an excellent understanding of the freight business from ground level. After emigrating to England in 1985 Charles spent some time in the catering industry before embarking on a degree in Mechanical Engineering at the University of the West of England at Bristol. Re-entering the railway industry in 1996 Charles worked for a preserved railway in the South of England before starting the MSc in Railway Systems Engineering at the University of Sheffield. As part of the course Charles did a one year placement with AEA Technology – Rail in Derby where he investigated rolling contact fatigue of railway wheels. Returning to the University of Sheffield to undertake a PhD, Charles lectures on short courses for industry and the MSc.

Simon Colbourne currently leads New Business development at English Welsh and Scottish railways. He has spent the last 10 year or so working in senior management roles in the supply chain industry, his last position being with Exel logistics. With experience in both the short sea shipping industry and the logistics sector his career has focused on the development of new solutions in the rail transport market from International intermodal services to the design new technology and services for the broader rail industry. Simon is a director of the RFG, member of the FTA rail freight committee and champion for the railfreight industry.

240

Alan Williams is Group Corporate Affairs Director at Royal Mail Group plc, and is a member of the Management Board. Previously, he was Chief Information Officer at the Department of Trade & Industry, where he was responsible for advising successive Secretaries of State and Ministers on all media issues. During this period he was also seconded to The Prime Minister's press office. His background is in journalism and broadcasting, and he has remained a regular writer and broadcaster on political and safety issues surrounding rail transport from the customer perspective for well over two decades. His monthly political column in "Modern Railways" recently celebrated 25 years of continuous appearance and he is the author of several books, including the satirical 'Not the Age of the Train'. He was invited to become an Associate of the Institution of Railway Signal Engineers in recognition of his writing on safety issues, and was an external Member of the British Railways Board Design Panel from 1985 until privatisation in 1994.

Following a family move from the Netherlands to the UK in the summer of 1998, *Ties van Ark* joined the Railway Consultancy Ltd., where he has been a key member of the team developing Railtrack's Access Rights Database. Ties's career with Dutch Railways was built on his degree in Management Economics, enabling him to understand and contribute to (strategic) business issues, and his interest in technical and logistical matters. The latter resulted in roles as Manager for Operational Control and Customer Services in both Rotterdam and Utrecht with NS Cargo.

David McIntosh has spent the majority of his career working in a railway environment, principally as a Senior Commercial Manager, through which he gained considerable business and operating experience. He is a versatile, imaginative and widely experienced executive with an established record of profit improvement on existing routes, and the creation of new services, for both passenger and freight. He has also been responsible for developing and negotiating third party funding and partnerships with a wide spectrum of private and public sector organisations. Following spells with two other consultancies, he now brings his railway operational experience to bear as a director of The Railway Consultancy Ltd.

Luke Ripley is a railway planner with experience in both Britain and South Africa, where he was involved in a number of strategic economic costing studies of various land transport modes. In Britain, he was involved in the WCRM project as a key player, monitoring the train performance of possessions. He has a wide range of other expertise, including in engineering and data analysis, and has an excellent railway geographical knowledge.

Matthias Beth graduated with a German Dipl.-Ing. degree in civil engineering. He has worked in several fields of rail transport, including tram and trol-

241

leybus operations, track construction and maintenance, as well as quality management. In 1997, he joined Kombiverkehr GmbH & Co KG, Frankfurt am Main, to work as Terminal Operations Manager for international intermodal rail transport and Consultant Civil Engineer. In 2001, he was additionally appointed Deputy Technical Director of Lokomotion GmbH, Munich, the first private company running freight trains between Germany and Italy.

Roland Niblett is a Director of Colin Buchanan and Partners and leads its railways group. He was previously Strategic Planning Manager for first the Greater London Council and then Network SouthEast, which was the sector of British Rail responsible for London commuter services. With CBP he has worked on rail freight issues for several Local Authorities, and has appeared as an expert witness at the Public Inquiry into the proposed London International Freight Terminal.

Note: All authors have written in their personal capacity, and their views should not necessarily be taken as representative of the organisations for whom they currently work.

Index